PARA-TRANSIT

Neglected Options For
Urban Mobility

PARA-TRANSIT

Neglected Options For Urban Mobility

Ronald F. Kirby
Kiran U. Bhatt
Michael A. Kemp
Robert G. McGillivray
Martin Wohl

This research was funded by the
DEPARTMENT OF TRANSPORTATION
Urban Mass Transportation Administration
and
Federal Highway Administration
Washington, D.C. 20590

THE URBAN INSTITUTE
2100 M Street, N.W.
Washington, D.C. 20037

The contents of this publication reflect the views of the authors, who are responsible for the facts and accuracy of the data presented herein. The contents do not necessarily reflect the views of The Urban Institute or the official views or policy of the U.S. Department of Transportation. This publication does not constitute a standard, specification, or regulation.

The Urban Institute is a nonprofit research organization established in 1968 to study problems of the nation's urban communities. Independent and nonpartisan, the Institute responds to current needs for disinterested analyses and basic information and attempts to facilitate the application of this knowledge. As part of this effort, it cooperates with federal agencies, states, cities, associations of public officials, the academic community, and other sectors of the general public. The Institute's research findings and a broad range of interpretive viewpoints are published as an educational service.

Library of Congress Catalog Card Number 74-84666
ISBN 87766-121-9
UI 171-4800-8-4
REFER TO URI 78000 WHEN ORDERING
List price: $4.95

The Urban Institute
2100 M Street, N.W.
Washington, D.C. 20037

CONTENTS

388.4
K58

v

116606

Page

TABLES

FIGURES

ACKNOWLEDGMENTS

This research was conducted under contract DOT-UT-20018 (Task 2.0) funded jointly by the Urban Mass Transportation Administration (UMTA) and the Federal Highway Administration (FHWA) of the U.S. Department of Transportation. The authors express their appreciation for the assistance provided by Jimmy Yu of UMTA in the technical direction of the research, and for the interest and encouragement of Stanley Price of UMTA and Thomas Hillegass of FHWA. John Schwellenbach of Urban Interface Group is also thanked for his assistance in the management of the contract.

In assembling the survey of existing operating experience for para-transit modes, the authors received a great deal of cooperation and assistance from a large number of people in all parts of the country. We are deeply grateful for their help. We also appreciate the generous permissions granted us to cite from various books and articles. Finally, we wish to acknowledge the valuable discussion and review provided during the study by Damian Kulash, Paul Jones, Charles Vidich, and Nigel Wilson. Special thanks are due to Janis Ackman and Virginia Weitzel for excellent secretarial support provided throughout our work.

FOREWORD

The pattern of village life, where residents traveled only a few blocks to obtain most of the goods and services they used in conducting their lives, has been largely obliterated in the present urban context. The variety and volume of goods and services—like the variety and number of real or assumed needs and desires—have multiplied dramatically, and while the urban dweller obtains some of those goods and services close at hand, most others must be found elsewhere in the city. The city tends to compartmentalize its residential, working, shopping, and entertainment areas in such a way that for most major activities the urban resident relies heavily on public or private transportation, or both.

For many urban residents, this function is served extremely well by the private automobile, which accounts for around 90 percent of all urban trips. But there are a number of drawbacks associated with private automobiles: they bear much of the responsibility for increased congestion and wasted traveling time, they raise the levels of noise and air pollution to the point of public hazard, and they consume large quantities of fuels. Moreover, there is increasing hostility at the neighborhood level to further highway construction. On the other hand, conventional public transit services —with fixed routes, overcrowding during peak hours, limited frequency and coverage during off-peak hours, and breakdowns and delays—only imperfectly satisfy the demand for public transportation in urban areas and, in the meantime, place government budgets at all levels under an increasing strain. Further, neither of these travel alternatives meets the needs of such groups as the elderly and the handicapped, many of whom are unable or unwilling to use public transit and have no ready access to private automobiles.

In attempting to deal with the various dilemmas of urban travel, planners and policy makers have been concerned almost exclusively with the private auto and conventional transit alternatives. Other near-term options have been suggested at various times but have been largely neglected. Some are concerned with the reduction or redirection of travel through land use policies, the staggering of work hours, or rationing the use of congested facilities through special pricing or other restraints. Others encourage greater use of less common highway modes of urban transportation, which the Department of Transportation (DOT) describes collectively as *para-transit*, and which includes car pools, rental cars, and specialized commuter bus services provided on a subscription basis, as well as taxicab and related services like dial-a-ride, jitney, and limousine.

In response to a request by the DOT, The Urban Institute has conducted a review and evaluation of the use of para-transit modes. In this study the Institute has assessed the pertinence of para-transit services to urban travel needs and has marshaled arguments for action aimed at taking greater advantage of these services. The study serves, at the least, to focus attention on an important and neglected range of travel options, and it also points to several specific ways in which para-transit might effectively substitute for or complement the private automobile and conventional transit. In particular, the study suggests that para-transit can play an important role in serving peak-hour travel, in meeting low-density travel demand (particularly by disadvantaged groups), in providing short access trips to conventional transit terminals, and in serving the demand for internal movement within business and commercial districts.

The study has already aroused widespread interest among other research professionals, journalists, and government officials. It has directly influenced the planning of a subscription bus service and a jitney service for Los Angeles, as well as the implementation of a more flexible taxicab service for Arlington, Virginia. It has been gratifying that the Department of Transportation recently initiated action on several of the study's recommendations: the development of detailed guidelines on the operation of subscription bus services, research on taxicab regulation, and a demonstration program to further explore the potential of taxicab, dial-a-ride, and jitney services.

We are very optimistic about the beneficial impact of our continuing research on para-transit, and our related efforts directed at congestion pricing, fare and service policies for conventional transit, cost analyses for transportation alternatives, and the use of transportation stamps for improving the mobility of the disadvantaged.

William Gorham
President
The Urban Institute

PREFACE

Improved mobility for urban dwellers has been the goal of the Urban Mass Transportation Administration (UMTA) since its inception in 1964. The immediate objective of the program was to preserve deteriorating urban transit systems; a decade later, UMTA is actively searching for better ways to move people. This exploration encompasses the development of new transportation systems and technology as well as the use of conventional transportation modes in innovative ways.

Para-transit potentially represents a major resource in this search. The diversity of travel patterns, user preferences, ridership densities and land uses suggests that a single mode of transit cannot serve all the travel needs of an urban area. An effective urban transportation system requires a mix of modes, vehicle types, and service characteristics to accommodate the urban transit user. Para-transit promises to become an essential element in a system tailored to meet the diverse needs of an urban area; it can operate in low-density areas not economically served by fixed bus or rail; provide feeder service to line-haul routes; and provide the backbone of small community and neighborhood transit service.

These possibilities are only a partial inventory of para-transit's potential. This study was designed to expand our understanding of the unique operating and service characteristics of the para-transit forms. The report's comprehensive analysis of the various services and its recommendations for future research efforts have contributed to a better understanding of the potential role of para-transit in addressing urban transportation needs. We hope it will stimulate others to pursue the yet unanswered questions of how para-transit can best be utilized to serve the urban community.

Frank C. Herringer
Administrator
Urban Mass Transportation Administration

PART ONE

PARA-TRANSIT POTENTIAL AND RECOMMENDATIONS FOR ACTION

The purpose of the first part of this book is to assess the potential of para-transit modes (those types of public transportation in-between the private automobile and conventional transit) for serving urban travel demands, and to recommend ways in which para-transit can be applied more fully and more systematically in supplying those services. The assessment and recommendations developed in this part of the report are based on the detailed review of para-transit operating experience presented in Part Two, some sections of which have been summarized in Part One to provide a suitable framework for discussion.

Chapter 1 describes the transportation services referred to by the term para-transit and groups them under three distinct categories— *hire and drive* services, *hail or phone* services, and *prearranged ride-sharing* services. The second, third, and fourth chapters address each of these categories in turn, discussing service characteristics, experience accrued to date, and existing methods of operation, and suggesting some promising innovations in service provision. The fifth chapter discusses the roles which para-transit services might fill in urban transportation systems and identifies several promising markets for para-transit. Finally, Chapter 6 discusses the steps which need to be taken to encourage worthwhile applications of para-transit services.

1

Chapter 1

Ronald F. Kirby

Introduction

In virtually all Western countries in recent years, a voracious appetite for private automobile travel within and between urban areas has run head-on into other social concerns: the desire for clean air, resistance to further neighborhood disruption from transportation facilities, the need to conserve energy, and irritation over the traffic congestion which continues to plague major cities. While considerable attention (but very little action) has been concentrated on the problem of traffic congestion, the more pressing issues at present are those of pollution and energy consumption. The Clean Air Act of 1970 together with recent gasoline shortages have suggested that some important changes in travel habits may be necessary within the next few years. Transportation professionals assisting urban policy makers have only very recently tackled directly the question of how public policy can deal with the conflicts inherent in trying to maintain or increase existing levels of mobility while limiting highway construction, air pollution, and energy consumption.

The most immediate response to these changing priorities in the United States has been to reinforce the cry for more bus and rail transit, presumably designed to reverse or at least slow down the increase in the proportion of urban travel by private automobile. (The urban passenger miles traveled by private automobile in-

3

creased by 74 percent from 1960 to 1970, accounting for 94 percent of total urban passenger miles in 1970 compared to 88 percent in 1960.)[1] Remarkably little attention has been devoted, however, to the potential of those transportation modes "in-between" private automobile and conventional transit services such as rental car, minicar, taxi, dial-a-ride, jitney, car pool, and subscription bus. These modes, recently termed *para-transit* by the Urban Mass Transportation Administration (UMTA), have been neglected in comparison with scheduled bus and rail transit, although in many respects they appear to be equally important.

The 1972 National Transportation Study Report pointed out that from 1960 to 1970, "taxicabs increased their revenue passengers by 30 percent while commuter railroads held steady; rail rapid transit decreased by 6 percent, and the combination of bus and trolley coach decreased by 24 percent." It has been estimated[2] that in 1970 fleet taxicabs traveled almost twice as many revenue vehicle miles in the United States as the transit bus, rail, and trolley coach modes combined, and that with passenger revenues of over $2.2 billion they accounted for almost 60 percent of passenger expenditures on intraurban public transportation.[3] Furthermore, car pooling and subscription bus service have often been recommended as two of the most promising short-term alternatives to private automobile use for many home-to-work trips, offering a relatively high level of service while helping to reduce congestion, pollution, and energy consumption.

Much of the activity by the federal government in the area of public transportation has resulted from the Urban Mass Transportation Act of 1964, as amended through October 1970, which authorized the Secretary of Transportation "to provide additional assistance for the development of mass transportation systems." The act has provisions for assisting states and local public bodies through capital grants, loans, and technical studies grants, and also provides for research, development, and demonstration (RD&D) projects, managerial training fellowships, and university research and training grants.

As shown in Table 1, capital grant expenditure under the act has been heavily oriented toward conventional bus and rail services. Through June 1972, 29 percent of the $1.5 billion spent had been directed to scheduled bus services, 65 percent to the rail

---

[1] U.S. Department of Transportation (1972b).

[2] Table 6.

[3] The term *public transportation* is used here to refer to passenger transportation services which are available to the general public: rapid rail, scheduled bus, taxicab, rental car, and so on. Many of these services are, of course, privately owned and operated.

Table 1

Capital grant expenditures through June 30, 1972

Mode of transportation	Projects	Vehicles purchased	Cumulative total federal funds	Percent
			(millions)	
Rail	52	2,450	$ 953	65
Bus	205	10,431	432	29
Ferryboat and other	3	N.A.	88	6
TOTAL			$1,473	100

Source: U.S. Department of Transportation (1972c).

mode (with 90 percent of the rail funds confined to four cities: New York, Chicago, San Francisco, and Boston), and the remaining 6 percent to ferryboat and other services. Until very recently no capital grant money had been committed for para-transit services. However, an UMTA grant has recently been awarded to Ann Arbor (Michigan) for the purchase of vehicles and communications equipment for dial-a-ride services.

Almost half of the RD&D expenditure of approximately $216 million under the act (Table 2) has been committed to "new systems" (including personal rapid transit, tracked air-cushioned vehicles, dial-a-ride, and minicar), a further 42 percent for improving technology for existing bus and rail services, and most of the remaining 10 percent for service development for limited mobility groups. In the para-transit category, dial-a-ride and minicar have been the subject of RD&D projects under the umbrella of "new systems" (although dial-a-ride services have actually been provided by a number of taxicab operators for many years). In addition, two demonstrations of subscription bus service have been conducted in Peoria (Illinois) and Flint (Michigan), although again a number of private services have been operating successfully for several years. A variety of specialized para-transit services have also been considered under the service development activity.

Near-term federal support for public transportation services has therefore been granted primarily to traditional bus and rail services, products of an era of much lower personal income and car ownership (during the past fifty years per capita car ownership in the United States has increased by over 400 per-

Table 2

Selected data on UMTA research, development, and demonstration activity since 1966 (dollars in thousands)

Category		Amount	Percent
Bus technology, systems, etc.		$ 22,635	10.5
Rail:			
Rail rapid vehicles & systems	$25,947		
Commuter rail vehicles & systems	20,368		
Light rail vehicles & systems	195		
Rail supporting technology	22,120	68,630	31.8
New systems:			
Morgantown system	52,714		
Dulles PRTs	11,221		
Dual-mode system	1,097		
Dial-a-ride	7,400		
Development engineering, requirements analysis, etc.	28,344		
Tracked air-cushioned vehicle	2,512	103,288	47.8
Planning, analysis, and service development		21,599	9.9
TOTAL		$216,152	100.0

Source: U.S. Department of Transportation (1973b).

cent).[4] Furthermore, the methodology employed by current transportation planning studies is ill-suited for even considering public transportation services other than existing forms of conventional transit. Yet recent studies of the effect of variations in transit fares stress that travelers are currently more concerned about the level and type of service than they are about the fares.[5] These studies have pointed out the need for increased emphasis on service, both for conventional transit and for other public transportation services such as para-transit.

WHAT IS PARA-TRANSIT?

In attempting to distinguish carefully between the various important public transportation services, we have placed consider-

[4] Motor Vehicle Manufacturers Association (1972).
[5] Kemp (1973), Kraft (1973).

able emphasis on defining the particular service features which characterize individual modes. Table 3 (which is discussed in some detail in Chapter 12) compares eight different service characteristics for para-transit modes, the private automobile, and conventional transit. (The minicar service is included under short-term rental car, for reasons which will be discussed later.) There are, of course, many other aspects of transportation service which are less useful for distinguishing between modes but which are certainly very important in their own right, such as comfort, schedule and route information, reliability, and safety.

Because the information in Table 3 is relatively complex and difficult to assimilate, some of the important structure in the table has been used to formulate a simpler categorization of the modes. Changes in a particular service characteristic between modes have been flagged by arrows, and the modes have been arranged so that the transition in service characteristics across the table is as gradual as possible. The result is a spectrum ranging from the most personalized mode—the private automobile—to the least personalized mode—conventional transit. The para-transit modes fall in-between these two more common modes and progress from daily and short-term rental car (the closest to the private automobile in service characteristics) through taxi, dial-a-ride, and jitney to car pool and subscription services (the closest to conventional transit). This is not to imply that the trend across the table is strictly one of declining level of service—for example, scheduled bus or rail service with short headways may be regarded by many travelers as superior to car pool or subscription bus services which have inflexible schedules.

As shown at the top of the table, the para-transit modes can be grouped conveniently into three categories: those you hire and drive, those you hail or phone, and those for which you make prior arrangements with other travelers. There is, of course, considerable variation within each of these three para-transit categories with respect to possible service levels, ownership, operation, and regulation. Nevertheless, by using the characteristic service features of each category we can considerably simplify our discussion of para-transit services.

In treating individual modes and groups of modes in terms of their distinctive service characteristics, we have regarded the particular vehicle or technology used to provide the service as a secondary consideration. This approach is in marked contrast to previous research on minicars, for example, which has automatically associated this service with specially designed vehicles and sophisticated computer technology for vehicle scheduling.

Table 3

General service characteristics by mode

		HIRE AND DRIVE SERVICES	HAIL OR PHONE SERVICES		PARA-TRANSIT MODES	PREARRANGED RIDE-SHARING SERVICES		
	Private auto	Daily and short-term rental car	Taxi	Dial-a-ride	Jitney	Car pool	Subscription bus	Conventional transit
Direct route (DR) or route deviations (RD)?	DR	DR	DR	RD	RD	RD	RD	RD
Door-to-door?	Yes	Maybe	Yes	Yes	No	Yes	Maybe	No
Travel time spent as passenger (P) or driver (D)?	D	D	P	P	P	P/D	P	P
Ride shared (S), or personal (P)?	P	P	P/S	S	S	S	S	S
System routes fixed (F), semi-fixed (S), or variable (V)?	V	V	V	V	S	S	S	F
Access determined by prior arrangement (A), fixed schedule (F), phone (P), street hailing (H), or at user's discretion (U)?	U	U	H/P	P	H	A	A	F
Vehicle parking required (PR) or not (NP)?	PR	PR	NP	NP	NP	PR	PR/NP	NP
Convenient for baggage?	Yes	Yes	Yes	Maybe	Maybe	Maybe	Maybe	No

Similarly, research on dial-a-ride has concentrated until very recently on advanced scheduling and routing techniques and on the use of specially equipped buses to provide the service, although neither of these features seems crucial to the provision of dial-a-ride services.

Some rearrangement of Table 3 shows that several new hybrid services can be defined which are realistic (if uncommon) forms of urban transportation. If in moving from dial-a-ride to jitney, for example, we retain the door-to-door and variable route system of dial-a-ride but change from phone to hail as the means of access to the mode, we have a form of shared-ride service which might be termed *hail-a-ride*. Similarly, if we change the hail characteristic of jitney service to access by prior arrangement and make the service door-to-door, we have a service which might be termed *subscription taxicab*.

It should also be noted that the same vehicle can provide different services at different times of the day or week. In Haddonfield (New Jersey), for example, small buses are used to provide dial-a-ride, subscription, and scheduled services as warranted by the demand. Similarly, a taxicab can provide regular taxi, dial-a-ride, jitney, and subscription services when regulations include suitable fare and service standards for these different services.

A careful consideration of Table 3 has resulted in the following formal definition:

> *Para-transit services are those forms of intraurban passenger transportation which are available to the public, are distinct from conventional transit (scheduled bus and rail), and can operate over the highway and street system.*

While this definition includes such hybrids as the hail-a-ride service defined above, it excludes strictly private services such as the private automobile, and systems such as personal rapid transit which require their own guideway. Those hybrid services qualifying as para-transit have been considered here in connection with the more common para-transit services to which they are most closely related.

DEFINING THE ROLE OF PARA-TRANSIT

Urban policy making which aims to improve urban mobility while minimizing accompanying congestion, pollution, and energy consumption should consider means of influencing

- the demand for urban travel, through land use policies and such institutional arrangements as working and shopping hours

- the availability of urban transportation services, through RD&D, and through financing, regulatory, legal, and pricing policies

This study has been concerned primarily with the second category, and has investigated ways in which the availability of para-transit services should be influenced relative to the availability of other urban transportation modes. None of the para-transit modes investigated is new in concept; many have been operating in various forms in U.S. cities for several decades, and others have been studied extensively by means of simulation. However, this study is, we believe, the first to look closely at these modes together, to examine the relationships between them, and to estimate their potential roles with respect to each other and the transportation system as a whole.

The role of para-transit in urban transportation will be greatly influenced by two important and related aspects of public policy in the next decade: prices or other restrictions directed at the congestion, pollution, and energy problems; and financial assistance provided to public transportation.

Public concern over congestion, pollution, and energy consumption may eventually be reflected in restrictions or special taxes on various transportation modes which will significantly influence the roles played by para-transit and other modes in serving urban travel needs. These restrictions and taxes will presumably encourage the use of high occupancy, low polluting types of transportation. In addition, resistance to the construction of new transportation facilities seems likely to favor those modes which can operate over the existing street and highway system. These trends, taken with the para-transit operating experience accumulated in this study, suggest that the role of para-transit will be greatly increased during the next decade. In particular, expanded car pooling, subscription bus, and high-occupancy hail or phone services seem likely to be important supplements to improved conventional transit services in encouraging high occupancy travel.

The influence of financial assistance provided to public transportation will depend largely on the form of assistance adopted by the federal government. As Table 1 shows, recent capital grant activity has assisted conventional bus and rail transit and not para-transit, with the result that state and local governments have had a rather distorted view of the costs of expanding various transportation modes. Under the existing act, capital grants can be used to assist para-transit services which are organized under public ownership, but the para-transit services which are privately owned are ineligible for such assistance. Other forms of subsidy to public transportation (such as transportation stamps) which might be instituted in addition to or in place of the present program could be applied to all public transportation modes, whether publicly or privately owned, and might help to ensure that para-transit modes play their proper role in the provision of public transportation services.

Chapter 2

Hail or
Phone Services

SERVICE CHARACTERISTICS

The three major services included under the *hail or phone* category are regular taxi, dial-a-ride, and jitney. Regular *taxi* services currently play a major (if little studied) role in serving demand for intraurban travel, accounting for over one quarter of the urban trips made by public transportation (excluding commuter rail) and for almost 60 percent of urban passenger expenditures on public transportation.[1] Taxicab services are operated by the private sector, but are publicly regulated with respect to entry control, financial responsibility, service standards, and fares. As discussed in Chapter 7, taxicabs serve professional and managerial workers, area residents and nonresidents of all income ranges, and in particular the economically inactive (homemakers, students, and the unemployed, retired, or incapacitated) who have no private automobile alternative.

The term *dial-a-ride* is one of many terms—including dial-a-bus, demand jitney, shared cab, and computer-aided routing system (CARS)—which have been used over the last decade to describe shared-ride, door-to-door service which is requested by telephone. Although this form of service has been provided by some taxi-

---

[1] Table 6.

cab operators for over thirty years (such as the Badger Cab Company described in Chapter 8), it was first investigated by researchers only about ten years ago, and has since received a great deal of attention as a promising form of public transportation intermediate between the more common taxi and scheduled bus services.

As shown in Table 2, the Urban Mass Transportation Administration has devoted $7.4 million to research, development, and demonstration projects on dial-a-ride services, culminating in a demonstration project in Haddonfield (New Jersey) which is testing operating techniques and public response to the service. Other dial-a-ride systems frequently reported are those in Davenport (Iowa), Ann Arbor (Michigan), Batavia (New York), and more recently Rochester (New York), in the United States; and in Bay Ridges (Ontario) and Regina (Saskatchewan), in Canada. It should be noted that all these systems actually offer a variety of services in addition to dial-a-ride, including subscription and, in some cases, package delivery. One of the most valuable contributions these systems have made is to demonstrate innovation and flexibility in providing public transportation services.

Jitney services have all but disappeared from U.S. cities after having spread rapidly during 1914 and 1915 as a strong competitor to street railways. Usually provided by large automobiles or small vans, jitney service is limited to relatively fixed routes (with occasional variations), is not formally scheduled, and is hailed on the street by potential passengers. Because of political pressure from street railways, jitneys were regulated out of existence in most U.S. cities by the early 1920s, and only Atlantic City and San Francisco still have formal jitney services of any size. However, considerable potential for these services is demonstrated by the continued survival of a number of jitney services operating without formal authority in Chicago, Pittsburgh, Cleveland, Chattanooga, and probably other cities as well.

An important operating characteristic of taxi, dial-a-ride, and jitney services is that, regulations permitting, they can all be provided by a common and very pervasive public transportation vehicle, the taxicab. As a rule, however, regulations strongly discourage taxicabs from providing formal dial-a-ride and jitney services by:

- requiring the driver to obtain the permission of passengers in the vehicle before picking up additional passengers (with some exceptions at places and times of very heavy demand—sports arenas, during rush hours, and during snow emergencies, for example)

- providing very little if any fare reduction for shared-ride services

- prohibiting taxicabs from displaying destination signs

These and related taxicab regulations are in our view the most serious obstacles to near-term implementation of worthwhile taxi, dial-a-ride, and jitney services.

TAXICAB REGULATION

Entry controls

Entry controls may take the form of numerical limitations on taxicabs, restrictions on the number of taxicab firms, or regulations allowing monopolistic operations in specific jurisdictions, with a great deal of variation from city to city. New York City, for example, has a limit of 11,787 on taxicab medallions (with buying prices which have ranged up to $35,000 each) and approximately 15,000 livery vehicles and informal taxis, while Washington, D.C., has "free entry" for taxicabs and 8,500 taxicab licenses, almost three times as many per head of population as the next highest city, Atlanta (which also has free entry). Los Angeles, on the other hand, has much stricter entry control, and the number of licenses per head is less than one twenty-fifth of the number for Washington.[2] The city is divided into six taxicab zones, and in each zone just one cab company has exclusive rights to pick up passengers. Many cities grant similar exclusive franchises for taxicab services from airports and rail stations: all cabs may deliver passengers to these terminals but only the franchised company may pick up passengers, resulting in much unnecessary deadheading.

Financial responsibility

Financial responsibility, in particular public liability insurance, has been regulated since the 1920s when many operators went out of business with unpaid liability claims, leaving unfortunate passengers to bear heavy losses. (It is estimated that in New York City public liability insurance for 1967 accounted for over 6 percent of total fleet cab expenses of 28 cents per vehicle mile.) While no detailed analysis of taxicab insurance rates has been undertaken in this study, conversations with industry representatives indicate that wide variations exist in the costs of the

---

[2] Table 7.

required coverage, and that an astute operator can achieve substantial savings by shopping around for coverage or by self-insuring.

Service standards and fares

Regulations relating to service standards include vehicle design and safety standards, driver qualifications, and prescribed methods of operation, including number of passengers, conditions for shared-ride, the use of cab stands, cruising and hailing restrictions, and conditions under which service requests may be refused. Fare regulations deal with the level of fare and the rate structure, the two main alternatives being the meter system and the zone system. The implications of various existing procedures for the regulation of service standards and fares are discussed in some detail in Chapter 7.

The need for regulatory revision

The regulation of taxicabs has a profound and complex effect on the type and quality of services they provide. While few will question the need for regulations regarding financial responsibility, vehicle condition, driver qualifications, and fare structures, direct entry controls and limitations on the services taxicabs may provide appear to deprive the public of needed services with little discernible benefit. In our judgment, substantial improvements in mobility could be achieved in many U.S. cities by relaxing entry conditions and permitting taxicabs to offer a wide range of services, including dial-a-ride, jitney, package delivery, and perhaps others.[3] In New York, Pittsburgh, Cleveland, and probably other cities inadequacies in formal public transportation services have been great enough to give rise to and support extensive taxicab services operating without formal authority.

A more flexible fare system is also needed to reflect variations in the costs of the different services provided by taxicabs. Dial-a-ride and jitney services can be expected to cost less per passenger than regular taxi services, and all these services are likely to cost more in congested rush hours than they do in the off-peak. Even with free entry conditions, Washington, D.C., suffers from an undersupply of taxicabs in the rush hours, largely because the fare structure fails to reflect the increased costs of operation during those hours. While the number of taxicabs operating is at a maximum during the middle of the day, passengers search in vain for a cab at 5:00 P.M.

---

[3] See Chapter 13.

Expanded taxicab services may have some drawbacks, however. Many will argue that strong curbs should be placed on taxicab operations because of their relatively large contribution to congestion, pollution, and energy consumption per passenger mile (taxicabs in Washington, D.C., are empty for 40 percent of their trips).[4] And indeed, to the extent that present concern over congestion, pollution, and energy consumption eventually results in enforceable disincentives or restrictions on urban vehicle movement, taxicabs—like other classes of vehicles—must somehow account for their contribution to these problems.

Pricing schemes or restraints which accurately reflect the congestion, pollution, and energy effects of each type of vehicle and service should favor high occupancy services such as car pooling, scheduled and subscription bus, jitney, and possibly dial-a-ride over regular taxi service and private automobile use, and should also encourage advances in vehicle technology and maintenance. Such schemes need not result in severe curbs on taxicab operations, however, if they are accompanied by regulations which actively encourage taxicabs to improve vehicle utilization and maintenance and to provide higher occupancy services, such as dial-a-ride and jitney.

TAXICABS, BUSES, AND VANS

The higher-occupancy dial-a-ride and jitney services can, of course, be provided by buses or vans operated by private or public agencies quite separate from the taxicab industry. Advocates of dial-a-ride services have been debating the different ways of operating the service for many years,[5] and a variety of different operational forms of dial-a-ride can presently be found in the U.S. and Canada. The question of who should provide dial-a-ride and jitney services should be considered from two points of view: efficiency and institutional feasibility.

Efficiency

If we ignore for the moment the question of institutional feasibility, and set aside special services—such as those provided by volunteer social service organizations, health care agencies, hotels, and so on—we can point to the substantial advantages which appear to be offered by the taxicab on efficiency grounds.

---

[4] Table 15.
[5] Highway Research Board (1973).

Of the six dial-a-ride systems we have studied in the U.S. and Canada, the Royal Cab Company in Davenport (Iowa)—the only taxicab system among the six—operates with the lowest cost per vehicle hour and is the only one of the systems operating at a profit. Costs per vehicle hour of between $3.60 and $4.90 in Davenport provide a dramatic comparison with costs of over $15.00 per vehicle hour for the federal demonstration project in Haddonfield (New Jersey), with the other systems falling between these two extremes. The differences are due to labor costs, vehicle operating costs, and system productivity, with the Royal Cab Company performing very well in each category.

While labor conditions vary considerably from city to city, a sample of nine major cities has shown hourly wage rates for bus drivers consistently 50 percent higher than wage rates for taxicab drivers (tipping excluded).[6] Labor agreements for bus drivers also include strict shift rules and additional compensation for split shifts, while taxicab operators are subject to very few constraints of this type. The taxicab industry offers an excellent environment for part-time labor, including students, low-skilled workers, moonlighters, and so on. Further, many taxicab operators (including the Royal Cab Company) are changing from a wage and commission scheme of operation to leasing their taxicabs to drivers under certain constraints regarding central dispatching and maintenance. This mode of operation allows the driver considerable freedom to operate as a private entrepreneur in seeking patronage, completely relieves the operator of minimum wage problems, and has resulted in increased driver productivity.

Private ownership of taxicab operations does, of course, present to regulators and policy makers the complexities of involved organizational structures created for tax advantages, and the involvement of the operator in other related business activities. These activities and methods of operation, however, achieve efficiencies in private operations which publicly operated systems cannot easily match. Intricate business deals with equipment suppliers, gas stations, and operators of complementary modes are the stock-in-trade of the private operator, and contribute greatly to his ability to provide public transportation services at much lower cost than public agencies.

Private ownership of taxicab operations is also potentially important for minority-owned business and would presumably qualify for special assistance by the Small Business Administration. The relatively low capital requirements would enable

---

[6] Table 12.

members of minority groups with the necessary skills and interests to enter a business which serves the public (including
large numbers of minority group members) and has a genuine
profit potential. Perhaps the strongest testimony to the opportunities in this area is the existence (as described in Chapters 7 and
8) of flourishing taxi and jitney operations which serve poor and
minority group neighborhoods in many major cities without formal authority.

Encumbered as it is by regulations limiting service and fare
adjustment, the taxicab industry still has much more operating
flexibility than conventional transit, and in a few cities such as
Davenport (Iowa), Madison (Wisconsin), and Richmond (Virginia),
where regulations encourage dial-a-ride operation, taxicab operators have demonstrated their ability to provide well-patronized
dial-a-ride services without public assistance of any kind. Indeed, the Royal Cab Company has made substantial independent
progress in the development of computer dispatching procedures,
even as the federal government sponsored academic research in
this area. And while the use of larger vehicles, such as vans and
buses, for dial-a-ride would be advantageous at high vehicle
occupancy levels, the vehicle productivities of the operating
systems discussed here do not appear to be high enough to justify
the additional costs associated with these larger vehicles over
those reported for taxicabs.[7]

In the case of jitney services, very little information is available on the costs of alternative operating schemes. To the best
of our knowledge, no taxicab companies in the U.S. are presently
providing formal jitney service (although shared-ride service
provided by taxicabs along some urban corridors in rush hours
closely approximates jitney service). Indeed, at present only Atlantic City and San Francisco still have formal jitney services of
any size, and in both of these cases the service is provided by
an operator licensed specifically for jitney service. Taxicab vehicles with adjustable route signs do provide extensive jitney
service in Caracas (Venezuela), however, accounting for 17 percent of the daily trips in the city,[8] and there seems to be no
reason why much of the taxicab fleet in the U.S. could not be
permitted (with suitable regulation) to operate in a similar way.

In the absence of reliable cost data on jitney operations, we
can only repeat some of the points made in our discussion of
dial-a-ride services. Taxicabs have advantages in cost per *vehicle*
mile over systems using larger vehicles, but only knowledge of

---

[7] Table 27.
[8] Table 36.

ridership will permit comparisons on the basis of cost per *passenger*. Until some experimentation is conducted with jitney service under typical urban conditions, we will have to reserve judgment on the efficiency of alternative ways of providing it.

Institutional feasibility

It must be recognized that there are major institutional obstacles to efficiency in many areas of urban transportation, and while, as a practical matter, we may have to accept many of them in the short run, it is important to keep in mind how they affect our urban transportation system. Inefficient taxicab regulation, already discussed, is one of the most important constraints on the expansion of efficient para-transit services. Perhaps equally important is the program of federal assistance for public transportation in urban areas, now proceeding at almost $1 billion per year under the Urban Mass Transportation Act described earlier. Substantial congressional pressure exists for expanding this program to include operating subsidies, and provisions have already been passed making part of the Highway Trust Fund available for mass transit.

Capital grants and loans under the act are limited to "states and local public bodies and agencies thereof" and consequently cannot be used to aid private operators directly. Some cities have recognized, however, that capital equipment obtained by a public body with federal assistance can be leased to a private operator for a nominal amount, thus passing on the subsidy, and Richmond (Virginia), for example, is considering a scheme of this type for assisting its bus operator. A similar scheme could in theory be adopted to assist taxicab operations, although as far as we know this has never been attempted.

Federal subsidies which are used exclusively for capital expenses for bus and rail services will certainly not encourage (and may actively inhibit) other forms of public transportation. Even within the context of conventional transit, the restriction of subsidies to capital equipment has been strongly criticized on efficiency grounds in an analysis by Tye (1973):

> The analysis indicates that the arguments for restricting direct mass transit aid to capital expenses are without basis. Furthermore, a grant to subsidize capital but not operating expenses encourages wasteful premature replacement, overcapitalized technology, and inadequate maintenance, which are likely to be extremely costly.

Federal assistance under the UMTA act also carries with it the labor constraints of section 13(c), which reads as follows:

(c) It shall be a condition of any assistance under section 3 of this Act that fair and equitable arrangements are made, as determined by the Secretary of Labor, to protect the interests of employees affected by such assistance. Such protective arrangements shall include, without being limited to, such provisions as may be necessary for (1) the preservation of rights, privileges, and benefits (including continuation of pension rights and benefits) under existing collective bargaining agreements or otherwise; (2) the continuation of collective bargaining rights; (3) the protection of individual employees against a worsening of their positions with respect to their employment; (4) assurances of employment to employees of acquired mass transportation systems and priority of re-employment of employees terminated or laid off; and (5) paid training or re-training programs. Such arrangements shall include provisions protecting individual employees against a worsening of their positions with respect to their employment which shall in no event provide benefits less than those established pursuant to section 5(2)(f) of the Act of February 4, 1887 (24 Stat. 379), as amended. The contract for the granting of any such assistance shall specify the terms and conditions of the protective arrangements.

In practice, this constraint has made it essentially impossible for UMTA to provide any assistance to public transportation which might result in reduced employment for conventional transit services, even though some of the transit services being provided might be highly inefficient. For example, the federal dial-a-ride experiment in Haddonfield used small buses and employed bus drivers largely because of section 13(c), when taxicabs might have been a better choice on efficiency grounds. Local officials may therefore be placed in the uncomfortable position of having either to support an inefficient transit system or do without federal funds for public transportation.

Many of these problems might be overcome if transportation assistance were provided in some form which would allow state and local authorities freedom to use the funds in the manner best suited to their areas. Any federal or state monitoring of expenditures under such a scheme would, however, still have to recognize the existence of *local* institutional constraints. In practice, the choice of an operator to provide dial-a-ride or jitney service in a particular area may turn as much on the competence and reliability of potential operators, or on the feasibility of obtaining necessary regulatory changes or local financing, as on concerns for efficiency.

In Ann Arbor, for example, the taxicab operators declined the opportunity to provide dial-a-ride service, and then sued the city (unsuccessfully) when a publicly owned service was initiated. In Canada, the dial-a-ride services have been closely coordinated with conventional transit services under public control, and little thought appears to have been given to the possibility of taxicabs operating these services.

The taxicab industry in the United States is often maligned as unstable (driver turnover is very high) and ill-suited to providing the carefully tailored para-transit services found in Batavia, Haddonfield, and Ann Arbor. It seems rather unfair to generalize in this way, however; in Richland (Washington) and Arlington (Virginia), for example, the taxicab operators cooperate closely with local government in providing subsidized services for limited-mobility groups.

In summary, we suggest that, in the interest of efficiency, government and regulatory bodies should actively encourage taxicab operators to provide needed para-transit services such as dial-a-ride, jitney, and subscription—in particular, specialized services for the elderly, handicapped, and other limited-mobility groups. Where the taxicab industry is unable for one reason or another to provide these services, however, other private or public agencies might be sought (or established) to provide the services.

PROMISING INNOVATIONS

The above discussion suggests that a number of specific innovations should be considered in providing para-transit services of the hail or phone category. The implications of these suggestions need to be explored further; many have never been tried (to the best of our knowledge), and, where they have been, virtually no evaluation has taken place.

- *Relax entry controls on taxicabs—*
  Relaxation of numerical limits on taxicabs and lifting of franchise restrictions should be considered as a means of expanding services and reducing deadheading (adequate compensation would have to be made wherever existing operators incur losses due to relaxed entry controls).

- *Peak-hour and shared-ride fares for taxicabs—*
  A new fare structure should be designed which reflects variations in the costs of taxicab operation between peak and off-peak hours and distinguishes between direct route taxi service and the shared-ride services (hail-a-ride, dial-a-ride, and possibly jitney).

- *Destination signs for taxicabs—*
  Taxicabs should be permitted to display destination signs to facilitate hail-a-ride and jitney services.

- *Subsidies to taxicab services—*
  At least two mechanisms for subsidizing taxicab services appear to have immediate promise: the distribution of tokens or stamps at reduced rates to target groups, and the acquisition of vehicles by a public body (with UMTA assistance) for lease to private operators.

- *Improved dispatching techniques—*
  Higher vehicle utilization might be achieved for taxi and dial-a-ride services with improved dispatching techniques. The use of computer technology to assist dispatchers is a promising innovation.

- *Advance request services—*
  Special rates might be offered for taxi and dial-a-ride service requests made several hours in advance of the desired trip time, since advance requests should facilitate dispatching, particularly for shared-ride services.

- *Package delivery—*
  In some cities taxicabs play an active role in package delivery, while in others they are prohibited by regulations from providing these services. The possibilities for allowing taxicabs to expand package delivery services should be explored.

Chapter 3

Ronald F. Kirby
Robert G. McGillivray

Hire and Drive Services

SERVICE CHARACTERISTICS

At first sight, the two para-transit modes referred to as *daily rental car* and *minicar* bear little resemblance to each other. *Daily rental car* describes the hiring of automobiles by rental agreement for a period of at least a day and at most a year, as provided by Hertz, Avis, Budget, and a number of other well-established private rental car companies. The term *minicar*, on the other hand, has been used to describe a proposed system of small electric cars which could be accessed by a computerized check-out system, driven for a short trip, checked in at one of the many system terminals, and then checked out shortly afterward by another user. The attractions of the minicar are described as the low polluting, low congestion properties of the vehicles, the labor savings achieved by the "drive-it-yourself" feature, and low per trip costs stemming from the expected high utilization per vehicle.

While the daily rental car and minicar services seem dissimilar, according to the characteristic features listed in Table 3 the services are indistinguishable. Consequently, we have considered the minicar concept as a special case of a more general service form, *short-term rental car*, which includes all rental car services available by the trip, by the hour, or by other periods shorter than one day.

The special features required by the minicar concept are an extensive terminal system, small low polluting vehicles, an extensive vehicle redistribution capability, and rapid check-out and check-in procedures. The specialized vehicle and the computerized redistribution system given so much attention in previous research do not appear to be absolutely essential to the minicar concept, and should be considered, along with other alternatives, as particular ways of providing the service if sufficient demand exists.

It is already possible (but not usual) in some areas to rent an automobile for less than a day, usually for four-hour time increments. Further, Hertz and Avis already have special clubs in which members are prescreened and able to bypass much of the long check-out procedure. As the daily car rental companies grow and diversify their services, it appears that the distinction between the daily rental car and short-term rental car services is likely to become less and less apparent.

DAILY RENTAL CARS

Daily rental cars are perhaps the most efficiently operated of all the para-transit services considered in this study. A growing market of business and tourist travelers (particularly the latter) has resulted in expansion and improvement of the rental car industry from 100,000 vehicles ten years ago to roughly 340,000 vehicles today. In sharp contrast to taxicab services, the absence of restrictive regulation of daily rental cars has resulted in vigorous competition between new and established firms and in diversification of service in response to demand.

A variety of special services are currently being offered by the daily rental car companies: clubs for special services (such as the Hertz Number One Club); daily, weekend and monthly rates; check-out and check-in at different locations; different vehicle sizes and types; and so on. Indeed, it is difficult to see how involvement by public bodies in the provision of this service could do other than hinder the progress being made by the private sector.

With respect to the transportation system as a whole and to congestion, pollution, and energy consumption, the behavior of the daily rental car and the private automobile is essentially the same; once the vehicle is checked out, it may be used as the traveler wishes. The daily rental car does not suffer from dead-heading problems and consequently should gain some advantage over taxicabs under pricing schemes or restrictions designed to curb congestion, pollution, or energy consumption. But there seems to be little potential for increased vehicle occupancy, since rental cars are currently used by businessmen and tourists with diverse travel patterns.

PROSPECTS FOR SHORT-TERM RENTAL CARS

The short-term rental car service, which provides vehicles by the trip, is not an operating mode in the United States and has been evaluated in this country only by some limited simulation studies. Some experience is available from Europe, however: a fleet of 35 Simcas with a unique prepayment scheme (the *TIPmètre*) has been operating in Montpellier, France, since 1971, and a system of small electric vehicles, *Witkars*, is in an advanced stage of planning for Amsterdam, Holland. The Montpellier experiment has not been encouraging: rental fees do not seem adequate (the user is charged only while the engine is running, not while the vehicle is parked and is inaccessible to other users); costs appear to be higher and utilization lower than expected; and it has been difficult to reserve parking space for the vehicles. The Amsterdam system is still at too early a stage for any evaluation but should eventually provide another useful case study.

The following discussion is offered as a judgmental evaluation of the short-term rental car concept at a time when very little operational experience is available. The reader is invited to consult the more detailed discussion of operating experience in Chapter 10. Our observations must clearly be tempered since usage of new transportation services is notoriously difficult to predict, and the short-term rental car concept certainly has not yet been given a fair trial.

Internal circulation

The major application considered to date for short-term rental cars—internal circulation within a business or commercial district—is aimed at travel demand which is now served largely by walking or taking a taxi. Simulation studies at the University of Pennsylvania have suggested a high degree of substitutability between taxi and minicar services, and the Montpellier system has diverted a large number of walk trips to rental cars, but very few from the private automobile. Under a pricing scheme which accounted fully for congestion, pollution, and energy effects, it is questionable whether short-term rental cars could compete with walking or with using taxicabs. Rental cars can be used only by those willing and able to drive, and since they must be redistributed in this application they lose much of their advantage over taxicabs.

Another consideration is the possible expansion of the shared-ride taxicab services discussed earlier, including dial-a-ride, hail-a-ride, and jitney. None of the demand studies undertaken to date has considered the degree of substitutability between short-term rental cars and these other para-transit services, and it seems likely that it would be relatively high.

As described in Chapter 10, some of the Pennsylvania research also considered the possibility of applying the short-term car rental concept to low-income groups. The idea was to set up the minicar service in an area in Philadelphia on a demonstration basis. However, the applicability of short-term rentals to the transportation-disadvantaged is limited in a number of ways: many people in these groups cannot drive, many live in areas where theft and vandalism would be problems, and many could not pass screening tests for credit and driving records. An alternative joint strategy of increasing automobile ownership (possibly through income supplements) and improving taxi and dial-a-ride services appears to be much more promising.

Feeder service

The second application for short-term rental cars, studied by Stanford Research Institute, is to use them as a feeder service to line-haul bus or rail transit. Here, as in the internal circulation case, it appears that alternative feeder services may leave too small a market for a large-scale rental car system. Taxi, dial-a-ride, jitney, scheduled feeder bus, subscription taxi or bus, car pool, private automobile (both driver and passenger), bicycle, walking, and, where the line-haul mode is bus transit, the extension of line-haul routes—all are possible means of access to line-haul transit service. Again the ability of a short-term rental car system to attract users appears to be suspect. The need for high utilization of the system, and the problem of shuffling vehicles from one location to another according to the incidence of customers, cast considerable doubt on the viability of the service.

A single location

Most of the proposals for short-term rental cars envisage a

large system of vehicles and terminals which would probably be under public ownership and operation. We suggest that a more promising initial application of short-term rental cars might be one based at a single high density residential location, with the rented vehicle being used for trips presently made by private automobile. The rented automobile carries higher insurance and administrative costs per vehicle than the private automobile, but these could be offset by higher utilization, to the point where the cost per trip for some users might be considerably lower than they would incur with their own automobiles.

The mix of transportation demands at a large apartment complex, for example, might permit very efficient use of a rental car fleet, especially where business and commercial centers lie within walking distance. Residents who need an automobile only for shopping and recreation travel might complement those who presently need a second car only for work trips. This service could be offered initially at independent locations with the possibility of cooperative agreements as warranted to permit check-in and check-out at different locations.

The utilization question

The key to successful short-term rental car services appears to be high utilization. If a large vehicle fleet, a large terminal system, and extensive vehicle reshuffling are required for a small number of users in the internal circulation application, the service will have difficulty competing with taxi, hail-a-ride, and jitney services, no matter how sophisticated the scheduling and vehicle technology. As a substitute for the private automobile, the short-term car rental service will have to achieve sufficiently high utilization to overcome the costs of system management and high vehicle insurance. In our judgment, the chance of success in the latter application is greater than in the former.

Many urban residents must spread the fixed costs of owned automobiles over only a few thousand miles of travel per year, so the potential exists for reducing these costs by some form of automobile sharing. In high density areas, this could presumably be accomplished with minimal inconvenience as far as vehicle availability is concerned. However, there are several important service attributes which are unique to the private automobile: ability to leave personal items in the vehicles, personal choice of vehicle and accessories, personal decisions on maintenance and vehicle condition, and so on. Even if substantial savings could be realized through short-term car rental, would they compensate for the loss of the personal attributes of the private automobile? This question can be answered only by experience.

PROMISING INNOVATIONS

Considerable innovation has taken place over the last decade or so in the provision of *daily* rental car services. Hertz, Avis, Budget, and a number of other private companies have expanded and diversified their services, offering a variety of special rates as well as package deals with airlines, hotels, and other organizations. Rental car services are still generally limited, however, to rental periods of at least a day, and relatively few locations are available for checking the vehicles in and out. The use of rental car services on a trip-by-trip basis within urban areas is thus virtually impossible, so the short-term rental car service discussed in this chapter must still be considered an untried concept and a possible candidate for innovation. In our judgment, potential for innovation in the provision of hire and drive services lies in the following general areas.

- *Short-term rental car services—*
  Any viable application of short-term rental car services in the U.S. would have to be considered a major innovation. As discussed above, daily rental car companies might offer these services at one high-density residential or business location as an experiment, and expand the service to other locations as warranted by demand.

- *Special vehicles—*
  The use of small electric vehicles has often been proposed for rental car services, particularly short-term services where the vehicles would be used for short trips. Developments in the problem areas of congestion, pollution, and fuel consumption might create special advantages and privileges for such vehicles over the next decade. (The vehicles would also be available, however, to such competing services as taxi, dial-a-ride, and jitney, and might even be purchased for private use.)

- *Automated check-in and check-out—*
  The check-in and check-out procedures for rental cars can be very time-consuming, and the development of automated procedures is a promising innovation in this area. Such innovation would be particularly important for any short-term rental car applications.

- *Cooperative arrangements for check-in and check-out—*
  Rental car services are currently available at only a very few locations. Arrangements with gas stations, stores, or other businesses to permit vehicle pick-up and drop-off would make the service much more accessible to potential users.

- *The club concept—*
  Special service clubs have been formed by some of the daily rental car operators (the Hertz Number One Club, for example). This concept would be useful for short-term rental car services, particularly where automated check-in and check-out procedures necessitate careful screening of users.

Ronald F. Kirby

Chapter 4

Prearranged Ride-Sharing Services

SERVICE CHARACTERISTICS

The term *prearranged ride-sharing* has been used in this study to describe services in which a number of travelers make an agreement to travel together on a regular basis. The two most common forms of this service are the *car pool* and the *subscription bus,* which in the spectrum of para-transit modes are closest to conventional transit service, as shown in Table 3. They can usually be operated at relatively high levels of vehicle occupancy and at quite low cost per passenger.

Services of this type involve some route deviation to pick up and drop off individual travelers, but, since this is usually confined to relatively minor collection and distribution patterns at the beginning and end of the trip, it accounts for only a small proportion of the total trip time. The schedule is fixed by agreement of the travelers and is essentially inflexible from the point of view of an individual traveler. Prearranged ride-sharing services can be considered superior to conventional transit in the sense that they provide essentially door-to-door service and the major portion of the trip is an express ride. They have the strong disadvantage, however, of schedule inflexibility, although for many of the trips this is not a problem since the travelers are already tied to fixed schedules because of trip purposes (work schedules, entertainment schedules, and so on).

A VARIETY OF OPERATING MODES

Of the three categories of para-transit services shown in Table 3, the prearranged ride-sharing category surely has the greatest diversity of current operating modes: common forms of car pooling, company-sponsored van pools, company-operated bus services, privately owned and operated bus services, services provided by neighborhood cooperatives, specialized school bus services with part-time or volunteer drivers, and, to some small degree, services provided by taxicabs and by conventional transit operators. The variety of service levels provided illustrates clearly that public transportation can take many forms other than scheduled bus and rail services, and that, when the incentives exist, the private sector can respond to certain types of travel demand with carefully tailored services.

Costs

The costs of providing prearranged ride-sharing services vary substantially with the mode of operation.[1] Specialty Transit, a privately owned and operated subscription bus service for workers at the McDonnell Douglas plant in St. Louis, operates rather like a large car pool with one of the passengers serving as driver and fare-collector (for which he receives compensation). The buses are parked during the day at the plant, so there is no deadheading, and costs are remarkably low at just over one cent per passenger trip mile.[2] Car pools and van pools operate at between 1.6 and 3.0 cents per passenger trip mile, but other forms of subscription bus service, using charter buses from transit authorities, can cost as much as 5.5 cents per passenger trip mile—the Washington Metropolitan Area Transit Authority (WMATA) recently requested an increase in the charter rate which would raise the cost of the Reston subscription bus service to over 8 cents per passenger trip mile.[3]

Perhaps the most crucial element in the costs of these services is labor; bus operator costs make up over half the cost of the Reston service and, at almost 3 cents per passenger trip mile,

---

[1] Table 48.
[2] The number of *passenger trip miles* produced by a service is given by the sum of the direct over-the-road trip lengths for the trips served.
[3] Table 58.

amount to more than twice the *total* cost of the Specialty Transit service in St. Louis. A cost analysis done for WMATA points out that the drivers and buses provided for the Reston service are not needed for other services during the remainder of the day, and that Reston subscribers must therefore pay the full cost of staff and equipment. WMATA goes a little further, however, in refusing to pass on any of its capital and operating subsidy to the Reston service and actually plans to charge a charter fee over and above the cost of providing the service. Comparison of Specialty Transit and the Reston service demonstrates the dramatic cost advantages of using a part-time driver.

A close look at costs per passenger trip mile for subscription services reveals other important influences on these costs—such as operating speeds and the degree of deadheading involved. Specialty Transit, for example, appears to produce over three times more passenger trip miles per vehicle hour than the Reston service,[4] partly because it operates at substantially higher speed and partly because it avoids the severe deadheading problems of the Reston service (for which buses average 58 miles to provide a 22 mile productive trip).[5] While speeds can be improved by the use of express lanes, and deadheading can be reduced somewhat by locating depots closer to the ends of the trip, for services like Reston some deadheading is unavoidable, and strict shift rules for drivers limit the labor savings which can be achieved. The "drive and park" forms of prearranged ride-sharing (car pools, van pools, and part-time bus services) thus have substantial inherent cost advantages over services provided by conventional transit authorities.

Regulation

Regulation of bus and van subscription services has not created any major difficulties to date. Interstate services are regulated by the Interstate Commerce Commission, and intrastate services by public utilities commissions. Safety and equipment standards, proper licensing, and financial responsibility have been required, but no major restrictions have been placed on the services which can be provided. Existing services have generally prevailed in suits of unfair competition filed by competing services. The Wayward Bus in San Francisco successfully fought off a court challenge by Greyhound, for example, and the Monarch Associates car pool scheme was authorized to operate certain routes

---

[4] Ibid.
[5] Washington Metropolitan Area Transit Authority (1973).

distinct from the conventional transit alternative.[6] School bus services are a rather special case in that state regulations usually specify vehicle and safety standards, and also usually limit the services to school trips.

Many of the smaller van pool services are not considered public utilities and are exempt from regulation. Share-the-expense car pools are similarly free from regulation and at present are covered by standard automobile insurance. If car pool riders were charged a fee, however, it appears that the service would have to be registered as a commercial enterprise and would then be subject to strict regulation and presumably higher insurance rates.

Financing

Owned and operated almost entirely by the private sector, subscription van and bus services have generally not been eligible for the subsidies and special privileges accorded most conventional transit operations. Along with taxicabs, these operations must pay fuel taxes (from which their conventional transit competitors are exempt) and are, of course, ineligible for direct assistance under the Urban Mass Transportation Act. Some subscription operations are subsidized in other ways, however: the National Geographic Society in Gaithersburg (Maryland) pays more than half the cost of providing subscription bus service for its employees living in Washington, D.C.; and the Golden Gate Bridge, Highway, and Transportation District helps to organize and subsidize a number of "Commute Clubs" in San Francisco.

Special privileges and services

Prearranged ride-sharing services can be expected to fare very well under well-designed charges or restrictions directed at the congestion, pollution, and energy problems. In fact, services like Specialty Transit are considerably more efficient than conventional transit because they avoid the deadheading problem, though they do pose special parking requirements. Van pools and car pools share this advantage, and as long as the pricing or restriction scheme reflects congestion, pollution, and energy effects accurately, prearranged ride-sharing modes are likely to gain substantial advantages over private automobile, taxicab, and even scheduled bus services.

In our judgment, experience with the variety of existing pre-

[6] Chapter 11.

arranged ride-sharing services provides valuable insight for conventional transit operators. To attract and retain ridership, extensive tailoring of bus services to demand has been found essential. Reliability, guaranteed comfortable seating, and even coffee and donuts are common service features, and routes and schedules are modified constantly as demand changes. Access is facilitated by route and schedule information, advertising, and various schemes for soliciting and matching riders.

By comparison, conventional bus transit often oppears an uninteresting, stereotyped, and poorly marketed service, and it would seem that substantial improvement in transit ridership could be achieved solely through innovation in management, operation, and marketing of existing facilities. Perhaps public assistance to conventional transit services should be directed in part to these areas of transit operation, with capital grants and operating subsidies disbursed so as to encourage innovation in service provision rather than simply to prop up existing services.

PROMISING INNOVATIONS

Suggestions for encouraging worthwhile prearranged ride-sharing services can be summarized in the six general categories defined below. Further evaluation of the various alternatives in these categories is needed to permit more precise recommendations on their potential; a good first step in this direction would be a more comprehensive evaluation of the variety of services already in operation.

- *Subscription services provided by transit authorities—*
  Transit authorities should consider providing specialized subscription services on routes which have suitable travel demand characteristics. The services could be provided in cooperation with neighborhood or company organizations and, if well-designed, could contribute substantially to increasing bus ridership.

- *Subscription services provided by taxicabs—*
  For shorter trips made on a regular basis, such as home-to-work trips, taxicabs could provide inexpensive subscription services to small groups of travelers. This type of service deserves greater attention from taxicab operators, and from local regulatory bodies.

- *Broader use of school buses—*
  The possibility of using school buses to provide additional services should be investigated. Travel to and from banks, shopping

centers, and health care facilities might be provided for special groups, such as the elderly and the handicapped, for example.

- *Special organizational schemes—*
Prearranged ride-sharing services can often be provided cheaply and efficiently by private operators, neighborhood cooperatives, and private firms. Government and regulatory bodies should be prepared to encourage and possibly assist the formation of well-designed services of this kind.

- *Matching of riders—*
Manual and computerized procedures have been used by some companies to facilitate the formation of car pools and van pools. These techniques could be used on a much larger scale to include several companies in adjacent buildings and also to group travelers within residential areas.

- *Special privileges—*
A variety of special privileges should be considered for high occupancy car pool, van pool, or subscription bus services. Use of express lanes, parking privileges, and even direct financial subsidies could be implemented, possibly in conjunction with firm disincentives for private automobile travel.

Chapter 5

Ronald F. Kirby
Robert G. McGillivray

The Role of
Para-transit

In discussing the potential role of para-transit services in urban transportation systems, we should note at the outset the degree to which urban passenger travel is currently dominated by the private automobile. Almost 90 percent of average weekday person trips in U.S. urban areas are made by private automobile, and this percentage is expected to increase over the next two decades.[1] With conventional bus and rail transit and commuter rail services accounting for most of the remaining trips, para-transit modes are currently used for only one or two percent of all trips made in urban areas. How significant a role are para-transit services likely to play in urban transportation systems when they serve only such a small fraction of urban trips?

We suggest that the importance of para-transit services over the next decade will stem from their ability to bridge the significant gaps between the transportation services offered by the private automobile and those offered by conventional transit. While 111 million Americans have driver licenses, there remain almost 100 million who cannot drive an automobile, and 20 percent of American households do not own automobiles.[2] The travel demand of much of this group is not sufficiently dense to

---

[1] Table 62.
[2] Motor Vehicle Manufacturers Association (1972).

be served economically by conventional transit, and many of those who cannot travel as auto passengers may have to rely on such para-transit services as taxi and dial-a-ride (in some cases using these modes as feeder services to conventional transit). Even those who have a private automobile often find themselves without it; in particular, business and tourist travelers rely to a large extent on rental cars and taxicabs.

Increased vehicle occupancy during peak hours to reduce congestion, pollution and fuel consumption can be achieved only to a limited extent by conventional transit. As a practical matter, urban bus systems simply do not have the system capacity to expand peak-hour services substantially in the near future. Para-transit services such as jitney, car pool, van pool, and subscription bus offer a promising means of reducing congestion, pollution, and fuel consumption effects per passenger trip while maintaining a relatively high level of mobility. It should be noted, of course, that higher occupancy travel in itself has only limited potential for reducing overall pollution and fuel consumption. While passenger cars account for almost 80 percent of all vehicle miles traveled on U.S. streets and highways,[3] 58 percent of passenger car miles are for family business, education, social activities, and recreation, and are already conducted with an average of more than two occupants per vehicle.[4] It is doubtful that transit or para-transit services (such as dial-a-ride) can achieve savings in pollution or fuel consumption per passenger trip for low density trips in this latter category; if such trips are to be made, the private automobile may well be the most efficient mode for the purpose.

PRICES AND RESTRAINTS

Our assessment of the role of para-transit comes at a time when several specific pricing, subsidy, and restrictive policies are being seriously considered (and in some cases, implemented) for tackling congestion, pollution, and energy consumption. If implemented on a large scale in the next decade, such policies could have a substantial effect on the role of para-transit and other modes in urban transportation systems. These policies range from a variety of sophisticated pricing schemes,[5] to parking or gasoline taxes or rationing, reduced transit fares, traffic signal priorities, use of express lanes, and exclusion of automobiles

---

[3] Ibid.
[4] U.S. Department of Transportation (1973a).
[5] Vickrey (1973).

from certain areas of the city. They appear to vary greatly with respect to their ease of implementation and their impacts, and considerable controversy still exists over their relative merits and demerits.

Some problems will almost certainly arise from imperfections in whatever pricing or restriction schemes are used. A heavy parking tax which shifted car poolers to taxicab or jitney service, for example, might have a perverse effect in reducing mobility while increasing the congestion, pollution, and energy consumption associated with those trips. Similarly, totally excluding other vehicles from an underutilized express bus lane may sacrifice potential benefits with respect to mobility, congestion, pollution, and energy consumption. There are also significant costs inherent in just the implementation of some of these schemes, and, perhaps more importantly, there are some serious equity questions.[6]

We suggest that to the maximum extent possible, pricing, subsidy, or restrictive policies should be sought which reflect accurately the negative effects of each vehicle and service type, so that within these policies all forms of transportation service can be encouraged to seek their full role in serving urban transportation demand, even where this will result in active competition between different services. Without the guidance of this goal, public concern over congestion, pollution, and energy consumption may be used in the next decade to justify expenditures on conventional transit services for travel needs which could be met more cheaply and efficiently by para-transit services.

POTENTIAL MARKETS FOR PARA-TRANSIT

Para-transit modes have demonstrated their suitability for serving a number of areas of the market for urban transportation services, and appear to have additional (but untested) potential in these and other areas of the market (Table 4). In particular, four major types of travel demand which are discussed below stand out as areas where expanded para-transit services could make an impact in the near term on urban transportation problems. The estimation of potential ridership for para-transit services is presently handicapped, however, by a generally poor state-of-the-art in understanding travel behavior (particularly in response to new services), together with considerable uncertainty about the manner in which the negative effects of different

---

[6] Zettel and Carll (1964).

Table 4

General markets for para-transit services

	PARA-TRANSIT MODES						
	Hire and Drive Services		Hail or Phone Services			Prearranged Ride-Sharing Services	
Demand Characteristics	Daily Rental Car	Short-Term Rental Car	Regular Taxi	Dial-a-Ride and Hail-a-Ride	Jitney	Car Pool	Subscription Bus
Spatial (location/trip length)	• Airport access • All types	* All types	• Short trips • CBD oriented • Airport access •* Small cities •* Line-haul feeder	• Short trips •* Intrasuburb •* Intersuburb •* Intra-CBD * Small cities •* Line-haul feeder	•* Tourist corridors * Home-to-work corridors * Business/commercial corridors	•* Long trips •* Home-to-work corridors * Line-haul feeder	•* Long trips •* Home-to-work corridors * Line-haul feeder
Temporal	• All hours	* All hours	• Midday (10 A.M.–4 P.M.) •* Early morning/late evening •* Peak hours	• Midday • Early morning/late evening	• Peak hours • Midday	•* Peak hours	•* Peak hours
Demographic (traveler/trip purpose)	• Out of town visitors • Business trips • Recreation trips	* Residents living in medium to high density areas—all trip purposes	• Professional & managerial workers • Out of town visitors • Housewives shopping • Low income * Limited mobility groups	•* Housewives shopping & personal business •* College students * Business trips * Limited mobility groups	•* Tourists * Workers of all income groups * Business trips • Shopping trips	•* Workers of all income groups •* Shopping in low-income areas	•* Workers of all income groups • School trips

KEY: • Present
* Additional potential
CBD=Central Business District

vehicles and services are likely to be transferred into prices or restrictions in the near future.

High density home-to-work travel

Perhaps the most important para-transit application for the immediate future is the increased use of high occupancy para-transit modes such as car pool, subscription bus, and jitney for high density home-to-work travel. By attracting the private automobile driver out of his car, these para-transit modes together with improved conventional transit can reduce the congestion, pollution, and energy consumption associated with each trip while offering high levels of service. Such services have succeeded in attracting between 20 and 70 percent of the home-to-work trips along their service routes in some locations.[7] Car pool and subscription bus services are particularly well-suited for relatively long home-to-work trips where trip origins and destinations are concentrated in small areas, desired arrival times are concentrated within a short period, and private automobile travel faces such disincentives as peak hour prices or restrictions, severe highway congestion, or parking difficulties.

The U.S. Department of Transportation (1973a) reports nation-wide average automobile occupancies of 1.4 for work trips and 1.9 for all purposes, with 74 percent of home-to-work automobile trips having only one occupant in the vehicle. Given the density of home-to-work travel, this suggests that substantial potential exists for increased vehicle occupancy for these trips. Trip purposes other than work include family and social travel where, of course, vehicle occupants are relatives or friends. Increased vehicle occupancy for home-to-work travel, on the other hand, involves matching travelers who may presently be strangers. How the public will respond to attempts to achieve such matching is rather uncertain at present; response seems to have been good within companies where travelers have some way of knowing about each other, but large scale matching attempts such as the Boston WBZ radio station scheme (Chapter 11) have not been successful to date.

Low density travel demand

Travel demand in many low density suburban and small town areas and at late evening and early morning hours in larger areas is often too low to support conventional transit service. While much of this travel demand is and will continue to be served effi-

---

[7] Table 51.

ciently by the private automobile, considerable potential exists for serving those who cannot use automobiles and those who might be persuaded by a high quality alternative service to do without a second or third automobile. Experience to date suggests that this travel demand can be served efficiently by dial-a-ride and regular taxi services, both of which can be provided by taxicabs (regulations permitting). Substitution of these types of service for conventional transit may be a good means of relieving existing transit services of unprofitable parts of their operation.

Limited mobility groups

A particular case of low density travel demand is that of limited mobility groups—traditionally classified as the young, the old, the unemployed, the poor, and the handicapped. Obviously *children* have inherently less mobility than adults and are dependent to a large extent on other family members or friends to transport them as passengers. Some of this travel demand might be served instead by expanded taxi or dial-a-ride services, especially where no scheduled transit is available at the time and place needed.

Elderly persons, whether living alone, with families, or in homes, are not necessarily limited in mobility. They may drive, have cars, have families who are willing to drive them, or have financial means to hire someone to take them. However, many elderly people are quite dependent upon the whims of others, and many are of limited financial means. Furthermore, some of them continue to drive beyond the time when they are physically able to do it well, largely because they lack suitable alternatives. The elderly have comprised an inordinately large fraction of mid-day ridership in dial-a-ride trials in Haddonfield, Batavia, and elsewhere. It is well known that elderly people value comfort, door-to-door service and ease of getting in and out of the vehicle. They are also more concerned than the average traveler with low fares,[8] and appear to have considerable flexibility with respect to time of travel. Taxi or dial-a-ride services which offer cheaper fares for travelers willing to adjust their schedules somewhat to suit the taxi or dial-a-ride operator appear to have considerable potential for serving the elderly.

The *unemployed* and the *poor* are considered to have limited mobility because they lack money to travel, are ignorant or inept in getting and keeping credit and a driver's license, or because inferior urban transit services are provided to their residential areas. The purpose in improving the mobility of both of these

---

[8] Kemp (1973).

groups is largely to give them access to employment. Much rail and bus rapid transit has been sold partly on its potential for serving the unemployed and the poor, while even a cursory inspection of the service provided shows that it is the middle- and upper-income suburban dwellers who benefit most from the service. In our judgment, the cheapest and best way to serve these groups is to facilitate their access to automobiles (either as drivers or passengers), *and* to make available such para-transit services as taxi and dial-a-ride—with subsidies if socially desirable.

The *handicapped* present a unique mobility problem. Different handicaps require different facilities. The blind and deaf are ambulatory but may require orientation aid. Other handicapped people, such as persons confined to wheelchairs, have no orientation problems but cannot climb stairs or use escalators. Unless special hardware is developed, many handicapped persons of all types will be unable to use transit or drive automobiles. Specially-equipped services provided by Yellow Cab of Phoenix and by the Haddonfield and Batavia dial-a-ride systems have shown that these para-transit services can successfully serve short trips by handicapped persons who need personal aid finding or getting in and out of vehicles. Serving travel demand for the handicapped by means of specially-equipped and subsidized para-transit modes would clearly be a great deal cheaper than equipping all the vehicles and stations of an urban transit system to serve them, and indeed would almost certainly result in a higher level of service.

In automobile-oriented cities of the U.S. where transit services are quite limited in frequency and coverage, one could characterize all urban residents *not having an automobile available* for use when they want it as having limited mobility. This may be due to automobile utilization within the household, where use of an automobile by one member may leave others with no automobile available. Even where such residents find transit convenient for going to work, it is still difficult for them to travel to parts of urban areas not served by transit. Para-transit services such as taxi and dial-a-ride can bridge these gaps between the services provided by private automobile and those provided by conventional transit.

In summary, limited mobility groups comprise three classes of members: those who could drive themselves around if an automobile were available, those who cannot drive but are able to use para-transit or conventional transit, and those who are inhibited from using an automobile, para-transit, or conventional transit because of physical handicaps. Improved access to an automobile would probably provide the most dramatic improvement in mobility for the first class, and the second class can be greatly assisted by increased opportunity to travel as auto passengers. However, taxi and dial-a-ride services can also play a major role in improving the mobility of these classes, especially where it is deemed socially desirable to subsidize them. Travel demand for the third class can be served cheaply and efficiently by specially-equipped taxi or dial-a-ride services, which can be provided by the operator of regular taxi or dial-a-ride services, or by health care or other agencies, whichever method is most convenient for each situation.

Feeder service to line-haul transit

The effectiveness of conventional transit services can be greatly increased by para-transit feeder services designed to collect and distribute transit passengers. Well-coordinated para-transit and transit services have improved the coverage and service levels of public transportation in Canada, and should have increasing application in the U.S. as major cities upgrade their line-haul transit systems. Car pool, subscription bus, and, to some extent, dial-a-ride and taxi services appear to be suitable for integration with line-haul transit, especially where high-speed line-haul service is provided along relatively few corridors with widely spaced stations.

Where para-transit feeder services are provided to a higher capacity mode, considerable potential exists for improved integration of the services. For example, any combination of trips made by different modes and linked together into an overall journey would be a candidate for a joint fare system designed to permit the traveler to transfer from one mode to another without paying a new fare each time. Such schemes have been implemented successfully in Hamburg (Germany) and are presently receiving serious consideration in the United States.

Several other aspects of intermodal integration deserve attention. Transferring from one mode to another can be greatly facilitated by well-designed transfer terminals which minimize the physical inconveniences involved. Coordinated routes, advertising, and traveler information are other features of a well-integrated system. Finally, considerable potential exists for package deals between different travel modes. Major airlines already offer joint air fare and car rental packages—why not offer similar arrangements with coordinated taxi and bus services?

Mobility in business and commercial districts

Mobility within business and commercial districts can be

greatly improved by well-regulated para-transit services, particularly taxi, dial-a-ride, and jitney. These services are well-suited to serving the short business and shopping trips made within business and commercial districts: taxi service offers the speed and schedule reliability required by the business traveler, and dial-a-ride and jitney services can provide the low cost mobility sought by the shopper. As discussed earlier, short-term rental cars have also been proposed for circulation within business and commercial districts, although we consider this application to be of doubtful potential.

Other important applications of para-transit include providing access to intercity travel terminals (where rental car and taxi presently account for 25 to 30 percent of the trips) and serving the demand for recreational travel by means of rental cars, sightseeing tours, and jitney service within tourist areas. In general, the availability of para-transit services can be varied much more readily than that of conventional transit. Para-transit consequently can respond more flexibly to variations in travel demand by time of day, week, or year, as well as to longer-term secular trends in the demand for public transportation.

Chapter 6

Robert G. McGillivray
Ronald F. Kirby

Recommendations for Action

One of the major frustrations to transportation analysts studying the operation and potential of para-transit modes is that while many ideas for expanding para-transit services have been suggested in recent years, there has been very little implementation of them. Perhaps the current problems with pollution and energy consumption will provide the impetus for expanding at least those services which could help relieve these problems—such as car pool, subscription bus, and shared taxicab service. This chapter delineates the next steps which we believe need to be taken to promote worthwhile applications of para-transit modes in urban transportation systems.

Some para-transit applications are understood well enough to require only the dissemination of carefully prepared guidelines to planners, policy makers, and active or potential para-transit operators. Others need the impetus of a demonstration program, because operating experience has been too limited to permit full assessment of their viability or to convince local planners and policy makers of their potential. And further exploratory research is needed where the potential of certain services is very uncertain and where regulatory and operational questions are not well enough understood.

For prearranged ride-sharing—the most promising near-term

service—effort should be directed at providing guidelines to policy makers, planners, and operators, based on the extensive operating experience accrued to date. The guidelines should deal in particular with possible incentives designed to reflect the efficiency of these services with respect to congestion, pollution, and energy consumption. The use of express lanes, parking privileges, and various forms of financial subsidy appear to be promising policies in this regard.

The hail or phone category offers greater mobility through taxi, dial-a-ride, and jitney services, and increased use of the higher occupancy dial-a-ride and jitney services could help reduce the congestion, pollution, and energy effects per trip. A demonstration program is needed to evaluate the potential of more flexible taxicab operations and to test the operation of jitney services. The latter services could be provided by taxicabs, small buses, or vans, and might even be offered informally by private automobiles.

The hire and drive category appears to be least in need of immediate attention as far as various levels of the government are concerned. Daily rental cars are operated efficiently by the private sector, and the short-term rental car concept does not seem promising enough to warrant high priority RD&D. Daily rental cars are rather like the private automobile where congestion, pollution, and energy consumption are concerned, and the only potential for improvement, apart from service restrictions, appears to lie in ongoing technological developments for the private automobile.

The activity proposed above should be supported by a continuing research program centering on the complex financing, regulatory, labor, and insurance issues related to para-transit services and on an evaluation of the much debated need for para-transit software and hardware development. In addition, this program should be accompanied by a broad project devoted to data analysis for urban transportation services, which would draw together new and existing cost and ridership data, develop inferences which these data permit, recommend the collection of new data as needed, and provide continuing empirical guidance for policy making in urban transportation.

GUIDANCE TO PLANNERS, POLICY MAKERS, AND OPERATORS

It is clear that there is widespread ignorance regarding all forms of para-transit. Local officials seem determined to replace failing private bus operations with subsidized conventional transit operations. With few exceptions no consideration is given to replacing conventional transit with taxis, jitneys, dial-a-ride, or the like, partly because current planning methodology is inadequate for considering para-transit alternatives. Subscription service is almost never organized by transit operators. Coordination of para-transit with conventional transit has never been seen as the role of areawide transportation authorities, even those with rather broad powers over roads and transit.

State highway or transportation departments generally have nothing to do with taxis or other para-transit modes. UMTA capital grants are not available directly for privately owned para-transit services. Jitneys have, by and large, been regulated out of existence by archaic city statutes. Taxis are traditionally controlled by cities or airport authorities, and are subject to the decision of local regulatory bodies whose interests are often strongly influenced by political considerations in other areas.

But there are some bright spots. Various forms of taxi, dial-a-ride, jitney, car pool, and subscription services have all performed very well in some locations in the country. We suggest that, based on these experiences and some ideas for changing local rules and institutions, manuals could be developed for planners, policy makers, and local operators for demonstrating or establishing promising para-transit services.

Manuals or how-to-do-it books, in addition to documenting successful operations elsewhere, could detail the steps or milestones for establishing service. There should probably be a manual for each potential para-transit mode, though there would clearly be overlapping materials and perhaps a set of materials common to all modes. They should probably be designed to permit additions to be made readily, based on the rapidly changing body of experience.

A number of different topics which should be included in the guidelines are discussed in turn below. Some of these topics are also mentioned in the final section of this chapter as appropriate for further research. Of course, any program to disseminate guidelines on these topics will need to keep up with new research as it is completed. Some effort needs to be undertaken in the short term, however, just to make current knowledge available in a suitable form.

Regulation

One topic for such a manual is the regulation of operators. Entry and discontinuance of firms and individuals would need careful consideration. The problem of service refusal and other unpleasant aspects of providing service should be discussed at length, since they are the primary reasons that services operate without formal authority in many U.S. cities. Regulatory conditions which have been evolving for new services, such as dial-a-ride and van or bus pools, should be specified for cities contemplating the implemention of these services.

Also covered under the heading of regulation would be the subject of pricing or rate-making. Cab drivers, in particular, have been observed not to provide service where the rate structure is unfavorable; this is illustrated by the scarcity of cab service during rush hours (Table 15). Rates should be such that needed service is provided, and operators should not have the right to delay people in emergency or distress situations. Fairness and honesty must be part of the service. The pros and cons of meters, zones, ride-sharing, and fare differentials by time of day must be explained. Procedures and rules for keeping track of operations would also need specifying, so that revenue and cost analysis could be used to indicate where rates or service levels were too high or too low.

A topic closely related to pricing policy is the demarcation of service boundaries, coverage, and basic service levels. In some demand-actuated cases this would be specified by service area, response speed, and route deviation permitted. For other services it would mean routes, frequencies, and reliability in maintaining those frequencies on the routes. It is restated here for emphasis that people appear to consider schedule frequency and reliability at least as much as travel time and price in making travel decisions.

Labor

Labor, work rules, and union participation pose extremely volatile, practical problems in all areas of transportation. Transit and para-transit are no exception. Taxicabs are operated by drivers under varying degrees of worker status, including fully unionized fleet drivers, nonunion drivers who lease cabs and operating rights for a period, and self-employed owner-drivers. Bus systems are usually operated by union drivers under working hour rules which make the provision of bus transit quite expensive relative to taxicab services. In particular, the provision of buses and drivers just for the peak hours and the operation of low-demand routes can build up heavy transit losses which are frequently passed on to the general taxpayer.

The federal subsidy program to bus and rail transit is specifically concerned with the labor problem. As we have discussed earlier,

An electrically-powered Witkar shares city streets with automobile and street-car traffic in Amsterdam, Holland.

Rental car companies often provide free transportation to and from off-airport terminals in order to minimize their use of high-cost airport space.

Computerized check-out procedures provide express service for customers with *Wizard of Avis* credit cards.

Arlington Red Top Cab Company

CONDITIONS OF ENTRY

1. PAY FEE OF 0.50.
2. DISPATCHER WILL ASSIGN ALL PASSENGERS.
3. A LIMIT OF ONE PASSENGER PER TAXICAB, EXCEPT FOR PRE-FORMED GROUPS TRAVELING TOGETHER AS A PARTY.
4. DRIVERS MUST REMAIN IN CABS EXCEPT TO LOAD BAGGAGE.
5. DISPATCHERS ARE IN CHARGE--THEIR INSTRUCTIONS ARE TO BE FOLLOWED.
6. DRIVERS WILL NOT SOLICIT PASSENGERS.
7. DEPART WITH PASSENGER AS SOON AS LOADED.

AIRPORT MANAGER

Michael Kemp

A supervisor (centre front), four telephone receptionists (rear), and two dispatchers receive and assign service requests for 165 taxicabs of the Red Top Cab Company in Arlington, Virginia.

While strict rules for taxicab operation are displayed prominently at Washington's National Airport (left) . . .

disputes between dispatchers and drivers still arise and have to be settled by police officers (below).

Michael Kemp

A convenient map and free teleph (left) assist users of the dial-a-service provided with 17-passe buses (below) in Haddonfield, Jersey.

Atlantic City Press Bureau

Ten-passenger vehicles provide jitney service along Pacific Avenue in Atlantic City, New Jersey. The vehicle number (61) and shift designation (C3) can be seen on the rear window of the vehicle.

Ervin

At the U.S. Department of Transportation matching boards are used to facilitate the formation of car pools.

Car pools with four or more passengers share express lanes with buses along the Shirley Highway in the Washington Metropolitan Area.

Ervin

Van pools have become a popular means of home-to-work travel for employees of the 3M Company in St. Paul, Minnesota.

A club-like atmosphere often develops as regular van pool riders get to know each other.

Ervin Poka

Passengers change buses at a transfer point of the subscription bus service between Reston (Virginia) and Washington (D.C.). In return for a free ride a "busmeister" (foreground) collects fares and insures that routes

section 13(c) of the Urban Mass Transportation Act of 1964 basically says that existing organized labor cannot be disturbed by UMTA capital grant projects. Guidelines are needed on the rules and practices of bus and taxi systems, the interpretation of the UMTA act by both the Labor and Transportation Departments in practice, and, in particular, the likely interpretation regarding shared cab or other para-transit experiments. Is it possible for the federal government to assist a more efficient para-transit service if this will result in a cutback of conventional transit services?

The role of labor in subscription buses and car pools deserves explicit attention in such guidelines. Casual observation suggests that allowing a passenger to drive a subscription bus (much as a strictly organized car pool operates) would enable subscription service to expand enormously at low cost; while having to use unionized bus drivers to provide just peak hour services can be prohibitively expensive. The full ramifications of this hypothesis should be explored. We need to know the existing situation, the barriers to more flexible rules, and the impacts of instituting them.

Management and organization

Astute management, in a number of respects not presently evident in existing transit operations, should be emphasized. Financing and insurance, maintenance procedures, provision of route and schedule information, integration with other services, and advertising should all be considered in some detail. Managerial techniques found valuable in existing efficient para-transit systems could be presented in a case-by-case format. Managerial controls over hardware and labor and over interfaces with governmental bodies and other suppliers should be covered.

Many factors outside the immediate control of the operator can affect the provision of para-transit service. It seems desirable to establish a relationship with other para-transit and transit operators in the area, and with highway operating and control agencies. For example, if subscription buses were allowed to use a bus facility from which private autos were excluded, agreements would be needed with the bus operator for sharing arrangements and priorities and with the traffic and police departments regarding enforcement of penalties for misuse.

Where a new para-transit operation is to be established essentially to replace an existing service, it will be necessary to determine how to phase out the existing service legally and smoothly. In many areas the value of a para-transit business is considerable, since monopoly rent or profit, as well as ordinary profit, is reflected in the selling price or capitalized value of the operation. Governments have shown themselves to be remarkably inept at purchasing declining bus or rail transit operations. What will they do about arranging compensation for a valuable taxi or limousine business which stands to lose a great deal from a proposed regulatory change?

A number of possible organizational forms ranging from a totally public to a completely private organization are possible for para-transit operations. Probably neither extreme is optimal—the former usually has built-in disincentives to perform well at low costs, while the latter has no incentive to *ever* provide non-profitable service, no matter how vital to the public interest. It is important to recognize that every para-transit vehicle is its own revenue and cost center to a great degree and that maximum advantage can be taken of this fact. Drivers *will* work on a commission basis where patronage provides revenue. If the costs of setting up and running a maintenance facility exceed those of contract maintenance of equal quality, maintenance should be contracted out. Leasing of vehicles may be better than ownership. If individual owner-operators provide as good a service as a large scale operator, they should be allowed to do so.

Guidelines on options for relationships between city government, state government, and operators need to be developed. The potential of special governmental units, such as districts or authorities, as well as state and city roles, should be covered. Integration of para-transit with scheduled transit, highways, parking, and intercity terminals are important components which operators and governmental agencies must negotiate. Current and potential methods for using special incentives to ensure a satisfactory level of para-transit service and for monitoring the financial responsibility of operators and the safety of their performance should be primary regulatory concerns of state and local government.

Planning

Planning and financing new facilities and operations is usually to a large degree a state or local responsibility. The task often involves obtaining and allocating federal funds, such as those available under the various components of the federal highway program and the UMTA capital grants program. However, para-transit is presently neglected in both state and local planning and in federal funding. No metropolitan or state transportation study has seriously analyzed trips made by different types of para-transit. Taxi trips are sometimes counted as part of origin-destination or traffic volume data, but no serious policy analysis has been done on a metropolitan or state basis. Para-transit services are seldom considered in the design of metropolitan transportation systems, largely because the role they could play in urban transportation is poorly understood and because they are much less visible than large-scale conventional bus and rail systems. Guidelines pointing out the potential of para-transit services should therefore be particularly valuable to planners.

DEMONSTRATIONS

Demonstrations are designed to find answers which cannot be reliably inferred from previous experience. Once found, that information can provide guidance to potential operators of the new service in other cities. It is important to recognize that a demonstration project may be a success even if the service being demonstrated does not perform as expected, since that information itself will be valuable in policy making.

A number of problems may arise if the duration and scope of the demonstration are too limited. First, people may resent losing a service to which they have become accustomed. Second, people may not react to a limited-term program as they would react to a long-term program or to one without a known termination date. Further, if the operating area of even a very good service is too small, it may be of limited use to travelers. These problems suggest that demonstrations should be confined to relatively small areas which are to some degree self-contained but are, at the same time, representative of larger areas where the service might be implemented. It would then be easier to implement a more or less permanent local demonstration of the service under consideration.

Monitoring responses to changes requires careful design, and collecting reliable information at a relatively low cost is crucial. If the demonstration causes changes of residence or changes in the number of private automobiles owned, reactions are extremely difficult to track, since they tend to be relatively long-term and are related to many other variables besides para-transit service, such as socioeconomic status, stage in life cycle, age, and family size. Determining the type of data to collect, the sample sizes, and the number and timing of the observations, is critical to a worthwhile demonstration, and should be treated fully in a design project carried out prior to the demonstration itself.

The most important subject which this study recommends for

a demonstration program is the provision of flexible para-transit services by taxicabs—including dial-a-ride, jitney, and subscription services, as well as package delivery—under carefully designed regulatory and pricing schemes. Since taxicabs are owned and operated by the private sector and are regulated by local authorities, much of the support for testing new service forms must clearly come from the local level. Reports of taxicab hearings in Washington, D.C., indicate that active interest in service innovation has existed for some time, and that some changes in the airport franchise scheme, rules for shared riding, and fare structures are likely in the near future. As a result, the opportunity for monitoring a permanent, large-scale, regulatory change may arise without any preliminary efforts to interest a community in the idea. A continuing para-transit research program which carefully monitored such activities would minimize the need for expensive, large-scale demonstration programs.

FURTHER EXPLORATORY RESEARCH

The preparation of up-to-date guidelines on the questions of para-transit regulation, labor, management, and organization should be supported by continuing research directed at these areas. Three other activities might also be undertaken as part of a near-term exploratory research program for para-transit: continued low-level investigation of the untried short-term rental car concept; analysis of ridership, performance, and cost data of new and existing para-transit services; and continued investigation of the need for para-transit hardware and software development.

Short-term rental cars

As discussed in Chapter 3, the short-term rental car concept is not among the most promising para-transit modes for expanded application in the near future. The most appropriate approach for the immediate future would probably be continued low-level exploration of this service concept. Considerable exploratory research has, of course, been completed in this country, one foreign demonstration has begun in France, and another is planned for Amsterdam. Although the service may be a desirable one under some conditions, whether it can be properly organized and priced to provide good service without requiring excessive subsidies is very much in doubt at this point.

The exploratory research we have suggested should keep abreast of foreign developments in the short-term rental car concept, and should also consider the two specific short-term rental car applications discussed in Chapter 3—i.e., short-term rental car services based at one or more locations, and a large-scale system of services for internal circulation within a business or shopping district. In evaluating the potential of these services the analyst should consider fully the alternative services available, particularly the private automobile and the various forms of shared-ride cab service.

Data analysis for intraurban travel

The conclusions of the present study were based largely on sketchy data on ridership, performance, and cost gleaned from a variety of operating para-transit systems. While some firm indications were obtained on the potential of para-transit modes, a great deal of uncertainty still remains, particularly with respect to such untried services as jitney and short-term rental car, and such untried policies as congestion pricing schemes and other restrictions aimed at alleviating our congestion, pollution, and energy problems.

A continuing, coordinated project of data analysis for intraurban travel is needed to monitor the ridership, performance, and cost characteristics of existing para-transit services, of special demonstrations, and of major policy changes such as fuel taxes or rationing, parking taxes, and travel restrictions. A variety of existing services and demonstrations can provide valuable empirical guidance for policy making if additional data gathering and analysis are carried out. Present fuel shortages may provide special opportunities for this kind of analysis, since new fuel prices and conservation incentives are apt to affect travel behavior in a manner never before studied.

Para-transit hardware and software needs

The present study has addressed the question of para-transit software and hardware development only briefly. It appears from this investigation that a number of areas warrant further investigation as possible candidates for new or reoriented research, development, and demonstration (RD&D). In particular, taxicab vehicle design, metering devices for single-fare and shared-taxi services, and computer dispatching for hail or phone services should be considered in the near future.

Recommendations have often been made that RD&D should be directed at the design of a special purpose vehicle for taxicab services. Although a strong argument can be made that regular automobiles are not of optimal design for taxi services, so many other vehicles of various sizes and designs are available both within and without the United States (some of which are used for taxi services) that it has been difficult to see vehicle design as a high priority item. With the current concern over pollution and fuel consumption, however, the argument for directing attention to taxicab vehicle performance carries some extra weight. Taxicabs provide services which are quite crucial to urban mobility and at the same time are perhaps the worst of all transportation modes with respect to congestion, pollution, and energy consumption per passenger trip mile (Table 58). Since restrictions on taxicab services could significantly reduce the level of urban mobility, an effort to improve vehicle performance seems warranted and should be considered a candidate for RD&D in the near future.

The development of computer software to permit automated vehicle dispatching for dial-a-ride services has been the subject of considerable government RD&D over the past ten years. Private companies have also been active in this area, particularly the Los Angeles Cab Company and the Royal Cab Company in Davenport, Iowa. These firms appear to have made substantial progress with automated scheduling procedures, although they report that a great deal still needs to be done. These reports suggest that there is little coordination of effort and that there may be unnecessary duplication. Consequently, a general review of the requirements for this area should receive high priority for continuing research.

PART TWO

A REVIEW OF PARA-TRANSIT OPERATING EXPERIENCE

The second Part of this book comprises a set of seven supporting chapters, written by various members of the study team. The first five—Chapters 7 through 11—describe in some detail the operational experience accrued to date with each of the principal para-transit modes. Chapter 12 draws together the most important features of this experience to identify the similarities of and differences between the modes. Finally, Chapter 13 discusses existing features of the public regulation of para-transit modes, and suggests regulatory innovations.

It has been our intention in these chapters to provide a succinct overview of the roles which para-transit services *currently* play in urban transportation in the United States, using the most up-to-date information available. Some para-transit modes (taxicab services, for example) are already very pervasive, and operational experience varies greatly from place to place. For such modes we have attempted to characterize both the national industry and its pattern of operation, and interesting variations within this national picture.

In other cases (dial-a-ride services and short-term rental cars, for example), current operational experience is limited to a handful of experimental systems. Case studies have been presented for the most important of these systems, both domestic and foreign, but in experimental situations operating changes tend to be made relatively frequently. The descriptions of case studies, therefore, present a snapshot at one particular point in time, usually early 1973. The reader should be aware that subsequent developments may have modified some of the data in our case studies.

Chapter 7

Michael A. Kemp

Taxicab
Service

INTRODUCTION

In this chapter the words *taxi, taxicab,* or *cab* are used inter-changeably to denote a form of transportation service by which any members of the general public may hire a vehicle and driver to convey them directly by road from one point to another as specified by the passengers. Typically the contract for the hire is informal and ad hoc, made by street hail or by telephone. Most commonly, passengers pay a fare for this service based on the distance (and sometimes duration) of the ride.

The taxi is predominantly an urban mode of travel, but suburban and rural communities often do have some taxi provision, par-ticularly where other forms of common carriers provide a very low level of service. Taxicabs are usually some form of auto-mobile, either standard production models (often adapted for use as taxis), or purpose-built. As will be described, the ownership, the methods of operation, and the regulatory environment of the taxi industry, all vary from city to city.

In most major cities, shared-ride service (in which additional riders may be taken on after the original hiring by the first party) is specifically prohibited by local ordinance. A particular form of shared-ride service along relatively fixed routes is often characterized as *jitney* service, which is discussed separately and in more detail in Chapter 9. A second form of shared-ride cab provides door-to-door service in response to telephone requests for a number of independently-traveling parties, by means of route deviations to accommodate the varying demands. This is a form of *dial-a-ride* service, and as such it is discussed in Chapter 8.

Our definition of taxicab service is sufficiently broad to em-

Table 5

Typical service characteristics of taxis

Service attribute	Comparison with other modes
Start from and end at any location	roughly the same as A, better than T
Availability at all times of day	no better than A, better than T
Waiting time before journey	short, but uncertain; no better than A, at least as good as T
Overall average speed in vehicle	at least as good as A, better than most T
Perceived money price per passenger-mile	higher than both A and T
Fare known before the trip?	usually not; roughly the same as A, poorer than T
Privacy and general comfort	poorer than A, better than T
Ability to do other things while traveling	at least as good as A, better than T
Ability to carry luggage	roughly the same as A, better than T
Convenience in coping with luggage	better than both A and T
Need for parking space at destination	at least as good as A, roughly the same as T

KEY: A denotes a typical private or rental automobile
       T denotes typical bus or rail transit service

brace so-called *public limousine* service. A limousine is a motor vehicle, usually large and prestigious, hired with chauffeur by the hour, typically under a contract made some time in advance; it is not hired by street hail. The service is relatively expensive and is mostly patronized by the affluent, by upper levels of business, or for some special occasion such as a wedding or funeral.

The so-called public *airport limousine,* however, is not a form of taxicab as the mode has been defined here. It usually operates a scheduled, relatively fixed-route service between an airport and the central business district of the city. It is much more akin to bus transit service or to jitney service than it is to taxicab service.

How do the service characteristics of a typical urban taxi system compare with the service provided by public transit and by the private automobile? Table 5 summarizes those aspects of service which, in varying circumstances, will probably enter into the traveler's decision whether or not to travel by cab. The contents of this table represent our general impressions of typical taxi service; much of the table will be substantiated subsequently in this chapter. In particular, we believe the most salient service characteristics of taxis to be the relatively high average travel speed (point-to-point) on urban journeys of, say, five miles or less; the route and time flexibility; the relatively high fare; the freedom from parking; and the general level of comfort and convenience which the cab provides.

THE SIZE AND ORGANIZATION OF THE U.S. CAB INDUSTRY

In all U.S. cities of which we have any knowledge, taxicab service is publicly regulated to some degree. The purposes and nature of this regulation are discussed later in the chapter; we will simply observe here that in several cities, particularly large ones, the regulatory agency defines two distinct types of taxi service:

- cabs licensed to accept hires by any method, and in particular, by street hail. For the purposes of distinction, we shall refer to these as *fully-licensed taxicabs.*

- taxis licensed to accept prior bookings only and, in particular, not allowed to accept street hails. As is the practice in a number of cities, we shall refer to these as *livery vehicles.* Limousine service, for example, is a form of livery service. When livery vehicles accept street hails, as is common practice in some areas, they are operating illegally and are sometimes designated *gypsy cabs.*

In addition to these two types of license, there exist in some of the larger cities significant numbers of completely unlicensed vehicles offering cab service illegally, particularly in poverty areas poorly served by fully-licensed vehicles.

The national trade association of the fully-licensed cab fleet operators is the International Taxicab Association, formed in 1966 by a merger of the American Taxicab Association, the Cab Research Bureau, and the National Association of Taxicab Owners. This association annually aggregates some data from its members which can be used to derive a broad estimate of the national size of the industry. Wells and Selover (1972) present the latest available figures (for 1970) derived from this source. It is estimated that there were roughly 7,200 fleets or associations operating in 1970 in some 3,300 local jurisdictions, with approximately 170,000 fully-licensed cabs. To these figures must be added an unknown (but much smaller) number of nonfleet owner-driver vehicles, the livery vehicles, and the illegal operations. The total size of the industry, therefore, is difficult to gauge. In New York City, the livery vehicles (roughly 15,000) outnumber the 11,787 fully-licensed cabs.[1] In Chicago there are 327 liveries to 4,600 fully-licensed vehicles, and it is estimated that there are an additional 300 illegal cabs operating in ghetto areas.[2]

However, even ignoring the unknown numbers of nonfleet and livery vehicles, the size and scale of operations of the fleet cab industry is impressive when compared with scheduled transit. Table 6 shows that taxi fleets operate almost three times as many vehicles as the U.S. transit industry (even counting individual rail cars) and in 1970 realized gross passenger revenues of roughly $2.2 billion, exceeding the combined revenues of the different transit modes by $600 million. It is obvious that taxicabs provide a very significant proportion of urban public transportation services.

The organization of the industry

At the level of the individual business concern, there exist principally *three* different organizational arrangements in the taxi industry—fleets, owner-drivers, and rental agreements. The majority of fully-licensed taxicabs operate in *fleets;* that is to say, they are owned by a proprietary organization (a single owner, a

---

[1] Lazar (1971).
[2] Kitch et al. (1971).

Table 6
National estimates of the fleet taxicab industry, 1970

	Fleet taxicab	Transit			
		Total a	Bus	Rail b	Trolley coach
Number of vehicles/cars (thousands)	170	61	50	11	1
Revenue miles traveled (millions)	3,420	1,883	1,409	441	33
Revenue passengers (millions)	2,380	5,932	4,058	1,746	128
Passenger revenue ($ millions)	2,200c	1,639	1,194	415	30
Mean employment (thousands)	110d	138	n.a.	n.a.	n.a.

KEY: a the total may differ from the sum of individual modes of travel due to rounding

b includes streetcars, rail rapid transit (subway and elevated), and grade-separated surface rail, but *not* commuter rail traffic

c this is significantly higher, but more credible, than the estimate of $1,411 million made by the Transportation Association of America (1973)

d believed to be understated

Sources: Wells and Selover (1972).
American Transit Association (1972).

corporation, a partnership) which operates more than one vehicle. Typically, the proprietor will operate a dispatching service for telephone hails (a proportion of the fleet cabs may be equipped with two-way radios) and centralized maintenance and repair facilities; sometimes, however, these functions are carried out by a separate enterprise.

Fleet operators in New York City, for example, have been described in the following way:

Taxicab fleets are normally a multicorporate structure, consisting of

- a single management company, which usually operates the taxicabs, receives the fare income, and pays the operating and maintenance expenses with a few exceptions. The net income of the management company is distributed, usually on a per cab basis, to the taxicab-owning corporations.

- various taxicab-owning corporations, which typically own two or three taxicabs, and pay such expenses as licenses, insurance, interest and minor other unpooled expenses. They are normally owned by the same principals who own the management company, but in several instances include corporations owned by others.

In some instances real estate companies owning the garage rented by the fleet are controlled by the same principals who own the fleet. The rent charged in such situations . . . bears a close relation to the depreciation, taxes and interest related to the garage.

This corporate structure affords several advantages, including facilitating the pooling of separately-owned taxicabs into larger fleets, limitation of liabilities for accidents to each taxicab-owning corporation, and possible reductions in federal income taxes.[3]

Fleets predominate in the industry for two principal reasons. First, as we shall describe subsequently, in several cities the cab regulations restrict the taxi supply entirely to franchised fleets, and in the majority of cities the regulations operate to inhibit the entry of nonfleet autos into the market.[4] Second, there are financial economies of scale in fleet operation, particularly with regard to insurance, financing, maintenance, and dispatching costs.

Fleets hire drivers who are compensated by some form of output-related incentive scheme, usually a commission on the gross receipts of their cabs. Customarily, this commission rate is on the order of 40 percent to 50 percent, sometimes varying with driver seniority. In addition, fleet proprietors often provide insurance, welfare, pension, and other customary benefits.

A smaller number of fully-licensed cabs are operated by *owner-drivers* (otherwise *owner-operators*); these are private entrepreneurs who own their vehicles, retain the gross receipts, and from them pay the full operating costs.

A third, but much less common, method of operation is the *rental* (or *horse-hire*) system. Under such an arrangement, a freelance driver will rent a vehicle from the owner (usually a fleet operator) for a flat per diem fee not including the cost of fuel, and will retain all of the passenger receipts. The owner provides insurance coverage, vehicle maintenance, and the services of a base depot. In New York City, rental arrangements appear to be more usual with livery vehicles than with fully-licensed cabs, but there are a number of other cities (Milwaukee and Washington, D.C., for example) where cab rental agreements are common.

In addition to fleet proprietors and owner-drivers, there are a number of other service enterprises and associations in the taxi industry. For example, one type of company provides dispatching services to both fleets and owner-drivers. Wells and Selover (1972) describe this form of service:

This type of company negotiates with the local government agency for the location of taxicab stands, advertises, and provides dispatch-

[3] Price Waterhouse and Company (1970).
[4] See Table 7.

ing service for a fee. The owner/operator benefits from group advertising and dispatching. The small fleet owner limits his capital investment by buying a service that he may not be able to support as part of his own fleet. Because some communities limit taxicabs to radio operation, the availability of dispatching service on a contract basis . . . enables the taxicabs of private owner/operators to function effectively.

Taxicab *associations* comprise owner-drivers and fleets banded together for economic or political reasons. Some associations (such as Taxicab Owners Cooperative, Inc., in New York City) purchase gasoline, oil, insurance, and other goods and services for their members at advantageous bulk prices. Other associations (the Metropolitan Taxicab Board of Trade, Inc., in New York City, for example) represent fleet owners in labor negotiations, and present the proprietors' position to regulatory agencies.

The implications of these differing organizational arrangements on the taxi service which is provided to the public will be discussed later in the chapter.

THE REGULATION OF TAXICAB SERVICE

We now turn to consider the public regulation of cab service— such questions as *who* regulates the industry, *what* aspects of operation and service are typically matters for regulation, and *why* the regulations were imposed in the first place. In this section we will confine our attention solely to a *description* of the regulatory environment in which taxis operate, together with some mention of the historical reasons why the public sector originally sought to regulate cab operations. We will leave until later in the chapter a discussion of how the typical regulations affect the service experienced by the public and a detailed discussion of the pros and cons of the most significant regulations.

The regulating authority

In the majority of U.S. cities, and certainly in the major ones, taxicab services are regulated at the city or county government level. Exceptions to this include Maryland and Pennsylvania, where state authorities are heavily involved.[5] In most instances one finds the cab regulatory power vested in the Public Utilities or Public Services Commission, or in the Police Department. Less commonly, taxi operations may be regulated by an authority which is principally responsible for regulating public transit services.

---

[5] Milwaukee Municipal Reference Library (1969).

Eckert (1968) has studied the question of whether *commissions* or *agencies* are more effective in regulating taxis. Commissioners are political appointees who hold office for a specified term, while agencies consist of career employees hired under civil service systems in police, public works, license, city clerk, or similar departments. Eckert's general thesis is that commissioners will tend to favor simplified, less time-consuming, albeit highly restrictive regulations, while agency officials are more apt to act in ways which justify the current levels of regulation and which tend to expand regulation. Thus, for example, he posits that commissioners would find it more rewarding than would officials to regulate a monopoly, prevent competition among sellers by dividing markets, reduce the number of service suppliers, require uniform rates, and avoid increasing the existing number of taxi licenses. His limited empirical data from a cross section of 36 large U.S. cities appear to bear this out.

There is no regulation of the cab industry at the federal government level. Unlike publicly owned bus systems, taxis are not exempt from federal or state gasoline taxes.

The nature of regulation

We may usefully classify those aspects of taxicab operations which the public sector has thought to be in need of public regulation in this way:[6]

- *Entry control into the market—*
  In particular, the number of cabs and/or cab fleets allowed to operate; the geographic description of areas of operation; the types of service to be allowed; and the rights reserved to the government.

- *Management and ownership control—*
  In particular, the financial responsibility of the cab owner.

- *Service standards—*
  In particular, vehicle standards, including the type and condition of the vehicle; driver standards; and methods of operation, including methods of hiring.

- *Fares and charges—*
  In particular, fare plans and the equity of charges among services and classes of users; the overall revenue performance of the industry.

---

[6] Following Banks and Associates (1972), who studied transit regulating practices.

Each of these four aspects of regulation will be described in turn in the sections which follow.

Entry control into the market

The historical rationale for limiting the numbers of taxicabs allowed to operate in a city has been discussed at some length (with particular reference to Chicago) by previous authors:

> Initial efforts to control entry into the taxicab industry came from the operators of mass transit rail facilities who correctly viewed the automobile as a threat to their business. They attempted to secure protection by persuading utility commissions and the courts that public service automobiles required a certificate of public convenience and necessity. The initial reaction of the taxi industry was, of course, to oppose legal limitations on its growth. But by 1929, when the National Association of Taxi Operators passed a resolution favoring entry controls, the established operators had set upon a policy of obtaining entry limitations. The mass transit operators became interested but largely passive bystanders.
>
> The resolve of the taxi owners to obtain entry controls in 1929 bore fruit quickly. Morris Markin, President of Checker Motors, pursued the policy with particular energy moving simultaneously in New York, Chicago, Minneapolis and Pittsburgh to unify control of the large operators while obtaining the introduction of entry controls in both Chicago and New York. Although the drive for entry controls was justified by reference to the public interest, the clear motive was lower costs and higher prices. In Chicago, a representative of Checker testified that entry limitation would stop taxi wars caused by too many cabs, and Yellow testified that limitations were necessary to insure financial responsibility. . . . [The] sponsor of the ordinance somewhat prematurely assured the Committee that the ordinance is practically a copy of an ordinance that is being passed in every large city in the United States.[7]

The principal arguments advanced in the early 1930s for the limitation of the numbers of taxicabs in New York, Chicago, and other major cities were financial responsibility, the effects of unlimited numbers of cabs on traffic congestion, the impact of low-cost service on mass transit ridership, and the (often veiled) hint that free competition in the industry leads to taxi wars—actual physical conflicts between rival drivers. In addition, it was claimed that entry controls would ensure that the compensation of drivers did not fall below "the minimum wage required for decent living," on the theory that an assured greater profit for the vehicle owners would trickle down to the drivers.

Entry controls to the industry came under strong attack at the end of the Second World War. Demand for taxicab service

---

[7] Kitch et al. (1971).

showed a sharp increase, principally because of the shortage of private automobiles, and returning war veterans organized a nationwide campaign to obtain cab licenses. In some cities suits were filed challenging entry restrictions as violations of the Sherman Antitrust Act. Many illegal cabs took to the streets, and in Chicago the legal and political battles between the established fleets and the veterans' associations lasted as long as thirteen years. In some cities special veterans' licenses, temporary and nontransferable, were introduced in limited numbers, but the *principle* of entry controls generally survived intact. Of eighteen major U.S. cities responding to a 1969 survey, only five indicated the existence of veterans' cab associations, and some of these were no longer comprised exclusively of veterans. Only one city of the eighteen, Milwaukee, gave the veterans any preferential treatment.[8]

How are the regulations limiting cab numbers usually framed? City or county ordinances restricting entry to the taxicab market typically adopt one or more of three different approaches:

- limitations on the total number of *taxicabs* which may enter the city's industry

- restrictions on new *firms* wanting to enter the industry

- regulations allowing monopolistic operations in specific jurisdictions or at specific points within the area served

Some examples will serve to illustrate each of these approaches:

1. *Numerical limitations on taxicabs*

Probably the best known example of taxicab numerical limitations is New York City where the number of taxi medallions, or licenses for a *vehicle* to operate by street hail in the city, is now set at 11,787, following the Haas Act of 1937.[9] Of this number, 6,816 medallions are owned by fleets, and the remaining 4,971 medallions belong to individual owner-drivers.

An annual license fee of $100 is paid for each medallion. In addition, the Haas Law allows medallions to change hands by private sale. The buying price in late 1972 appeared to be about

---

[8] Milwaukee Municipal Reference Library (1969).

[9] See Eckert (1968) or Vidich (1974) for a more detailed history of cab regulation in New York City. The Haas Act actually permits a total of 13,566 medallions, but since 1937 nearly 1,800 of these have been surrendered and not reissued. The figure of 11,787 medallions represents the ceiling number frozen by the Taxi and Limousine Commission in 1971. In 1927, before any entry controls were imposed, there was an all-time high of 30,450 medallions outstanding.

$6,000 for a fleet medallion, declining from a high value of $35,000 in late 1964. Individual medallions are currently sold for around $20,000, a figure which has stayed relatively constant over recent years. These price differentials presumably reflect variations in the supply and demand patterns for the two different types of license. The decline in the fleet medallion price since 1964 has closely paralleled a rapid growth in the nonmedallion cab industry over that period, and also a decline in the profitability of fleet operations.[10]

The values attached to a medallion indicate the degree to which the entry limitation restrains the force of the free market at a given fare level. Thus they provide an index of the degree to which prices are increased, taxicab availability is decreased, or both, as a result of the entry limitation. The high medallion prices in New York City indicate that consumers of taxi services pay a relatively high penalty in these price and service terms. We shall expand on this point later in the chapter.

Similar situations exist in Chicago, where the number of taxicabs is set at 4,600, and where independent licenses sell for about $15,000;[11] in Boston where there are 1,525 medallions and an average price of about $27,000; and in Detroit where there are roughly 1,360 cabs licensed, and where a cab and license together typically sell for about $7,500.[12]

Another type of numerical limitation links the maximum number of vehicle licenses to the population of the jurisdiction, on the theory that expansion of supply should only be allowed if the population increases. Such an ordinance is in force in Seattle, where the total number of taxis is in theory limited to one per 2,500 population—in practice, the number of licenses is higher than this. Similar regulatory practices exist in Cleveland, Miami, Milwaukee, and New Orleans.[13]

2. *Entry restrictions on new fleet operators*

When the total number of cab licenses is fixed as it is in New York City, it is possible for new firms to enter the industry by buying up fleet medallions from existing firms. Some other cities (for example, Cleveland, Dallas, and Pittsburgh) franchise fleet owners, and restrict the market to the franchised firms. In some cases the regulatory agency may also place limitations on the number of vehicles each franchisee may operate, thus creating

---

[10] Vidich (1974).
[11] Kitch et al. (1971).
[12] Rosenbloom (1968).
[13] Milwaukee Municipal Reference Library (1969).

an overall numerical limitation on the industry as well. In other cases, franchisees may be free to operate as many cabs as they see fit.

It is usual, in cases of this form of entry control, for the regulatory agency to adopt a so-called *public convenience and necessity* clause which allows for additional franchises to be issued if a condition of unmet demand can be established. Such a clause might typically read:

> Licenses shall be issued for public convenience and necessity and the safety of existing vehicular and pedestrian traffic requiring such limitations. Public hearings shall be held to determine if additional licenses should be granted to meet the demand for service.

The actual criteria applied in establishing the existence of unmet demand appear to vary from one regulatory agency to another. In practice, in those cities with a history of highly concentrated ownership of the taxicab supply, few new franchises are ever licensed.[14]

3. Monopolistic franchises to serve particular facilities or jurisdictions

A logical extension of restricting the cab market solely to franchised fleets is for the regulatory agency to franchise only one company to serve a particular area or facility—in other words, to create and protect a monopoly supplier. Probably the best known example of this situation is in Los Angeles. That city has been divided into six zones, and in each zone one single cab company has the exclusive rights to operate—each franchisee is allowed to solicit or originate business only within his own territory. It is interesting to note that this monopoly system is not formalized in the law, since none of the city's legal instruments specifies any restriction on the number of firms which may be franchised. Although the city authorities could legally franchise any number of fleet operators with or without territorial restriction, the Board of Public Utilities and Transportation Commissioners has always acted to reinforce the current monopoly system whenever it has been faced with the option of permitting additional suppliers. Eckert (1968) shows that this history is supportive of his general theory of Commission behavior—that the monopoly situation simplifies the task of regulation.

Another common example of monopoly franchises granted to

---

[14] Eckert (1968).

a single company occurs at airports or other intercity travel terminals. The reasons supporting this practice include:

- Revenue—
  Probably the central force in most exclusive franchises at specific locations is the pressure to produce revenues for the site owner. For example, the privilege of parking at the Greater Pittsburgh Airport is sold to the highest bidder, and typically sells for $1,500 per month.[15] Passenger fares must cover this cost in addition to a direct charge of 25 cents per trip levied on top of each airport fare. Similarly, at Union Station in Washington, D.C., where an exclusive taxi franchise was discontinued in 1972, station managers have subsequently incurred expenses of $6,000 to $8,000 per month. These expenses include the cost of starters, theft and liability insurance in the dispatch area, and management of the dispatch service.

- *Operational simplicity*—
  Frequently starters are employed at busy taxi boarding points to load people into cabs in some equitable way and to promote efficient cab sharing by combining persons with similar destinations. Paying for this starter, and enforcing a fair policy in the distribution of lucrative and not-so-profitable trips to the companies competing at that point, are likely to be operational problems.

- *Cross-subsidization*—
  In some cases companies may be granted an exclusive franchise at a particular location on the condition that they provide a certain minimum level of service at all times. Thus, the lucrative busy periods partially subsidize the slack times when drivers may occasionally wait for long periods before carrying a passenger.

- *Minimization of jurisdictional disputes*—
  Airports are frequently outside the boundaries of the central city jurisdictions which generate and attract most cab journeys to and from the airport. The regulatory authority may therefore be unable to prescribe uniform rates of fare, and it is not uncommon in the U.S. and many other countries of the world for cab drivers to extract extortionate fares from unsuspecting out-of-town visitors for rides from the airport into town. Franchising the fleets permitted to pick up passengers at the airport allows the airport authority or the regulatory agency to

---

[15] Rattien and Duckett (1971).

specify fare rates, and to withdraw the franchise from cab owners against whom abuses are proved.

Three major cities in the United States—Atlanta, Honolulu, and Washington—do not have numerical limitations on taxicabs. In Washington the number of vehicle licenses issued approaches the number of operative New York City medallion cabs. However, these numbers can be misleading because the number of Washington cab *drivers'* licenses is less than the number of *vehicle* licenses, and in practice there apparently are never more than 2,500 taxicabs operating on the Washington streets at any one time. The reasons for this will be examined later when we consider the impacts of regulation on service provision.

Management and ownership regulations

The principal aspect of public regulatory concern in the ownership and management of taxicab fleets is that the cab operator should provide evidence of a minimum level of financial responsibility, usually in the form of public liability insurance. The need for this facet of regulation was highlighted in the 1920s and 1930s when many operators went out of business, leaving behind many unpaid and uncollectable liability claims.

The insurance industry does not publish data which would enable one to examine the insurance premium rates for taxicabs on a national basis. However, conversations with members of the cab industry (together with other evidence) suggest that a median premium for 1970 would be on the order of $600 to $700 per vehicle, although the rates do appear to vary highly from cab company to cab company, presumably reflecting different claims experiences. Public liability insurance accounts for a significant proportion of each vehicle's operating costs,[16] and it is to the obvious advantage of large fleets to retain control over the substantial assets which they must set aside for insurance purposes. So in New York City, for example, it is common practice for fleets to be self-insured for public liability claims. Such a fleet is required to make deposits with a bonding agent to cover outstanding claims, and these deposits are usually in the form of tax-free municipal bonds. In Chicago two insurance companies, Calumet Mutual and City Mutual, are wholly-owned subsidiaries of the dominant fleet owners.

---

[16] See Table 10.

Regulation of service standards

Taxicab regulations typically are concerned directly with certain aspects of the service provided to the passenger. The ordinances will usually include rules relating to vehicle standards, to driver standards, and to permissible methods of operation.

1. *Vehicle standards*
Aspects sometimes prescribed by regulation include:

- vehicle type or design (standardization of vehicle type by regulation is, however, less common in U.S. cities than in Europe)

- regular vehicle safety inspections

- standards for external appearance (in particular, color schemes and permitted markings)

2. *Driver standards*
The following factors are commonly specified by ordinance as relevant to the granting of a cab driver's license:

- satisfaction of a minimum age requirement

- possession of a driver's license, with no invalidating record of driving convictions

- demonstration of sound physical condition

- demonstration of "good moral character" (the applicant has no invalidating record of criminal convictions)

- provision of photographic and fingerprint records

- demonstration of an adequate knowledge of city geography

It is interesting that very few U.S. cities place much emphasis on a driver's geographic capabilities in granting licenses. By contrast, in London (where there are no numerical limits on cab numbers) adequate geographic knowledge is the hardest driver qualification to fulfill, requiring on the average between 12 and 15 months of study.[17] Where fares are computed by meter on the basis of distance traveled (as is common practice), a driver's knowledge of city geography may be of some significant financial importance to the passenger.

3. *Prescribed methods of operation*
Regulations frequently address such matters as:

---

[17] Few other British or European cities, however, place such emphasis on this driver skill. London appears exceptional in this regard.

- the maximum number of passengers allowed in the vehicle

- the conditions (if any) under which group riding may be allowed

- the conditions under which the driver may refuse to accept a hire

- permissible modes of solicitation, including the displaying of such signs as "For Hire," "On Call," and "Off Duty"; and the acceptance of street hails

- the use of cab stands

- local restrictions on cruising certain streets or certain other facilities, with a view to minimizing taxicab contribution to traffic congestion

- the visible display of the driver's taxicab license or badge

In addition, the ordinances may specify that fleets must provide service for at least a specified minimum number of hours per day, and that owner-operators must fulfill minimum road time quotas.

Regulation of fares and charges

City cab regulations will typically prescribe a mandatory fixed scale (rather than maximum or minimum levels) of charges for conveyance and other ancillary chargeable services. They will specify the method by which the appropriate fare is to be calculated. They will call for the visible display of the fare scale details within the vehicle; and, if a meter is used to compute the fare, they will typically prescribe the calibration, sealing, and regular testing of the meter.

What are the historical motives behind the regulation of fares? Writing of Chicago, Kitch et al. make the following observations:

> On first inspection this regulation of fares appears to be typical utility rate regulation, designed to substitute regulated for negotiated prices and limit the regulated firms to a reasonable profit. But further examination of the regulation has led us to conclude that in fact the original purposes of the fare regulation were quite different. Prior to 1934 the fare regulation was apparently designed to put maximum limits on the negotiating position of the driver. In 1934 the fare regulations were converted to minimum price provisions designed to eliminate price competition and make taxicab operations more profitable.

A further motive was to protect the traveling public by pre-
venting the extraction of extortionate rates:

> The design of the regulation appears to be to remove the power of
> the . . . driver to charge more than the going rate by informing the
> user of the rate and to undercut the driver's bargaining power by
> imposing a duty to convey. The regulation protects strangers—those
> who do not know the ordinary rate of fare—and others compelled to
> use the service—those who, because of the urgency of their needs,
> are unable to bargain effectively.[18]

Local ordinances typically give the regulatory authority very broad
powers in determining both the appropriate *level* of fares (and
hence the profitability of supplying taxi service), and the rate
structure to be applied. We shall discuss each of these two aspects
in turn.

1. *The overall level of fares*

The range of considerations which the regulating agency may
take into account when fixing fare levels may be very broad.
For example, the 1971 ordinance creating the New York City
Taxi and Limousine Commission specifies:

> In determining the rates of fare, the commission may consider all
> facts which in its judgment have a bearing on a proper determina-
> tion, with due regard among other things to the time and distance of
> travel, to the character of the service provided, to the gross revenues
> derived from operation, to the expenses of operation including the
> income of drivers or operators, to the return upon capital actually
> expended and the necessity of making reservations out of income for
> surplus and contingencies, to the number of passengers transported,
> to the effect of fares upon the public and in relation to the fares for
> other forms of public transportation, and to the fares and practices
> with respect to similar services in other cities of the United States.
>
> No determination by the commission changing the rates of fare
> shall be made except after a public hearing before the commission,
> at which evidence shall be taken. . . . The burden of proof to show
> that existing rates are not reasonable shall be upon such segment of
> the business or industry affected by this chapter as is involved in the
> change in rates.[19]

In assessing the "reasonableness" of a proposed rate structure
for a regulated utility with respect to the rate of return it provides the supplier of the service, it is common practice to use
one or both of two indices.[20] These are:

- The *operating ratio* (the ratio of total operating expenses to
  gross revenues) is the index most commonly used in assessing

---

[18] Kitch et al. (1971).

[19] New York City (1971), sec. 2304.

[20] Peck and Meyer (1965).

taxi, transit, and interstate passenger and freight rates. It is considered to be most applicable to competitive industries with a relatively high rate of capital turnover, industries with a relatively large year-to-year variation in performance, and industries with a high operating ratio indicating a significant risk.

- The *rate of return on a rate base* is the ratio of net operating income to the capital invested in a *rate base* calculated following some standardized practice. The rate base is usually stated either at *original cost* or alternatively at some estimate of current *reproduction cost*. This index is considered to be most applicable to protected monopoly industries with a relatively low rate of capital turnover and a relatively low operating ratio. It is used extensively to assess rates for monopoly public utilities such as gas and electricity supply and telephone service.

In order to determine what rates of return are considered by taxicab regulatory agencies to be within the bounds of reasonableness, Price Waterhouse and Company searched for and reviewed rate-making decisions relating to urban passenger transportation between 1951 and 1967.[21] They reported on four taxicab rate cases and on ten transit rate cases drawn from eleven different cities. In all cases, the operating ratio was deemed to be the more appropriate index of profit margin for consideration.

It was concluded from this evidence that the range of operating ratios acceptable to regulatory authorities in such cases appears generally to be 88 percent to 96 percent, before income taxes and interest. In the four taxi rate cases, the acceptable operating ratios (before taxes and interest) were between 90 percent and 96 percent.

In nine of the fourteen cases, a rate of return on the rate base had also been considered as a secondary indication of profit margins. Acceptable values (based on a reproduction cost valuation of assets) had ranged from 6 percent to roughly 18.5 percent; all of the low values related to *transit* rate cases.

In Chicago, the entry controls into the market are linked directly to the profitability of the industry. The ordinance specifies that the number of licenses may not be increased unless the operating ratio (before tax) falls below 84.5 percent. In addition, the Municipal Code also specifically allows fare increases whenever the operating ratio is above 86 percent. In recent years the ratio has

---

[21] Price Waterhouse and Company (1967).

been over 94 percent for the two leading fleet operators; as one analysis points out, under existing conditions the ordinances appear to protect all licensees against further entry and to entitle them to fare increases unless they have a return on capital of roughly 47 percent or more.[22]

2. *The rate structure*

The great majority of cab systems calculate fares by use of a pre-set sealed *meter* permanently fixed in the vehicle. These typically compute fares on a basis which takes account of both the time and the distance of the hire, but not both simultaneously. There is a minimum fare (or *flag drop*) which is shown on the meter when it is initially activated, and which pays for an initial distance. Subsequent distances are usually charged for at a linear rate in discrete steps of, say, 10 cents.

To compensate the driver for time spent almost stationary in congested traffic while conveying passengers, most meters contain a *live clock* which computes an additional charge based on the time spent when the vehicle's speed falls below a certain minimum level.

A second system, in use in Washington, D.C., and in several small and medium-sized cities, dispenses with meters and calculates fares on a *zonal* basis. In the District of Columbia the jurisdiction is divided into a total of 26 geographical zones, and a charge is specified for trips which originate and terminate completely within a zone, and for trips between any pair of zones. Two fare tables are used: one applies to single passengers, and the second is a lower per capita charge for group riders. While the system and the full zone-to-zone matrix fare table sounds and looks complicated, it is in fact quite easy to understand and not difficult for a passenger to check whether he has been charged the correct amount.

Both systems may be modified slightly by a scale of charges for services outside the normal call of duty. For example, it is common for an extra charge to be assessed on large items of luggage. Under the meter system, the fare is usually the same no matter how many passengers travel in the cab, but some cities add a small, fixed, per capita increment for every rider after the first. There are sometimes incremental charges for late night service or for telephone hails. Under the zone system in Washington, there is an extra fee for significant deviations from the direct route.

---

[22] Kitch et al. (1971).

The advantages and disadvantages of these two types of pricing schemes will be discussed later.

THE SUPPLY OF TAXI SERVICES AT THE LOCAL LEVEL

We have discussed the size and organizational characteristics of the national taxicab industry and described in a general fashion the regulatory environment in which cabs typically operate. We now turn to consider the characteristics of the industry at a more local level, to attempt to explain local variations in the level of supply and in the methods of operating, and more importantly, to consider how the regulatory and organizational features which have been described actually affect the service offered to the traveling public.

Numbers of cabs

From our earlier description of the prevalence of entry controls to the cab market, at least in the major cities of the country, it should be obvious that the number of taxicabs available for hire in a particular metropolitan area is likely to be largely determined by the nature of the locally regulated entry controls. Table 7 presents broad estimates of the number of vehicle licenses extant in 1970 in the major urban jurisdictions of the country, together with the 1970 resident populations and areas of those jurisdictions. These data must be considered with care, since the city boundaries and the populations actually served may be quite different. Moreover, the data sources from which this table was compiled vary slightly in their estimates of license numbers.

Furthermore, it should be noted that the number of cab licenses issued is a very simplistic measure of supply, in that there are known to be variations between cities in the degree to which licenses are used. In Washington, D.C., for example, it appears that many vehicles with cab tags are rarely if ever used as taxis,[23] and moreover, Washington taxi drivers average half or fewer hours on the road than the national industry average. We expect that if the vehicle license figures could be normalized to take account of differing vehicle utilization rates, the observed variations between cities would be greatly reduced.

---

[23] There are some purchase price and financing advantages in buying a cab rather than a private automobile. And although liability insurance for cabs is several times more expensive than for a private car, cab insurance has an advantage for the poor in that it can be purchased on a weekly basis.

Table 7

Taxicab licenses for a number of major cities, 1970

Jurisdiction	Population served (a) (thousands)	Area (sq. mi.)	Population density (thou/ sq. mi.)	License restriction (b)	Number of vehicle licenses (c)	Licenses/ thousand population	Licenses/ square mile
New York City	7,895	300	26.3	N	11,754	1.5	39.2
Chicago	3,367	223	15.1	N	4,600	1.4	20.6
Los Angeles	2,816	464	6.1	C	1,024	0.4	2.2
Philadelphia	1,949	128	15.2	C	1,750	0.9	13.7
Detroit	1,511	138	10.9	N	1,358	0.9	9.8
Houston	1,233	434	2.8	C	473	0.4	1.1
Baltimore	906	78	11.6	N	1,151	1.3	14.6
Dallas	844	266	3.2	C	507	0.6	1.9
Washington	757	61	12.4	None	8,500	11.3	139.3
Cleveland	751	75	10.0	C	560	0.7	7.5
Indianapolis	745	48	15.5	—	482	0.6	10.0
Milwaukee	717	95	7.5	N	423	0.6	4.5
San Francisco	716	45	15.9	N	756	1.1	16.8
San Diego	697	317	2.2	—	304	0.4	1.0
San Antonio	654	184	3.6	—	518	0.8	2.8
Boston	641	46	13.9	N	1,575	2.5	34.2
Memphis	624	217	2.9	—	400	0.6	1.8
St. Louis	622	61	10.2	C	1,267	2.0	20.8
New Orleans	593	197	3.0	C	1,500	2.5	7.6
Phoenix	582	248	2.3	C	95	0.2	0.4
Columbus	540	135	4.0	C	351	0.7	2.6
Seattle	531	84	6.3	C	316	0.6	3.8
Jacksonville	529	766	0.7	—	270	0.5	0.4
Pittsburgh	520	55	9.5	C	550	1.1	10.0
Denver	515	95	5.4	—	317	0.6	3.3
Kansas City	507	316	1.6	N	542	1.1	1.7
Atlanta	497	131	3.8	None	1,900	3.8	14.5
Minneapolis	434	55	7.9	N	248	0.6	4.5
Miami	335	34	9.9	N	431	1.3	12.7
Honolulu	325	84	3.9	None	1,400	4.3	16.7

KEY: a Resident population of the jurisdiction licensing the taxi services
b N denotes a numerical restriction on the total number of vehicles
C denotes a limitation to franchised fleets, and possible overall numerical limitation as well
— denotes information not available
c Data of varying reliability

Correlation coefficient of number of cab licenses with
population   0.78 (significant at 0.1% level)
area   −0.02 (not significant)
population density   0.68 (significant at 0.1% level)

Sources: Wells and Selover (1972); Rosenbloom (1972); U.S. Department of Commerce (1972); Milwaukee Municipal Reference Library (1969).

There is yet another complicating factor. We have noted that in some cities fully-licensed cabs are augmented by significant numbers of livery vehicles and illegal taxi services. So New York City, to cite an extreme example, probably has roughly two and a quarter times more vehicles providing taxi service than the number of vehicle licenses entered in Table 7 would suggest.

But imperfect as vehicle license statistics are as a measure of the supply of taxi services, they are, unfortunately, the best measure which is available, since data on the relative levels of vehicle utilization and the degree of illegal service provision in different cities have not been collated. And Table 7, despite these limitations, highlights several features which are worthy of note.

First, in Washington, Atlanta, and Honolulu—three cities which do not restrict either the total number of cabs or the permitted fleet companies (a situation we can describe as *free entry*)— the ratio of taxis to the resident population is markedly higher than in any of the other jurisdictions. In fact, the Washington ratio is so high that, even were it to be divided by four to take account of a relatively low vehicle utilization rate, it would still be higher than the ratios for restricted entry cities. This fact strongly suggests that entry barriers in the majority of cities are actively inhibiting the growth of the industry, and that there are fewer cabs on the streets than would be found under free entry.

However, since in some of the cities which restrict taxis to franchised fleets those companies could further increase the size of their fleets without restraint, it follows that it is not only numerical limitation which inhibits growth. Presumably franchised companies fix their fleet sizes in a way that they believe will maximize profits. This suggests that the most significant inhibition on taxicab supply is the restriction, under both forms of regulatory barriers, on the entry of individual owner-drivers into the market.[24]

Second, Table 7 shows that the number of cab licenses appears to bear no significant relation to the area of the jurisdiction served, but is correlated positively with both the resident population and the population density of the jurisdiction. One analyst attempted to relate the number of taxis in those cities without an overall numerical limitation to ten selected indices of economic activity, tourist activity, auto ownership, and household income. The results were largely inconclusive.[25]

Moving beyond the large cities to look at the national picture, it appears that seven out of every ten jurisdictions with cab fleets

[24] Rosenbloom (1972).
[25] Rosenbloom (1968).

have a ratio of cab licenses per thousand population of less than
0.8. Table 8, based on International Taxicab Association data
from a sample of 741 jurisdictions, illustrates the distribution of
the vehicles-to-population ratio.

Table 8
Distribution of the cabs-to-population ratio, 1970

Cab licenses per thousand population	Proportion of sample jurisdictions
	%
Under 0.2	10
0.2 to under 0.4	20
0.4 to under 0.6	23
0.6 to under 0.8	16
0.8 to under 1.0	10
1.0 to under 1.2	8
1.2 to under 2.0	9
2.0 and over	5

Based on a sample of 741 jurisdictions
Median licenses per thousand population $= 0.57$

Source: Wells and Selover (1972)

Rosenbloom (1972) has also investigated how the ratio of cabs
to three selected indices of economic activity has changed over
time in a number of cities. She found that in seven cities with
numerical limitations every calculated taxi-to-index ratio decreased (even if only slightly) in the five-year period from 1963
to 1968. In the three free entry cities the ratios all *increased* over
the same period. Rosenbloom concludes:

> Clearly the number of taxis is increasing in some relationship to
> the increase in economic activity in the unrestricted cities. It seems
> clear that increased economic activity caused an increase in demand
> for taxi service. The unrestricted cities have been able to fulfill this
> increased demand for taxi service while the restricted cities have
> been prevented from doing so.

This finding is fully consistent with our conclusion that the
supply of cabs is relatively greater in the free entry cities than
in the cities with entry controls.

Details of fleet operation

Data compiled by the International Taxicab Association from
samples of its member companies give some indication of how

fully-licensed taxicab fleets typically operate.[26] From a sample of 194 jurisdictions, it appears that in the "typical jurisdiction" in 1969 taxicabs averaged roughly 40,000 miles and 14,000 passengers per cab per year, with an average load of 1.6 persons and an average trip length of about 4.5 miles (including the associated deadhead mileage).

These figures, however, could possibly be highly misleading. They are averages only in the sense that they are mean values for a distribution of *jurisdictions,* and any sample of jurisdictions is dominated by the large number of relatively small cities and suburban areas.[27] To be able to draw meaningful conclusions about the average *vehicle,* on the other hand, requires that we know the distribution of *vehicles* rather than jurisdictions. And, in contrast to the jurisdiction distribution, the distribution of the nation's taxicabs is highly skewed towards the large cities— the thirty major cities listed in Table 7, for example, account for over one-fifth of the national fleet of fully-licensed cabs.

Because of this rather complicated but nevertheless important statistical distinction, we suspect that the average utilization of a taxicab, nationally speaking, is somewhat higher than the 40,000 miles and 14,000 passengers per year which is superficially suggested by the ITA sample.[28]

Some more detailed operating data are available for 1970 from a much smaller ITA sample of 27 fleets.[29] The sample has broad geographic coverage but is biased slightly towards the larger fleet operations. These data are summarized briefly in Table 9.

It can be seen from the table that during each nine-hour shift the average cab in the sample fleets travelled about 85 miles. The paid mileage averaged about 50 percent of the total mileage, generating gross revenues of roughly $37 per shift. Of this, about 44 percent was paid to drivers in the form of commissions —equivalent to a wage rate of roughly $1.85 per man-hour, not including fringe benefits or tips. There appears to be relatively little seasonal variation in these data.

It is interesting to observe that across this sample of fleets roughly 86 percent of all trips originated from telephone orders. It seems that relatively little revenue is generated from cruising,

---

[26] Wells and Selover (1972).

[27] Although the data source does not indicate so specifically, circumstantial evidence suggests that the median population for the jurisdictions in this sample is probably less than 50,000.

[28] This is because there is limited evidence to suggest that, with the exception of Washington, D.C., the utilization rates are higher in the large cities than in small cities and suburban areas.

[29] Wells and Selover (1972).

Table 9
Medians of selected fleet operating statistics, 1970

Ratio	Approximate median for 27 fleets
Total cab mileage	
per cab per day	115
per man-hour	12
per cab trip	6
per gallon of gas	11
Paid mileage per cab trip	3
Cab trips per man-hour	2.2
Passengers per cab trip	1.35
Gross receipts ($)	
per mile	0.31
per paid mile	0.65
per man-hour	4.1
per cab trip	2.0
per shift	37.0
Hours per shift	9.0
Phone orders	
per shift	15.6
as percentage of all trips	86%

The word *trip* is used to denote not only the time the cab is occupied by a hiring party (that is, *paid mileage*) but also the deadhead and cruising mileage associated with that hire.

Source: Wells and Selover (1972)

although the proportion of hails which are made on the street does vary quite a lot from area to area. A priori, one might expect that the ratio of street hails to telephone orders is a function of city density primarily, and also city size and cab availability. The limited circumstantial evidence available appears to bear this out—in Manhattan the proportion of telephone hails is low, while in suburban areas and small or less dense cities cruising is not very productive and most hires are made from cab stands or by telephone hail.

One consequence of this is that in the suburban areas and the less dense cities the proportion of cabs equipped with two-way radios is relatively high, certainly so when compared with cab fleets working predominantly in the central areas of the large cities where cruising is more profitable. Examination of some Washington data derived from cab-driver manifests [30] suggests that, when the operations of radio-equipped taxis in Washington are compared with those of vehicles without radios, the radio vehicles serve slightly longer passenger trips but do not differ significantly from nonradio cabs either in vehicle occupancy or in the proportion of their time spent without passengers.

Operating costs of fleet taxicabs

There are available three sources of detailed data on fleet cab operating costs. These are:

- Financial surveys for the New York City fleet taxicab industry for financial years 1967 and 1970. These surveys were carried out by auditors for the trade association of New York fleet owners (the Metropolitan Taxicab Board of Trade, Inc.) and are based on samples representing 63 percent (1967) and 80 percent (1970) of the fleet-operated fully-licensed cabs in the city.[31] For the sake of convenience, we shall identify these data bases as NYC67 and NYC70 respectively. To reduce annual totals to a per mile basis, we have assumed an average gross mileage per New York fleet cab of 75,000.[32]

- A study of the operating costs of Washington taxicabs [33] derived largely from data for nine months of 1968 for 222 fleet cabs operated by four companies. We shall identify this source by the code DC68.

- Data for 1970 collated by the International Taxicab Association from a sample of 27 fleet operations with a wide geographical distribution.[34] The statistics quoted are median values for the 27 fleets. This source is identified as ITA70.

Table 10 presents estimates of fleet cab expenses per gross mile derived from these three sources. Despite the sketchiness of the data, the estimates appear to be reasonably consistent. Total driver costs in New York City in 1970 accounted for 60 percent of gross revenues and 63 percent of the total operating

[30] The base data which are summarized in National Capital Region Transportation Planning Board (1970).

[31] Price Waterhouse and Company (1967); Price Waterhouse and Company (1970). Verkuil (1970) has questioned the accuracy of these data.

[32] Utilization of vehicles in New York City is known to be higher than the (possibly suspect) national average of 40,000 miles per year derived from an ITA sample. Our assumed value of 75,000 miles per year may, however, be an overestimate.

[33] Gramza et al. (1969).

[34] Wells and Selover (1972).

expenses. Driver costs from the 1970 ITA national sample seem, as far as can be judged, to account for roughly the same proportion of revenues, but this data source does not appear to include the costs of employee-related benefits.

The value of interest expense quoted for New York City fleets includes the current interest expense for the financing of both vehicle and medallion purchase. These capital costs are usually financed by borrowings from one of a number of New York City banks, the loans being secured by the entire fleet stock of cabs and medallions and the capital stock of the corporations. Vehicles will typically be replaced in 18- to 24-month cycles, but as New York fleet operators have increasingly come under a

Table 10

Estimates of fleet cab expenses per mile

	cents per gross mile [a]			
	NYC67 [b]	DC68 [c]	NYC70 [b]	ITA70
Gross fare revenue	28.0	—	32.6	31.7
Total expenses	27.8	—	33.3	28.2
depreciation	1.6	1.5	2.1	1.7
interest expense	1.0	—	1.2	—
Total operating expenses	25.3	—	30.0	—
driver cost —	16.0	—	19.3	—
commission	13.0	15.2	—	15.6
benefits, etc.	3.0	—	—	—
vehicle operation —	2.6	3.6	2.8	—
gasoline	1.9	3.0	2.2	2.2
tires	0.3	0.2	0.3	0.3
licenses, etc.	0.3	0.4	0.3	—
maintenance —	1.6	2.4	2.1	2.0
labor	0.7	—	1.2	1.1
parts, etc.	0.9	—	0.9	0.9
garage	0.8	—	1.1	—
public liability insurance	1.7	1.2	1.8	1.6
general & administrative	2.5	—	2.8	—

KEY: [a] Since paid miles average roughly 50 percent of gross mileage, the costs per paid mile are about twice those in the table.

[b] NYC data assume an average annual utilization per fleet cab of 75,000 miles, possibly an overestimate.

[c] DC data relate to full-time operation (40 hours per week).

Blanks (—) in the table denote data not available.

strong financial squeeze (to be discussed later in this chapter), there is evidence that increasing numbers of fleets have lengthened their replacement cycles up to as long as three years.[35]

The 1970 financial survey of the New York fleet industry reports that

> The vehicle and medallion purchase loans are repayable in installments over 18 to 24 months, which amortize a portion of the loan over that period, with the unpaid balance refinanced at the end of the period. Personnel of major lending banks have informed us that they will refinance already existing medallion loans if necessary but they are reluctant to extend new lines of credit for the purchase of fleets.
>
> The average loan balance, based on information received from the principal lending banks representing 3,149 cabs (46% of the taxicab industry), approximates $8,400 per cab. Banks are generally charging interest at 6% discounted (equivalent to over 11% effective rate) on vehicle loans and 11% add-on interest on the medallion loans. The overall average effective interest rate on existing loans appears to be approximately 11%.[36]

Thus the accountants estimated that in 1970 the mean annual interest expense for a fleet cab (and medallion) in New York City was roughly $920 per vehicle, based on an average loan balance of $8,400 per cab.

Insurance premium rates appear to vary widely throughout the industry, and they impinge far more heavily on the independent owner-operator than on fleet vehicles. In New York City in 1970 it was estimated that public liability insurance expense for fleet cabs averaged out at about $1,800 per vehicle per year—although the actual cost to the fleet owner is roughly 5 percent less than this because of the interest which his securities bonded for insurance purposes are able to earn. We have, unfortunately, no information about insurance costs for independent owner-drivers in New York City.

In Chicago, insurance costs of the dominant fleet operators averaged $720 per cab in 1968—the insurance is provided by mutual companies which are wholly owned subsidiaries of the fleets. For the smaller fleets and the independents, by contrast, the cost of public liability insurance was $1,500 to $1,600 per vehicle.[37]

We have evidence from conversations with fleet operators that careful management and investment in driver training can help to reduce insurance costs substantially. For example, we know of one operator who has been able to cut his annual public

---

[35] Vidich (1974).

[36] Price Waterhouse and Company (1970).

[37] Kitch et al. (1971).

liability premiums from $1,250 per cab in 1967 to $640 per cab in 1972, mainly by instituting an education program on defensive driving and an annual medical checkup for drivers.

Examination of the NYC67 operating cost data on a per vehicle basis by fleet size (Table 11) suggests that the main economies of scale in fleet expansion occur in insurance costs, maintenance costs, and executive salaries. We might also intuitively expect some scale economies in dispatching costs.

Labor aspects of cab operations

Driving a taxi requires relatively little special skill. Drivers must generally be over a minimum age, in good health, have good driving records, be without criminal records, and be able to pass an examination on street locations, insurance, regulations, accident reports, meter rules, and so on.[38] Many persons are clearly qualified to work as taxi drivers, and the number who elect to perform that service is dependent on vehicle entry restrictions, fare regulations, and arrangements between taxi fleets and drivers—as well, of course, as the local economic conditions and the availability of other forms of unskilled employment.

Consider first the relatively rare situation of a free entry taxi market, such as prevails in Honolulu or Washington, D.C. In such a case, the number of cab drivers entering the market is likely to be primarily determined by their expectation of financial remuneration relative to other jobs available to them—and this level of remuneration is largely determined by the fare levels fixed by the local regulatory agency. Such a situation has been described succinctly by a British government departmental committee:

> Fixing fares, the primary purpose of which is to prevent exploitation of taxi users, in fact determines the profitability of the taxi trade in relation to other enterprises and so influences the number of taxis which are available on the streets. Generally speaking, raising fares has some discouraging effect on use, but has a more important immediate effect on taxi drivers' earnings and the profits of the taxi owners. Higher earnings bring more people into the trade and increase the supply of taxis. This means that taxis will spend less of their time engaged and more of their time looking for fares, and that the public consequently will find it easier to get taxis. If, on the other hand, the fare structure is not adjusted to meet rises in costs, taxi driving or owning will become less profitable, drivers will leave the trade or not enter it in sufficient numbers to fill natural wastage and the number of taxis will decline.[39]

---

[38] U.S. Department of Labor (1965); U.S. Department of Labor (1970a).
[39] U.K. Home Office (1970).

Table 11
Estimates of New York City fleet cab expenses per vehicle, 1967

	Size of fleet		
	less than 50 cabs	from 50 to 99 cabs	100 cabs or more
	$ per vehicle-day	$ per vehicle-day	$ per vehicle-day
Driver-related costs:			
commission	26.46	26.62	26.97
bonus & vacation	0.98	0.79	0.80
health & medical	1.97	1.95	1.98
pension plan	0.85	0.84	0.86
payroll taxes	1.58	1.56	1.56
compensation insurance	0.62	0.60	0.61
employee welfare & insurance	0.28	0.33	0.42
Total driver costs	32.74	32.69	33.20
Vehicle operation	5.55	5.35	5.37
Maintenance	3.77	3.54	3.10
Garage costs	1.91	1.49	1.81
Public liability insurance	3.85	3.24	3.25
Depreciation	3.03	3.59	3.46
Executive salaries	2.46	2.12	1.69
General & administrative	3.54	3.03	3.39
Total expenses	$56.85	$55.03	$55.26
Sample sizes:			
fleets sampled	4	26	18
cabs in sample fleets	151	1790	2352

Source: Price Waterhouse and Company (1967)

In the free entry cities (Washington, in particular), there is some evidence that taxi driving is seen by many drivers as a casual option to earn money if and when they want to do so. The proportions of autonomous owner-drivers and of daily rentals in Washington are much higher than in most other cities.

On the average day, about 22 percent of all licensed drivers do not work. Of the *drivers working,* almost 60 percent work for four hours or less; of *all drivers,* this proportion is almost 70 percent. The mean work day across all drivers is slightly greater than three hours.[40] Many of these drivers are probably using part-time cab driving as a supplement to a regular job, or are retired from another job, or are students earning money for their education. Free entry Honolulu faces no shortage of drivers either; in fact, there is a city limit of two drivers per taxicab. Both in Washington and in Honolulu there is a limited market for semiskilled and unskilled labor. Even in London, where there is no numerical limitation on entry to the market but drivers' licenses involve a heavy personal investment of time in training for a stringent geographical test, there is evidence of numbers of part-time drivers.[41]

One of the attractions of taxi-driving under these conditions is undoubtedly the freedom and flexibility the job affords. The British government committee described it in these terms:

> He is to all intents and purposes a free agent; he may look for work wherever and at whatever time of day he pleases. His earnings are related to the number of hours he works, the acquired ability to be in the right place at the right time and a certain amount of luck. Taxi drivers, each reacting to the challenge in his own way, choose all times of the day and night to start and finish work, and similarly there is a wide variety of standard methods of operation.[42]

In addition, a large number of Washington drivers own their own cabs and use them while off duty as family automobiles.

Under the more usual regulatory environment, where numerical limitations or franchises inhibit the entry of owner-drivers into the market, the number of drivers working is likely to be determined predominantly by the financial arrangements between fleet owners and drivers, which in turn are affected by the regulated fare level. There is some evidence that fleet owners in some regulated cities think it to their advantage to operate on a smaller scale than regulations would actually allow.

For example, Rosenbloom reported in 1967 that

> A spokesman for the International Taxicab Association claims the entire industry is suffering from a 20% manpower shortage, the New York Mayor's Taxi Panel claims there is a current shortage of 5,000 drivers in New York, the New York Metropolitan Taxi Board claims it keeps 1,000 cabs idle at all times for lack of drivers, the Philadelphia Yellow Cab Company pays a bonus to any employee staying

---

[40] National Capital Region Transportation Planning Board (1970).
[41] U.K. Home Office (1970).
[42] Ibid.

over 90 days, and the Los Angeles Yellow Cab Company claims a 60% annual turnover.

But the author goes on to remark:

> It should be remembered that this shortage of drivers is only a shortage at the current salary being offered by taxi companies. In spite of the fact that the industry complains the loudest about the lack of drivers, they have not seen fit to raise either wages or commission percentages to attract further applicants. It is apparent then that with the current fare structure and demand for taxis, companies consider it in their best interests to operate at below maximum level, or they would not continue to do so.[43]

A possible major reason why these companies do not raise wages is that it is often difficult to persuade the local regulating agency to increase the regulated fare levels, and in some cities those fare levels may not allow them a fair return on the capital employed. For example, the audited accounts of the fleet industry in New York City in 1970 suggest that (for reasons to be detailed subsequently in this chapter) the industry suffered an operating loss in that year of nearly $7 million.[44]

Reliable data on individual driver earnings are difficult to come by, and the available estimates may not be accurate because tips and other off-the-meter income are likely to be underreported. The 1970 International Taxicab Association national sample of 27 fleets revealed commission rates of between 41 percent and 47 percent, equivalent to a median wage of $1.85 per hour exclusive of tips and fringe benefits. This seems very low. However, it is not much below the estimates made by Rosenbloom from conversations with union officials in three cities—she suggests that a typical fleet-employed cabbie works between 50 and 60 hours a week for a salary probably in the range of $100 to $125 each week. Independent owner-drivers work the same or longer hours for about $150 a week.[45]

Table 12 summarizes two other sources of taxi driver income data for a number of cities in 1967 and 1969.[46] The wage rates for bus drivers or similar occupations in the same cities are given for comparison. Even allowing for substantial reporting error and adding a 10 percent tip increment, it seems apparent that bus drivers are considerably better paid than cab drivers.

There are a number of reasons for this discrepancy in pay. Most importantly, the taxi industry is not heavily unionized—

---

[43] Rosenbloom (1968).
[44] Price Waterhouse and Company (1970).
[45] Rosenbloom (1970). The earnings figures probably relate to 1967/68.
[46] Gramza et al. (1969).

Table 12
Taxicab and bus driver hourly wage rates in selected cities

	Taxi		Bus	
	1967	1969	1967	1969
Baltimore	$1.65	$2.15	$3.13	$3.78
Boston	1.85	2.50	3.55	4.22
Cleveland	1.37	2.25	3.26	3.67
Chicago	1.84	2.40	3.41	4.10
New Haven	1.21	2.25	3.01	3.30
New York	2.12	2.75	3.50	4.16
Newark	1.48	2.45	3.17	3.66
Philadelphia	1.80	2.45	3.11	3.66
Washington	2.00	2.40	3.37	4.16

Sources: Gramza et al., 1969 (columns 1 & 2); U.S. Department of Labor, 1968 (column 3); U.S. Department of Labor, 1970b (column 4).

except in the biggest cities drivers tend to be nonunion, probably as an outgrowth of the "you-can-be-your-own-boss" psychology which is one of the attractions of the job to many cabbies. Even in the cities where the majority of drivers are union members, the unions have not been particularly strong. Moreover, restricted entry controls in many cities mean that the monopoly which fleet owners have over taxi supply also makes them monopolists of labor demand. Since the fleet operators are collectively the only employers of drivers, they are in a strong position to dictate drivers' remuneration levels.

THE IMPACT OF ORGANIZATIONAL AND REGULATORY ASPECTS ON SERVICE

Thus far we have been content simply to describe the organizational characteristics of the taxicab industry and the regulatory environment in which taxis typically operate. We now turn to consider how these factors influence the level and nature of the cab service which is available to the general public, and to discuss the pros and cons of some of the features which have been described.

Entry control into the market

The first and most obvious effect of entry restrictions to the taxicab market is a lower supply of cabs than would be available under free entry conditions. This conclusion seems a fairly safe one in the light of Table 7 and our earlier discussion of that table. And such an undersupply is readily acknowledged—for example, the chairman of the New York City Taxi and Limousine Commission writes that "a shortage of medallion taxi service plagues all residential neighborhoods throughout the city, and virtually all business centers outside of the central business district of Manhattan." [47]

Taxicab entry controls have frequently been called into question by transportation economists as a clear case of unwise government policy.[48] This argument is based primarily on a fairly standard result of theoretical supply/demand analysis which suggests that when the supply is constrained at an artificially low level, it is impossible to fix on a price which optimizes the public interest. The situation can be represented, albeit imperfectly, by the model shown in Figure 1.

Within the framework of classical supply/demand analysis, let SS and DD represent respectively the aggregate supply and demand schedules for taxi rides under conditions of unrestricted supply. The equilibrium price and output would be P_e and Q_e respectively, at the intersection of the supply and demand curves.

However, when the total output is artificially constrained so as not to exceed Q_r, the supply schedule is represented by SS′; no matter how high the price rises above P_r, no further output can be made available. If the administered fare is set at any value less than P_s, the price at which the demand curve and the constrained supply curve intersect, then there will be unsatisfied demand. If the administered fare is greater than P_s, there will be unutilized output but still pressure to enter the market from potential suppliers. The most advantageous price for the favored suppliers allowed in the market is P_s—this is where all output is fully utilized at the highest price which the market will bear.

Any price above P_e assures the favored suppliers of some monopoly profit, implying a higher price *and* less output than would prevail under competition. At price P_s all of the favored suppliers maximize their monopoly profits (represented by the cross-hatched area in Figure 1), and they have no reasons to compete with each other over price. So, depending on the level of the administered price, entry restrictions are likely to imply a mixture of unsatisfied demand and monopoly profit.

---

[47] Lazar (1971).

[48] See, for example, Meyer et al. (1966); Kitch et al. (1971); and Beesley (1973).

Figure 1
Simple model of constrained supply

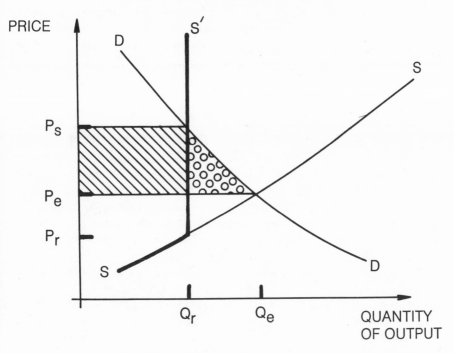

A move from this situation to one of a free entry market would clearly be to the benefit of the riding public. *First,* the people who are now riding at a price of, say, P_s will be able to purchase the same output (Q_r) at the reduced price P_e—the monopoly profits (cross-hatched rectangle) would be diverted to the consumers. *Second,* the public would be allowed to expand consumption from Q_r to Q_e, doubtless resulting in resource savings elsewhere in the economy. *Third,* the new riders entering the market are also better off than they were without the service. These benefits can be represented by the dotted triangle.

While this simple model does not perfectly characterize the market for taxicab services for a variety of reasons, we suggest that the above conclusions are valid. Orr (1969) provides a more realistic but more complex model and concludes that

Apparently the (independent) taxi drivers assess the situation correctly when they contend that an expansion in the medallion supply depresses the individual operator's profits. In the case of fleet operations, drivers should hail an increase in the number of medallions, since such an increase implies an expansion of output in the industry and hence an expansion in the derived demand for their services.

Moving from theoretical analysis to the real world, what are the actual impacts of entry restrictions on the service experienced by the traveling public? *First,* undersupply of taxicab services means that it is harder for the intending passenger to hail a cab on the street—the average waiting time is longer than it would be if more cabs were allowed; service refusal is likely for the less lucrative trips; and some level of demand will go completely unfulfilled or diverted to other travel modes (private automobile, for example). *Second,* entry restrictions are one of the main reasons why extralegal cab services can be found in many cities, and why, for example, New York City supports such a large nonmedallion livery cab industry. *Third,* we have seen that for a given level of operating costs the fares are higher than the competitive fare level in a free entry market would be, other factors being equal. *Fourth,* operator capital costs are increased by the amount of the entry price into the market (the medallion prices); these costs are ultimately borne by the travelers, and from the point of view of the public at large they represent a completely nonuseful expenditure of resources.

If the economic value of entry restrictions is suspect, how about some of the other reasons which are advanced to justify those restrictions? We have already set out the arguments advanced to support the original introduction of entry control ordinances in the 1930s. What reasons are advanced in the 1970s for the retention of the entry barriers?

The President of the Yellow Cab Company of Chicago (and then President of the International Taxicab Association) set out the association's position regarding entry controls in 1972:

The position of the International Taxicab Association concerning the theories of unlimited entry into and exit from the taxicab industry

A. Regulation of entry into and exit from the taxicab industry, including regulation of the number of licenses to be issued, is a necessity for the welfare, safety and protection of the public in general and the public who ride in taxicabs. No regulation or no limitation on the rights of entry and exit from the industry will (in addition to grave injury to the public) provide less, poorer quality and more expensive service in the long run.

B. Unlimited entry into and exit from the industry will force an operation of fly-by-night (financially and otherwise) irresponsible operators who will not even be able to provide insurance as a substitute for assets.

C. The taxicab industry is affected with a public interest; it is not in the public interest to permit chauffeurs to set their charges at will, or according to the time of day, or according to the weather, or according to the trip, or according to the wealth of the passenger.

D. Freedom of exit is also not in the public interest. It only means abandoning the business, leaving the public the obligation to pay the debts.

E. Taxicabs are an essential part of the transportation system of any city and, as such, should provide service at all hours and in all locations. Unlimited entry would create such intense competition as to drive the cabs into the area of greatest demand at the hours of greatest demand, out of low demand areas, and off the streets entirely at low demand hours. A sort of Gresham's Law in action. That advocates of unlimited entry recognize these facts is evident from their suggestions for higher fares in dangerous neighborhoods, outlying areas, cold weather, hot weather, rain, snow, late at night and on and on. The Association believes that unlimited entry will result in poor service even if some or all of these suggestions could be made effective.

F. The public is best served by responsible, reliable taxicab operators who are and intend to remain a part of the community which they serve and where they maintain an investment which is:

   (1) sufficient to purchase and maintain safe, comfortable vehicles appropriate for use as public conveyances;

   (2) sufficient to provide garages, equipment and employment for mechanics, washers, etc.;

   (3) sufficient to provide employment of administrative supervisory personnel; and

   (4) sufficient to provide proper and adequate insurance.

G. The public is best served by taxicab operators employing trained, reliable and responsible drivers and supporting employees; that [sic] unlimited entry and exit would render such employment impossible.

H. The public is entitled to be served by taxicab operators who shoulder their share of the public burden: be it paying taxes, keeping records, participating in civic affairs. None of this would be possible if anyone could come into the industry and anyone could leave without let or hindrance.[49]

Several of the points in this statement are not arguments for entry control *per se* so much as arguments for other facets of public regulation. For example, paragraphs B, D, and F deal more with the public concern for the financial responsibility of taxicab operators than with limiting the numbers of legal suppliers of the service. Similarly, paragraph C is an argument for regulated fare levels rather than entry controls.

The validity of the remaining assertions (paragraphs A, E, G, and H) can best be assessed by comparing actual experience in the few free entry cities with that in the cities which do impose entry restrictions. We will examine the detailed empirical evidence relating to the principal arguments for entry controls

---

[49] Samuels (1972b).

in the paragraphs which follow; later in the chapter we do this in a more general way by providing case studies of cab service in New York City and Washington, D.C.

The most frequently offered argument for entry limitation, both in the original debate in the early 1930s and today, is the public need to ensure that cab operators are financially responsible. This was a very genuine concern in the 1930s, given a history of fly-by-night operations in the 1920s. Indeed, the taxicab industry, by its nature, has a background of casual labor and often short-lived fleet operations, so there are compelling reasons for the public to limit cab operation to those firms or individuals who are financially sound and can bear responsibility for the liabilities they are likely to incur.

But this is palpably *not* the same thing as limiting the *number* of cabs allowed to operate, or limiting the market to those fleet operators who already hold monopoly franchises. It is not clear that there is any strong connection between entry limitations and financial responsibility. The free entry cities typically require just as much (and, equally true, just as little) evidence of financial responsibility from cab operators as do the cities with numerical limitations or franchises. Nor, indeed, have entry control ordinances done anything to solve the problems of fly-by-night operations, when they are not coupled with adequate financial responsibility ordinances. For example, it has been pointed out that in Chicago

> The problem of financial responsibility of . . . cabs was, and is, attributable not to "competition" but to the failure to require reliable insurance coverage. Even in 1970, after entry had been barred for thirty years, when the right to do business was worth more than $15,000 and insurance was required by the ordinance, financial responsibility remained a problem among independent Chicago cabs.[50]

Similarly, there is evidence that in New York City, another city with numerical limitations, the financial responsibility requirements are not fully adequate to protect the public interest—but we will discuss this problem further when we turn to consider explicitly the impact of financial responsibility regulations on cab service.

A somewhat related argument for entry limitations [51] suggests that only by entry controls can the public ensure proper business practices in the industry, including full accountability for tax-paying, record-keeping, and compliance with workmen's compensation laws, social security laws, and so on. This argument

---

[50] Kitch et al. (1971).
[51] Paragraph H in the ITA statement.

is surely as much a red herring as the argument regarding financial responsibility. It confuses entry limitations with the need for public agencies to ensure full registration and to oversee business concerns for taxation and other related purposes. Why should the taxicab industry be considered any different from other businesses in this regard?

In fact, the registration of the suppliers of taxicab services, and the collection of taxes from them, might well be more comprehensive in the free entry cities than in those cities where numerical limitations or franchise arrangements have led to a sizable number of totally illegal cab operators.

A third argument advanced in the ITA statement[52] suggests that entry controls provide some answer to the problem of service refusal, a major problem in the provision of cab services and one we will later discuss in some detail. But service refusal arises primarily because the driver thinks that certain types of passengers or destinations will not be profitable or might even place him in physical danger. Thus, many drivers refuse to accept these hails, even though ordinances (both in free entry and limited entry cities) typically specify that the driver has a legal obligation to convey the would-be passenger. And the question of entry controls is really irrelevant to the factors at work in this problem —it is at least as difficult to persuade a New York cabbie to take a passenger to Harlem as it is to persuade a Washington or Atlanta cabbie to drive into the high-crime areas of those cities.

But paragraph E of the ITA statement claims more than that free entry would aggravate the service refusal problem. It suggests that under free entry conditions drivers will concentrate on the areas of greatest demand at the times of greatest demand, and will neglect to provide service to low-demand areas or at low-demand times. Again, it is difficult to see the relevance of entry control ordinances to this argument. Whatever the entry conditions to the market, an independent cabbie can be expected to work at those times and in those places he perceives, rightly or wrongly, to be most economically productive. Similarly, there is no incentive for fleet operators to keep drivers on the road under conditions of very low demand.

There are, indeed, at least two regulatory provisions which *might* help to ensure some minimum level of service provided to all parts of the jurisdiction at all times of day. One is the type of regulation adopted when exclusive franchises are granted to serve particular facilities such as airports—the owner grants a monopoly franchise in return for a commitment by the fran-

---

[52] Paragraph E.

chisee to provide service at all necessary times. A second regulatory approach, which presumably helps to provide most parts of the city with some level of service, is to divide the city into zones and to grant a monopoly franchise for each zone as is done in Los Angeles.

Both of these forms of regulation contain the notion that monopoly privileges are being granted in return for some agreement to provide services which possibly would not otherwise be provided. But the monopoly aspects of these types of regulation are *not* an essential element—the essential element of the arrangement is that operators must have *licenses* to do business at a particular facility or in a particular area, where the granting of such a license depends on a commitment to provide the desired level of service. The *number* of licenses issued need not be restricted. As long as the licensed taxi operators are allowed to charge enough to provide an acceptable level of profit (which will not include, of course, the monopoly profits which currently accrue to the exclusive franchisee), presumably they will want to obtain a license even though it places obligations on them to provide some services at unremunerative times.

So while it may be possible to devise regulations which ensure that relatively unremunerative demands are served as well as the more lucrative ones,[53] it is not at all clear that entry restrictions to the market are either necessary or helpful in doing this.

There are other arguments for entry controls beyond those spelled out in the ITA statement. One of these, propounded both in the 1930s and today, is that unlimited numbers of cruising taxicabs might increase traffic congestion. It is very difficult to evaluate the strength of this argument—its validity will depend on a number of factors such as the physical form of the city, the nature of the demand induced by increased cab supply,[54] the relative importance of street and telephone hails, and so on. Doubtless there are some cities where taxis do contribute greatly to street congestion, and where increasing the number of cabs might exacerbate the situation unless accompanied by a reduction in the number of private automobiles on the street. Studies in London and New York City have shown that traffic speeds increase significantly during strikes of taxi drivers.[55]

---

[53] Service at otherwise uneconomic times or places could, of course, attract a legitimately higher price, in accordance with sound economic theory.

[54] If new cab trips were mostly diverted from auto drive-alone, for example, congestion might be expected to *decrease*—as might the demand for parking space in the congested areas.

[55] Marlowe (1967).

This is a difficult problem because it is in the most dense, congested downtown areas that the ability to hail a cab quickly on the street (which implies slowly cruising vehicles with frequent stops) is most important to the potential passenger. On the other hand, it can be argued that drivers of occupied cabs will usually try to avoid traffic congestion if it slows them down significantly, and that in the free entry cities of Atlanta and Washington taxicabs do not appear to be a major source of congestion.

A relatively recent refinement to the traffic congestion argument concerns the contribution which cruising taxicabs make to air pollution. Indeed, at the time of this writing, New York City is considering a ban on taxi cruising on Manhattan streets in response to the 1970 Clean Air Act.[56] However, the effects of entry controls on the levels of air pollution are as difficult to assess as the relationship between entry controls and traffic congestion—and for the same reasons.

Related to concerns over the congestion and pollution implications of expanded cab service is a concern over public safety. One argument that has been advanced for entry controls suggests that taxidrivers are relatively accident-prone, and that free entry would consequently impair urban transportation safety levels. In this context, a Milwaukee study investigated in detail the relative frequency of vehicle accidents and injuries in that city from 1966 to 1969, and concluded that

> Despite the fact that the number of taxi-involved accidents is increasing and is a continual cause for concern . . . there is no reason to believe that an increase in cab permits will induce a greater than proportional increase in traffic accidents.[57]

On a national basis, too, the sketchy evidence available does not support the notion that taxi drivers are accident-prone. The National Safety Council has compiled transportation-related accident data for a sample of 16 states,[58] and, on a per vehicle-mile basis, neither the number of accidents nor the number of fatalities appears to differ much between taxis and private automobiles. And, in the free-entry cities of Honolulu, Atlanta, and Washington, the 1972 motor vehicle accident death rates do not

---

[56] An informed decision on this proposal would require more data about New York's cab operations than are readily available. However, the prohibition of cruising would reduce significantly the taxi service available to the public unless large areas of curb space are given over to cab stands. We suspect that other alternatives to a cruising ban (such as compulsory standards for cab maintenance) are more likely to lessen air pollution by cabs, without so greatly reducing cab availability.

[57] Milwaukee Department of City Development (1971).

[58] National Safety Council (1973).

differ significantly from the mean rates for other cities of their size.

Yet another argument for entry controls suggests that unrestricted numbers of taxis would reduce the patronage of other forms of public transport. This is not *necessarily* bad if taxis can provide an equal or better service for a lower level of costs;[59] but the argument will probably find some support in current popular debate, since many people appear to believe that increased public transit ridership is always a worthy end in itself, regardless of the costs or the alternatives.

It is certainly true that a good, easily available cab service will reduce transit ridership if the two modes are in direct competition. But for transit routes where the level of traffic is already too low for profitable transit operation, expanded taxi services may allow the transit operator to curtail services and thus improve his financial situation. In other words, a free-entry taxi market has the potential for helping as well as for worsening the net revenue position of local transit.

Finally, it has been argued that entry restrictions prevent *taxicab wars*—physical violence between rival driver groups—sometimes common during the depression years of the 1930s. Indeed, there is more recent evidence that highly competitive conditions can lead to acrimony and violence; as gypsy cabs have encroached more and more on the territory hitherto reserved to medallion cab drivers in New York City, for example, hostility between the two groups has grown:

> The first major battle in the industry came in the summer of 1968 when 13 medallioned taxis were burned in Bedford-Stuyvesant as a threat of "hands off." Since that time innumerable skirmishes have broken out throughout the city pitting the medallion taxi drivers against their ghetto enemies. . . . Further warnings . . . took place during the summer of 1971 when over 100 cab windows were smashed and one taxi burned at a Bronx taxi fleet. These overt gestures of hostility . . . have been quite effective deterrents to the presence of the medallion taxi.[60]

While the immediate cause of these actions is a dispute over turf rights, it is not immediately clear that the presence or absence of entry controls to the cab market really plays a causative role. New York City has a numerical limitation on vehicles; Washington, on the other hand, has been relatively free of this type of occurrence.

---

[59] That is, costs broadly construed to include both social and financial costs.

[60] Vidich (1974).

Whether or not the lack of entry controls contributes to taxicab wars, it does seem likely (judging from the New York City experience and similar acrimony between different driver groups in other cities) that the overnight abolition of entry controls in a city would create problems of this kind, particularly in the short run. Any proposal for deregulation in this respect would do well to protect the financial interests of the existing drivers and fleets to the fullest extent practicable.

It is, however, significant that the threat of violence arises from within the ranks of the protected industry. When abolition of entry controls was under consideration in Milwaukee, a local report placed this threat in its proper political perspective:

> To argue that the possibility of anti-social conduct is so imminent in this industry that violence is likely to occur if it is returned to a normal competitive status is to propose that threatened lawlessness should be permitted to determine the level of commerce that city residents can have available to them. Acceptance of this argument by governmental bodies in the determination of policy is not only a tacit admission that a semi-organized threat is an effective political tool, but also that law enforcement agencies are not equal to the task of enforcing the existing laws governing the threatened behavior.[61]

In summary, then, what can one conclude about taxicab entry controls and the public interest? The main weight of available evidence suggests that the entry controls found in most large cities are *not* in the public interest, leading to an undersupply of taxi services, to higher fares than would otherwise obtain, and, often, to the creation of an extralegal unlicensed cab market. In particular, the public are likely to benefit from opening markets to more independent owner-drivers who satisfy adequate and effective tests of financial responsibility.

At the same time it is recognized that abolishing existing entry controls could indeed create problems, the magnitudes of which are difficult to foresee with any precision. Increased numbers of cabs *might* exacerbate traffic congestion and air pollution in some city centers, and could possibly lead to more traffic accidents. Judging from past experience, the removal of entry barriers may spark increased acrimony between different groups of drivers. Undoubtedly, some sections of the taxicab industry will be harmed financially by the dissolution of their monopoly rights. These matters are considered further in Chapter 13.

Financial responsibility requirements

Evidence of adequate financial responsibility is required from

---

[61] Milwaukee Department of City Development (1971).

fleet operators and owner-drivers to ensure that the public can obtain due financial redress for damages adjudged against the operators. There is some evidence that the regulations in this respect often do not have sufficient bite to protect the public adequately.

As a case in point, it is common practice for fleet owners in New York to establish a separate corporation for every two or three cabs in the fleet, the group of corporations in turn being controlled by a fleet holding company. This corporate structure minimizes the vulnerability of the fleet owner to liability claims since his assets are spread over the individual corporations. No matter how large the liability claim against him, the owner can be assured that he will never lose more than two or three cabs and the $10,000 bond he filed for liability insurance. Incorporation enables the owner to "avoid placing the true value of all his medallioned assets in the hands of every careless driver employed by his fleet." [62]

A 1958 court case revealed that there had been increasing concealment of New York City fleet assets through this device over the years. In 1937 a total of 8,424 fleet cabs were owned by 380 corporations; by 1958, the existing 6,816 fleet taxis were formally owned by as many as 2,120 corporations. [63]

In deciding that case, the court found that

> Although the increase in the number of corporations and the reduction of the number of taxicabs registered in the name of each may, in some instances, have been partially motivated by the legitimate desire to reduce federal income taxes, it is clear that the predominant motive generally has been the desire to avoid recovery of more than nominal or negligible amounts on judgments obtained for negligent operation of the taxicabs. . . . The public is inadequately protected with respect to compensation for personal injuries sustained through negligence of taxicabs . . . and the state and the city are unwitting accomplices of a legalized racket to avoid liability for payment for the negligent maiming and killing by taxicabs. [64]

In a similar connection, a 1959 court declared:

> The industry generally has demonstrated an appalling lack of concern for the public and has been guilty of so shameful an exercise in immorality that it almost defies description. [65]

Similar problems in ensuring adequate compensation of the public for liability claims are reported in Chicago. [66] It is not

---

[62] Vidich (1974).
[63] Ibid.
[64] Teller v. Clear Service Co., 173 NY Supp. 2d 183 (1958).
[65] Mull v. Colt Co., Inc., 178 Fed. Supp. 720 (1959).
[66] Kitch et al. (1971).

easy to suggest remedies which would solve the problem completely and would yet fall within the range of powers legally vested in the taxicab regulating agency. However, at least a partial remedy would be to raise the minimum liability insurance coverage required of taxicabs to a level which more realistically reflects both the frequency and magnitude of claims for damages. The $10,000 coverage required in New York City is equivalent to the minimum coverage required of private automobiles in that state, despite the much greater utilization (and possibly higher accident rates) of cabs.

The regulation of fares

Given that the taxicab regulating authority sets the *overall level* of fares in such a way as to provide what it regards as a "fair" rate of return to the taxi industry, some discussion is warranted on the way in which individual fares paid by the public can be related to the features of their rides—in other words, the fare *structure*. A Committee of Enquiry into the London taxicab trade approached the question of fare structures in this way:

> The Committee . . . considered the optimal structure of fares, as distinct from the general level of fares. Our approach has been in terms of the principles of marginal cost pricing, which are widely accepted as a basis for a rational allocation of resources, and of an equitable pricing system in which the user of any good or service pays that sum for its enjoyment which is equal to the cost to the rest of society of the resources absorbed in the production of the good or service.
>
> The main elements in the cost of providing a taxicab service can be classified into three groups:
>
> • Annual costs: mainly taxicab costs, such as depreciation, insurance, cost of capital tied up in the vehicles.
>
> • Hourly costs: mainly labour costs, which in most industries would be the driver's wages, but in this industry are its equivalent in the form of the hourly earnings he must expect to make in order to choose to stay in the trade.
>
> • Mileage costs: mainly fuel and tires; also some element of depreciation and repairs.
>
> It can be seen, therefore, that the costs of providing a journey in a taxicab are positively related to two variables: to the time taken for the journey, which leads to the two sets of time-related costs; and to the mileage of the journey, which leads to the distance-related costs. Except when the taxi is stationary, both of these kinds of cost accrue simultaneously; a journey of a mile in three minutes (at an average speed of 20 m.p.h.) involves three minutes' worth of time-related costs and one mile's worth of distance-related costs. It fol-

lows, therefore, that a rational pricing system, based on the principles outlined above, would use a meter which operated simultaneously on a time-and-distance basis. This would, for example, mean that a journey at a fast speed in uncongested conditions would cost a good deal less than a journey of the same length in moderately congested conditions. This makes sense, since the user of the taxi is depriving others of its use for a longer time if his journey takes longer. One consequence might be to help relieve the shortage of taxis at busy times, when traffic is more congested, because some users would not find it worth their while to pay the relatively higher journey costs at such times and so would make the taxis more easily available for those with pressing needs.[67]

The British report goes on to give a more detailed discussion of the implications of marginal cost pricing principles for the structuring of cab fares, and the interested reader is recommended to refer to the source. Vickrey also agrees that the *simultaneous* incrementing of fares based both on time and on distance traveled would be a more efficient method of pricing, but he points out that even such a change is less than optimum:

> A more rational fare structure that would stay within the overall confines of existing practice would be a fare that would include an initial charge for cabs responding to a call only (in some areas, indeed, the mileage from the hack stand to the pickup point is charged for), and would charge separately and on an additive overall basis for time and for mileage, with 50 to 80 percent of the charge being levied on the time basis, or possibly even no mileage charge at all. However, if the charge were entirely on the time basis, this might be thought to lead to excessive dawdling on the part of drivers. Some move to reduce the present pressure on drivers to accomplish their trips in the shortest possible time would be desirable from a safety standpoint.
>
> Even such a fare structure would be far from the ideal, however. One difficulty is that rational and knowledgeable cab drivers would tend to distribute their cruising more or less in proportion to the density of fares along various possible cruising routes, whereas minimizing the total time that potential riders would have to wait for a cab would call for distribution of cruising in proportion to the square root of the fare density. . . . This is in addition to the general public interest in reducing the cruising of empty taxis in areas of high traffic congestion. Another element that should be taken into account in an ideal fare structure is the pattern of back-hauls. At any given time of day, there will be areas with an excess of trip terminations over trip originations, and other areas where the reverse is true, requiring the movement of empty cabs from the first area to the second. The cost of a cab ride in this direction would thus be substantially less than the cost of a ride that takes a cab from a deficiency area to a surplus area. . . . A fare structure that took this element of cost into account would be fairly complex. It would have to look a lot more like a

---

[67] U.K. Home Office (1970).

multiple set of zone-to-zone fares than anything that could be implemented with the usual type of taxi-meter.[68]

Obviously, attempts to adhere completely to the principles of economically efficient pricing could well create an administrative nightmare for drivers, passengers, and the regulating agency officials alike. Moreover, we know of no existing taximeter on the market which does operate simultaneously on a time-and-distance basis, and the London Committee was told that it was technically impossible to convert the existing stock of London meters to such a basis. However, for both zone fare systems and existing meter systems it is possible to introduce some fairly simple fare differentials which constitute steps in the direction indicated by marginal cost pricing considerations.

For example, a simple, flat fare increment for cab journeys which start during rush hours (an extra 25 cents, say) would reduce the pressure of demand at those times and also reduce the frustrated demand of people willing to pay for peak hour cabs but unable to find them. Under a zone fare structure it would provide an incentive to drivers to stay on the streets in the rush hours.

The additional fee charged in some cities for telephone hails is presumably meant to compensate for the extra costs of operating 2-way radio equipment,[69] as well as to provide an incentive to drivers to respond to telephone hails when street hails are abundant. In Mexico City, cabs engaged from street taxi stands have a higher fare than those hailed while cruising, presumably justified by the extra costs of maintaining stands. The economic basis for such rate differences, and their wider implications, merit some investigation.

Among the details to be considered in discussing fare structure are the pros and cons of different methods of computing the fare—in particular, the choice between *meter-based* and *zone-based* fare structures. The principal advantages of each of these two methods of charging are:

Meters

- Meter-computed fares more closely approximate the marginal costs of providing the service in that they take the duration of the journey partially into account. Under the zone system the driver usually receives no compensation for time spent in congestion delays, and therefore rush hour periods are less profit-

---

[68] Vickrey (1973).
[69] These costs have been investigated by Gramza et al. (1969).

able to him. This explains why there are markedly fewer cabs on the streets during the rush hours in Washington, D.C., than during the middle of the day.

- In addition, meter-computed fares more closely reflect the distance-related costs of the journey. A zone system can often create fare anomalies near the boundaries of the zones, where passengers may be charged relatively high fares for very short journeys. Further, zone boundaries may not be changed sufficiently frequently to reflect areas of new residential or commercial development, again leading to possible anomalies in fares.

- Meters are better able to charge for time spent in waiting at the origin or destination of the trip under orders from the passenger.

- Meter-displayed fares probably are easier to understand, and lead to less argument between driver and passenger than zone fares. Meters are reasonably tinker-proof, and afford protection to the public against fraud.

- Meter-computed fares may be more equitable in the sense that zone boundaries can be drawn in such a way as to benefit politically powerful groups of the population. For example, the zone boundaries used in Washington ensure relatively cheap cab fares to and from the U.S. Capitol building, and it is sometimes claimed that this fact is more than coincidental.[70] On the other side of the same coin, however, a zone system could be used fairly flexibly by a local government to allow fare discrimination in favor of worthy population groups (such as residents of poverty areas)—this would be more difficult to do with a meter-based system.

Zone system

- A zone system ensures that there is no incentive for the driver to take an unsuspecting passenger by a deviously lengthy route or to attempt to be stopped by red lights in order to increase the fare.

- The zone system obviates the capital costs of meters, not a small consideration over a large fleet of vehicles.[71]

---

[70] Fried (1970).

[71] A representative of the dominant manufacturer of meters informed us in 1973 that prices for a new unit range from $200 to $700, with the average meter probably costing between $300 and $400.

- The traveler is often in a better position to judge the exact fare before taking his trip.

- Meters limit the flexibility for adjusting fares (particularly by small increments), since the process of adapting them to a new fare scale is often a time-consuming and costly one.

Of course, meters and the conventional zone system are not the only options for basing charges. The adoption of a "moving" or "floating zone" structure has received some consideration in Washington, D.C.—such a fare system is also contemplated for conventional transit modes in the Rhine-Ruhr metropolitan area in West Germany.[72]

Organizational features and taxicab service

We have noted previously that, nationally, the most common organizational arrangement within the taxicab industry is for a fleet to employ drivers who are paid a fixed commission on the gross receipts of their vehicles. Less commonly, fleets may lease vehicles to drivers by the day under either a short-term or long-term rental agreement which typically requires the lessee to purchase gasoline, oil, and maintenance and dispatching services from the fleet operator.

These leasing arrangements appear to be common in the New York City livery cab industry, and in the fully-licensed cab industry in a number of other cities. It is fairly easy to understand why leasing is common in the free entry city of Washington where there are large numbers of casual cab drivers. It is not so easy to understand why there are some other cities (Milwaukee, for example) where leasing arrangements for cab drivers appear to have been more common than employee/commission arrangements for many years.

A number of progressive fleet owners (particularly in medium-sized cities) are switching from employing drivers on commission to leasing out their vehicles. These owners tend to be very enthusiastic about the results of the change. They claim that big improvements in the drivers' productivity (as measured, say, by gross receipts per mile) typically ensue. In addition, drivers appear to take a much greater interest in the welfare of their passengers when they see themselves as entrepreneurs rather than merely as fleet employees.

However, it is possible that under leasing arrangements the independence of individual drivers may lead to some degrada-

---

[72] Gutknecht (1974).

tion of service. For example, if the lessee has the right to refuse some of the radio calls channeled to him by the central dispatcher, the telephone hail system may break down. This is not an uncommon occurrence at peak hours in Washington where one cannot be confident that a cab hailed by telephone will actually respond. The remedy might be to give drivers a financial incentive to accept telephone hails in preference to street hails by incorporating a significant telephone surcharge in the fare structure.

A CASE STUDY:
Cab service in New York City and Washington, D.C.

It is instructive to compare and contrast briefly the nature of taxicab services in New York City and in Washington, for both cities illustrate many of the points we have made about the ways in which regulatory and organizational features influence service. We do not wish to imply, however, that the transportation systems and problems of New York City and Washington are strictly comparable—they differ greatly in many ways. Nor should New York City be viewed any longer as a typical example of a city with numerical limitations on entry to the cab market—as we shall see, in recent years there has been a de facto breakdown of entry controls in that city.

New York City [73]

We have already noted that the 1937 Haas Act, as currently enforced, limits the number of medallions for fully-licensed New York City cabs to 11,787, of which 6,816 are specifically reserved for fleet owners. In addition the city supports probably 15,000 private livery vehicles,[74] which are licensed by the state rather than the city and which require no medallions. Legally the private liveries can respond only to hires made by telephone requests or on the premises of the livery operator.

However, over the past few years the pattern of vehicle-for-hire services in New York City has changed markedly, due primarily to the advent of the gypsy cab. Gypsies may be either licensed private livery vehicles illegally accepting hails on the street, or drivers operating taxis without official licenses of any kind.

Historically, medallioned cabs and private liveries have tended

---

[73] Material in this section is derived largely from Vidich (1974).
[74] Lazar (1971).

to serve different areas of the city. For economic reasons and for reasons of personal safety, medallion drivers usually prefer to work in Manhattan's central business district. The rapid growth of the private livery and gypsy cab operations can be traced largely to black or Puerto Rican poverty areas—it is estimated that nearly 95 percent of all private livery drivers are black or Puerto Rican compared with no more than 35 percent of all medallion cab drivers.

Other factors have contributed to the large increase in gypsy operations since the mid 1960s. The present medallioned drivers' union, chartered in 1966, managed to raise the drivers' commission rate from 45 percent to approaching 50 percent. This increased the incentives for medallion cabs to serve only short hires in the central business district, thus diminishing service to black and Puerto Rican communities even more. Further, legal enforcement of the regulations against gypsy operations appears to have broken down entirely.

The increase in gypsy cabs has had several important consequences. Gypsy drivers are now encroaching on territory which has long been the exclusive domain of the medallioned industry. Many disenchanted fleet drivers have defected to become gypsy drivers (or part-time gypsies). The turnover rate for medallion cab operators has grown,[75] and the negotiating strength of the drivers' union has been weakened by the increased transient nature of the profession. Moreover, gypsy drivers have demonstrated their willingness to take over the medallioned cab market during any strike, which has further weakened the union's bargaining position. Since 1971 fleet drivers have been working in New York City without a ratified contract.

The economics of fleet operation have also been adversely affected by the rapid growth in gypsy operations, as well as by the initial bargaining power of the newly formed taxidrivers' union in the mid 1960s, by labor shortages, and by cheating on the part of the drivers. The decline of the fleet industry is reflected in the change in the resale value of fleet medallions—from an all-time high of $35,000 in late 1964, the buying price had dropped to $6,000 by late 1972. The bankruptcy of ten fleets in September 1971 highlights the severity of the problem.

In response to the gradual dissolution of their monopoly empire, fleet owners have tried to make significant reductions in their costs. Replacement cycles for vehicles have been lengthened, and vehicle maintenance has been cut back. Cabs have been

---

[75] Over the last five years over 50 percent of all new drivers have left the industry within three years of receiving their first hack license.

fitted with so-called *hot seats* to thwart dishonest drivers,[76] although this measure has been outwitted by some cabbies and there is other evidence to suggest that off-the-meter transactions with passengers are increasing. Moreover, the fleet owners have been successful in forcing back the commission rate for new drivers to 42 percent and in establishing production quotas for fleet drivers.

In 1971, the newly organized Taxi and Limousine Commission set out to inhibit further growth in gypsy operations by trying to institute mandatory $200 fines for the acceptance of street hails by nonmedallioned vehicles. The measure has had little success:

> This technique has not been supported by the courts, which have been extremely lenient with the gypsies, reducing their fines to nominal levels and condoning their activity in light of the woefully inadequate taxi service in the ghetto. The courts have worked to undermine the letter of the law in order to compensate for the inadequacies caused by the existing law which determined the monopoly of the medallioned industry. Rather than censuring the activities of the gypsy, the courts have been implicitly disagreeing with the lawmakers.[77]

It is not difficult to trace the current troubles of the New York City taxi industry, at least in large part, back to the numerical entry limitations imposed by the Haas Act. The growth of gypsy operations came about chiefly because a large volume of demand for cab services, particularly in the black and Puerto Rican areas, was not being satisfied by the medallioned industry. That industry could not expand, and in particular, a private entrepreneur wishing to respond to the unsatisfied demand could only do so legally by raising upwards of $20,000 to buy a medallion from an owner-driver.

Moreover, the medallion system has ironically exacerbated the difficulties of the fleet industry as the monopoly has been assailed by gypsy operations:

> . . . The sale of fleet medallions has had the most profound consequences on the cost efficiency of the industry. The transfer of the medallion cost from one operator to another has meant that new operators automatically have had economic disadvantages over those who have owned their medallions since 1937. The medallion cost as a result has become a large part of the overhead of the most recent individuals and companies entering the taxicab industry.
>
> The additional overhead of the medallion has aggravated the financial well-being of the entire taxi industry. . . . The financial ruin of the taxi industry has not been a private affair. The industry has

---

[76] A *hot seat* is a pressure-sensitive device installed in the cab's passenger seat which turns on the meter when the passenger sits down.

[77] Vidich (1973).

consistently passed operating costs on to the public. Instead of eliminating inefficient producers of service, the fleet owners have banded together . . . and have legislated for fare increases which have allowed these inefficient operators to stay in business. For the first time in fifty years the price of a taxi ride relative to the consumer price index has begun to climb. . . . The rise in the price of taxi service reflects the growth of inefficient producers of service. The medallion has been the key to the whole problem. It has been transferred from one owner to another like a hot potato. Those who have held onto the hot potato too long have gone bankrupt; those who have passed it along have eventually passed it to the public. Nobody wanted to get stuck with the cost of paying off an overpriced medallion. However, those who did, and didn't have the sense to sell it and recoup some of their losses, have attempted to turn their loss into profit at the public's expense.[78]

Washington, D.C.

Washington, on the other hand, is an example of a city with no numerical entry controls on the provision of cab service. However, it is important to note that, with the exception of the lack of entry controls and of certain provisions permitting shared riding, the public regulation of taxicabs in Washington differs little from that in most other major cities. Vehicles must be properly identified and maintained, and drivers must satisfy tests of financial responsibility, character, and driving ability.

We have seen earlier that the provision of cab service in Washington is significantly greater than in any other major city in the United States. However, there are some important deficiencies in the service provided by the District of Columbia cab system, and these deficiencies have sometimes been used to denigrate the free entry arrangement in that city.[79]

The shortcomings most often cited with respect to the Washington cab system are:

- the difficulty of obtaining taxis at certain periods of the day, particularly during the afternoon rush hour and after midnight

- the unreliability of the telephone hail system

- the difficulty of ensuring adequate levels of financial responsibility for, and of collecting taxes from, the many independent cabbies in the city

The lack of cabs on the streets at certain periods of the day cannot logically be imputed to the free entry arrangement. Cab drivers find it uneconomic for them to work in the afternoon peak

---

[78] Vidich (1974).
[79] See, for example, Samuels (1971) or Witkin (1971).

principally because the zone fare system, which does not take account of the duration of a hire, is particularly unremunerative when the taxi has to move in highly congested traffic. Likewise, relatively few cabbies work through the night because the overall level of demand at these hours is very low—Washington has few night clubs or other major sources of taxi demand after midnight. In both cases, during the afternoon traffic peak and during the early morning hours, the current situation could be ameliorated by imposing a flat fare increment for hires made at those times—say 25 or 50 cents. This type of incentive would induce more drivers to work at the times which are currently least remunerative. Post-midnight surcharges are, in fact, included in the fare structures of several cities.

The telephone hail system breaks down in Washington because most fleet drivers are not employees of the fleet owner but are independents operating under vehicle rental agreements. This is partly a result of the free entry arrangement, although several cities which do have entry controls also have extensive renting of cabs. A Washington newspaper explained the situation to an enquiring reader in this way:

> The manager said you should have been told that they no longer can guarantee a cab. Most of the drivers are independent owners who pay rental fees and dispatch fees to use the cabs and radios. When a call comes in, the dispatcher puts it on the air and then the drivers bid (by stating their locations) on that job if they want it. If there is no cab nearby, or no one bids on the job, the company cannot make a cab come to your home. However, in emergencies, the dispatcher does have some reliable drivers to call on.[80]

Again, the situation could be improved by making it more financially attractive for drivers to respond to telephone hails—particularly at times when street hails are plentiful. An increase in the surcharge for telephone hails, currently 25 cents, would make telephone service more reliable.

Washington, like New York City, has trouble in ensuring adequate financial responsibility of taxicab operations. That the problems are very analogous to those in New York can be seen from a 1957 Congressional hearing:

> It appears that a large number of the taxicabs now operating on the streets of the District of Columbia were placed there as a result of the activity of car dealers, irresponsible fleet owners, and finance companies without regard to public service. . . . The sellers and lessors of these vehicles desire to escape liability in any way that is possible. Therefore, the vehicles are often painted with the color scheme and titled in the name of a small cooperative or practically

---

[80] *Washington Evening Star & Daily News*, April 5, 1973, p. B2.

insolvent corporation so that in the event any accident should occur in which liability above insurance limits is incurred, the corporation may be dissolved and the judgment creditor defeated thereby.[81]

As in New York City, the problem could be partially alleviated by requiring higher levels of insurance for each licensed taxicab —current liability is limited to a maximum of $20,000.

THE SERVICE REFUSAL PROBLEM

Cab regulations usually include some concept of *compellability*— that is, a driver breaks the law if he refuses to convey a passenger under certain specified sets of circumstances. However, these ordinances are extremely difficult to police, and there is much evidence that in a number of cities service refusal on compellable journeys is widespread. Drivers will deliberately "fail to see" pedestrians who hail them; they will display "On Call" signs until they spot a potential passenger whom they wish to accept; they will sometimes make oral refusals in open defiance of the law.

Glick (1971) documents the extent of formal complaints lodged about service refusal in New York City. Service refusal (along with numerical limitations on cab licenses) has been cited as one prime reason for the existence of illegal taxi and jitney systems and for the operation of livery vehicles as gypsy cabs, particularly in ghetto areas.[82]

Service refusal arises for three main reasons:

- Taxi drivers fear for their safety in various areas of the city. To avoid going to areas in which they think they may be financially or even physically at risk, they do not respond to hails from people who *look* as if their destinations might be in those areas. Since many of the high crime regions are poverty zones in the inner city, this type of service refusal unfortunately has racial overtones. The main clue a cab driver may have to a potential passenger's destination is skin color, and the news media have conducted experiments which often show that drivers (both black and white) will stop for white patrons after ignoring black ones.

- Drivers do not like to accept hails which will take them to areas (usually out of the central city) where they think they will have

---

[81] U.S. Congress, House of Representatives (1957).

[82] Lazar (1971); Rattien and Duckett (1971); Lee et al. (1972); and Marbury (1972).

difficulty in finding their next passengers, or into areas where (for franchise reasons) they are not allowed to accept hails. For obvious financial reasons, they wish to avoid long, nonproductive deadhead journeys back to the profitable area.

- Drivers going off duty are happy to accept riders heading in the direction of their own destination, but balk at accepting hires which require a significant detour.

From the driver's viewpoint, each of these reasons has some justification, as recent firsthand descriptions of cab driving have graphically documented.[83] The deadheading problem might be solved by providing some form of financial remuneration under the fare structure for journeys which entail a high probability of empty return trips. It is more difficult to suggest institutional or financial arrangements which might effectively solve the security problem.

THE DEMAND FOR TAXI SERVICES

We now turn from considering the *nature* of taxi service (and the way it is shaped by organizational and regulatory factors) to examining the demand for cab services. First, however, a note of caution. A number of studies have tried to characterize taxicab demand and present a picture of the market. This is difficult to do with any certainty in view of several problems of data collection and interpretation which we will discuss briefly before returning to summarize the existing evidence.

A good detailed description of the market for taxi services would require knowledge of taxi passengers (their demographic and socioeconomic characteristics) and of the cab journeys they make (the origin and destination points, the trip purposes, the distribution by time of day, and so on) under varying patterns of urban passenger transportation supply. There are three main data sources for such information:

- *Data from metropolitan area home-interview, origin-destination studies—*
  This source typically provides a very detailed description of the cab trips of residents of the metropolitan area under study. However, in many cities one might reasonably expect non-residents of the area to comprise a sizable portion of the taxi market, and this segment is typically not included (or included

---

[83] See, for example, Lasson (1971) or Wallace (1972).

only very inadequately) in the coverage of this type of data base.[84]

- *Data from records of trips compiled by cab drivers—*
This source may provide an accurate record of taxi trips distinguished by origin, destination, and time of day, but only very limited information is available about the cab passengers or their purposes in traveling.[85]

- *Data from special postcard surveys of passengers—*
A limited number of attempts have been made to collect information about passengers and their trips from surveys using driver-distributed postcards.[86] However, the response rates for these surveys have been very low, and the representativeness of the data must be open to serious question.

All of these sources of information, by and large, describe only legal taxi operations and hires; in some cities, illegal operations cover a large segment of the total market. Despite these many difficulties, the data collected in different cities by varying and imperfect methods do show some consistencies, qualitatively if not always quantitatively, and this evidence is summarized in the sections which follow.

Taxicab patrons

In any particular city the personal characteristics of taxi passengers will be determined fairly obviously by a number of factors: particularly important are the socioeconomic composition of the population at large, the spatial distribution of economic activity, and the availability and price of alternative forms of transportation, both public and private. However, the available empirical evidence suggests that taxi users are predominantly of working age (18 through 64 years old), and that there are a number of different population subgroups with a relatively high propensity for taxi usage. These subgroups are:

- professional and managerial workers

- persons from high-income households

- nonresidents of the area

[84] The market descriptions given by Beimborn (1969), Lee et al. (1972), and the Tri-State Transportation Commission (1969) are based on home-interview surveys.

[85] The data cited by the National Capital Region Transportation Planning Board (1970) are of this nature.

[86] Rattien and Duckett (1971) and the U.K. Home Office (1970) collected information in this way.

- people traveling to and from interurban transportation terminals

- economically inactive people (homemakers, students, retired people, etc.), particularly those without drivers' permits

- low-income residents of poverty areas

The available data are generally too sketchy to identify differing patterns of usage associated with each of these subgroups. However, it is possible to make some hypotheses which appear to be intuitively reasonable and also compatible with the available empirical evidence:

- *Professional and managerial workers* account for a large share of all cab trips—approaching 50 percent of the (legal) cab trips within the New York metropolitan region,[87] over a quarter of all cab trips in the Chicago city region,[88] and one in six of all cab trips in the Pittsburgh area.[89]

The differences in this proportion between cities partly reflect the varying proportions of professional and managerial workers in the metropolitan resident populations: in the New York SMSA 26 percent of employed persons are in those occupational categories, 23 percent in the Chicago SMSA, and 23 percent in the Pittsburgh SMSA.

These occupational categories use taxis for job-related journeys, and probably more for travel in the course of work than for travel to and from work. The service characteristics of the taxi make it particularly suitable for someone who, say, has to attend meetings at various geographical locations within the central area of the city during the working day. If the working time of employees in professional and managerial positions is valued at the direct wage rate, then taxis will invariably prove to be a cheaper method of central area door-to-door transportation (in time and money terms) than typical bus or rail transit services. The cab may also be preferred to private automobile for traveling in congested areas during the working day because time spent in the taxi may be used productively—preparing for a meeting, for example—and because parking is no problem.

This type of demand, therefore, is heavily oriented toward areas of high office development (usually central areas), and is predominantly limited to normal office working hours. In Chicago, for example, where 42 percent of all cab trips have central

---

[87] Tri-State Transportation Commission (1969).

[88] Beimborn (1969).

[89] Harris (1963).

area destinations, 60 percent of the taxi journeys by professional/managerial workers terminate in the central area.[90]

• Taxi patrons are drawn disproportionately from upper income households. In the New York City metropolitan region in 1966, 45 percent of legal taxi users came from households with a gross annual income of $10,000 or over; by comparison, only 22 percent of the region's households had incomes this large.[91] In Pittsburgh in 1970, 43 percent of cab passengers were from households with a gross annual income of $10,000 or over.[92]

Of course, since professional and managerial workers are among the highest paid, there is a great deal of duplication between this market segment and the professional/managerial one just discussed, and many of the cab journeys of the relatively wealthy are probably made for business-related purposes. However, there is a sense in which the taxi can be regarded as a luxury mode, and those who are willing and able to pay a money premium for on-call, door-to-door, private, chauffeur-driven service may enjoy these benefits for all their urban traveling requirements when they have no wish to drive themselves. So members of high-income households, the economically inactive as well as the employed, may use cabs for a wide range of purposes: to and from work, to shop, to eat, to visit, to go to entertainment and other recreational activities. This type of demand will be spread throughout the day and will be oriented toward major shopping and entertainment sections of the central area.

• For visitors from out of town who arrive without their own automobile, the taxi represents a very attractive way of achieving mobility. If most of the visitor's travel will be in the center of the city, using cabs will probably prove cheaper and more convenient than the principal alternative, a rental car. The cab is particularly suitable for providing access to interurban terminals,[93] or for traveling between terminal and hotel when the visitor is carrying bulky luggage. Consequently, cab stands are always in evidence at airports, downtown airline terminals, main line railroad stations, and principal hotels.

The size of this segment of the market will probably vary markedly from city to city, depending on the city's importance as a tourist or business center, or as an interurban transporta-

---

[90] Beimborn (1969).

[91] Tri-State Transportation Commission (1969).

[92] Rattien and Duckett (1971).

[93] This applies equally to residents and nonresidents of the area, of course.

tion interchange point. It is, however, very difficult to find any data to illustrate the importance of the nonresident demand for taxis, except in the most indirect and circumstantial fashion. In Pittsburgh, between 10 percent and 20 percent of all cab trips are to or from the airport; these account for about a third of the city's (legal) cab revenues.[94] Twelve percent of Pittsburgh taxi users live outside the county. In London in summer, it is estimated that roughly a third of all cab passengers are visitors to the city.[95] In a survey of taxi trips made to and from Boston cab stands, hotels accounted for 32 percent of the hires, and transportation terminals for another 11 percent.[96]

The pattern of demand for taxi travel to and from interurban transportation terminals during the day is obviously likely to mirror the fluctuations in arrival and departure volumes. At airports, for example, the peaking characteristics differ from city to city,[97] but the greatest passenger volume is typically in the early evening, with a slightly less pronounced early morning peak. Friday and Sunday evenings are often an airport's busiest periods.

- A number of studies have shown taxis to be used relatively heavily by the *economically inactive* (homemakers, students, unemployed, retired, or incapacitated persons), particularly those who for one reason or another have no private automobile alternative. So, for example, in 1956 in Chicago, 45 percent of all cab trips by residents of the area were made by housewives.[98] It is reported that 60 percent of the residents' legal taxi journeys in Pittsburgh are made by the economically inactive; 34 percent are made by housewives.[99]

In the Chicago sample, 55 percent of taxi passengers did not have drivers' permits. In the 1970 Pittsburgh sample,[100] 42 percent of users were without drivers' permits, and 52 percent claimed that their immediate family did not own a car. Similar data for some of the subgroups of the (statistically suspect) Pittsburgh sample are presented in Table 13.

Hence, large proportions of taxi users appear to be without a private automobile alternative, possibly out of deliberate choice. One would hypothesize that they are most likely to use cabs for those trips which are least well served by conven-

---

[94] Rattien and Duckett (1971).
[95] U.K. Home Office (1970).
[96] Barbera (1972).
[97] Whitlock and Cleary (1969).
[98] Beimborn (1969).
[99] Harris (1963).
[100] Rattien and Duckett (1971).

Table 13

Auto availability for Pittsburgh cab passengers

Subgroup of sample	Passengers with no driver's permit (by group)	Passengers whose family does not own a car (by group)
Proportion of	%	%
total sample	42	52
females	57	68
passengers over 55	56	56
nonwhite passengers	69	85
annual household income under $7500	70	85
regular cab users (50+ times per year)	49	58

Source: Rattien and Duckett (1971)

tional transit modes. Since most transit systems are designed to serve best the flows to and from the central area of the city, they typically provide a relatively poor service (in door-to-door time and convenience) for travel between two noncentral locations. Thus intuition suggests that the cab trips made by homemakers, students, and other economically inactive categories are probably less oriented towards the central area than those made by, say, the professional/managerial subgroup. Data from Chicago indirectly support this hypothesis, as is illustrated by Table 14.

• The *low-income residents of poverty areas* have been found to make a relatively intensive use of taxicabs. There is evidence for this from a number of different cities. One Boston study[101] suggested that households with annual incomes under $4,000 contributed a fifth of the city's cab revenues. Another Boston study found that, when car ownership was controlled for, those with an income under $4,000 used cabs as often as those with incomes over $10,000.[102] In the 1970 Pittsburgh study, 44 percent of cab users had annual family incomes below $7,500.[103]

Data from a home interview survey of residents of the Central Brooklyn Model Cities (CBMC) area have been used to examine cab usage in this type of poverty area in some detail.[104] Whereas households with an annual income of $4,000 or less

[101] Herr and Fleisher (1968).
[102] Rosenbloom (1971).
[103] Rattien and Duckett (1971).
[104] Lee et al. (1972).

Table 14
Cab trips of Chicago area residents

	Proportion of person trips with noncentral area destinations (by group)
	%
All riders	58
Male riders	46
Professional/managerial workers	39
Female riders	66
Housewives	70
White riders	55
Nonwhite riders	82
Riders with a driver's permit	43
Riders without a driver's permit	70

Source: Beimborn (1969)

constitute about a fifth of all households in the New York metropolitan region, their share of the region's taxi trips amounted to only about 8 percent. In the CBMC area, on the other hand, 40 percent of all households had an annual income of $4,000 or less, but these households accounted for 43 percent of the cab trips generated by the area.

The CBMC study compared the reasons for traveling for the cab trips of the poverty area residents with the taxi journeys of all metropolitan area residents. Relatively speaking, very few of the cab trips of the CBMC area residents were related to work or school; they were much more likely to be for shopping, recreational, or personal business (including medical) purposes. One in three trips was made within the immediate community. Seventy-two percent of the cab riders came from households without automobiles.

The researchers estimated that there were 1,500 cabs registered in the CBMC area, all but 200 of which were nonmedallion livery vehicles. Accordingly, about 85 percent of all the taxi trips recorded were made in nonmedallion cabs.

The most obvious reason for relatively heavy taxicab usage in some poverty areas is the lack of any cheaper nonautomobile transportation alternative with comparable flexibility. In many cities, ghetto areas are as well served by traditional transit modes as any other part of town. Many transit routes into and out of poverty areas are among the most profitable routes in their systems. However, transit's fixed route and departure time inflexibilities mean that the transit modes cannot adequately serve many types of travel demands such as shopping and recreational trips. Where the middle- or upper-income person might drive his own automobile, the poor person has to take the taxi. This makes sound financial sense, too. By examining annual money outlays and depreciation costs, it is very easy for most city dwellers who own cars principally for intraurban travel to convince themselves that on strict financial grounds they would be better off by selling their own cars and using cabs extensively instead—the urban automobile owner is paying a high price for the service differential between the private car and the taxi.

There may well be other contributing reasons for the relatively heavy use of taxicabs by the poor; the following contribution by a sociologist at a 1968 conference on poverty and transportion is of interest here:

> I had occasion to attend meetings weekly . . . at a public housing project in Roxbury. One of the things that startled me about this area . . . was the number of taxicabs I saw coming to and from the housing project. After a while it began to dawn on me that I did not understand at all why people were using cabs so much. I started asking a few of the people who lived there and came up with a set of notions having to do with the style of life of the people who lived there which I think might be useful. For one, a term which is used by sociologist David Caplovitz comes to mind, "compensatory consumption." That is, some people, including Caplovitz, have a sense that the poor people—when they find themselves continuously blocked in their mobility aspirations —tend to pick one or two items like a television set or taxicab or something else with which they will indulge themselves as a way of compensating for other things they want but cannot have. One woman in the project told me that one of the reasons she and some of her friends (these were black women) liked riding cabs was that it was the only occasion they had where someone was serving them. She also told me that some women rode cabs at night because the neighborhood was dangerous, and even a block or two walk from a busline was something they did not want to risk. Finally, from other impressions, I did have a sense that cabs are used often in emergencies and that emergencies are defined more broadly and loosely by lower-class people. I think one would make a mistake in trying to find a single reason why cabs are used by poor people.[105]

We suggest that the aggregate patterns of taxicab demand observed in cities is substantially the result of the mixture of the demand profiles for the five population subgroups just described.

---

[105] Gordon Fellman (Brandeis University), recorded in American Academy of Arts and Sciences (1968b).

We now turn to look briefly at some other aspects of the aggregate demand patterns.

The spatial pattern of demand

We have hypothesized that for a number of the population subgroups which use taxicabs most heavily, travel in cabs is oriented towards the central area of the city. The empirical evidence does indeed suggest that in large metropolitan areas the demand focuses heavily on the downtown areas. Metropolitan area transportation studies typically reveal that a very high density of taxi trips begin or end within the central business district, falling off rapidly as one moves radially outwards. In New York City, for example, Manhattan accounts for nearly half of the taxi journeys within the city region. Within a radius of half a mile from the junctions of Fifth Avenue and 50th Street, five times more taxi trips than auto trips begin each day. In this area the density of taxi trip destinations exceeds 40,000 per square mile per day. But few areas (other than the airports) outside a five mile radius from Manhattan have trip destination densities exceeding 5,000 per square mile per day.[106] Similarly, in Chicago about 58 percent of all cab trips originate or terminate in the 4.5 square mile central area.[107]

The temporal pattern of demand

While some peaking of taxicab demand during morning and evening rush hours may be detectable in major cities, it is typically much less pronounced than the peaking observed for other travel modes. In the New York City region very slight peaks are noticed around 8 A.M. and 5 P.M., with secondary peaking over the lunch hours.[108] In Chicago, and particularly in the central area, taxi traffic is greater at lunch time than at any other time of the day.[109] A similar midday peaking is observed in Washington.[110]

One possible reason why there is no pronounced increase in cab usage during the morning and evening rush hours is that the supply of cabs is fully utilized at those times, and that, because of regulated supply limitations, no more taxis are available to cope with any increase in demand. Another possible contributory

---

[106] Tri-State Transportation Commission (1969).
[107] Beimborn (1969).
[108] Tri-State Transportation Commission (1969), from which Figure 2 is taken.
[109] Beimborn (1969).
[110] National Capital Region Transportation Planning Board (1970).

Figure 2

Peaking characteristics of New York City region travel modes

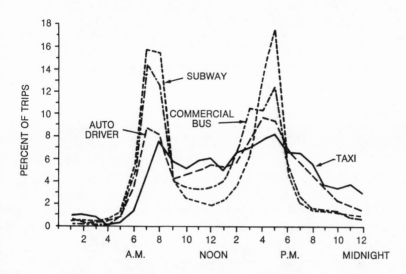

factor is that during peak hours transit modes offer some of their best service characteristics—in particular, short headways.

The situation in Washington is interesting in this regard. In that city there are typically fewer cabs on the streets during

Table 15

Weekday availability of cabs in Washington, D.C., 1968

	7 A.M. to 9 A.M.	9 A.M. to 4 P.M.	4 P.M. to 6 P.M.
Mean number of cabs in service	1,400	2,200	1,600
Mean number of taxi trips			
with fares (per hr)	2,950	5,180	2,860
without fares (per hr)	2,080	4,030	2,270
Rough availability ratio			
(taxi trips without fares/all trips)	0.41	0.44	0.44
Mean fare trips per hour per cab			
in service	2.1	2.3	1.8
Mean duration of fare trips	16 min.	15 min.	14 min.
Mean passengers per fare trip	1.2	1.2	1.2

Source: Basic data used for National Capital Region Transportation Planning Board (1970)

rush hours than during the rest of the day (for reasons which were discussed earlier). However, the *proportion* of cabs on the streets which are empty and available for hire in the rush periods does not appear to be significantly lower than during the period from 9 A.M. to 4 P.M. according to cab manifest data (see Table 15).

Trip length

Journeys by taxicab in the major cities tend to be short—at least in comparison with journeys by other urban modes. In the New York City region, for example, almost three in every four hirings are under two airline miles [111] in length. The mean trip length in Manhattan is 1.5 airline miles, with a mean duration of 10.2 minutes. For the New York City region as a whole, the mean trip length is 2.1 airline miles—this compares with mean trip lengths by bus of 2.5 airline miles, by private automobile of 3.9 airline miles, and by subway of 5.75 airline miles.[112] No data are available for the length of walk trips.

The data from Chicago show a very similar picture. The mean airline distance for cab trips was 2.9 miles, compared with an overall average trip length recorded by the home interview survey of 4.3 airline miles. Work-related cab trips and trips oriented towards the central area tended to be still shorter. The average Chicago area cab trip took about 20 minutes, implying a mean speed of roughly nine airline miles per hour, very similar to average cab speeds in Manhattan.[113] The mean cab speeds in Washington, D.C., appear to be a little faster—12 airline miles per hour in the rush hours, and 14 airline miles per hour at other times.[114]

However, a brief word of warning is necessary in interpreting broad averages like these. They may give a particularly deceptive picture when the trip length distribution is skewed or multimodal. This is likely to be the case when, for example, a significant proportion of cab trips are of relatively long length at relatively higher speeds—say, to an airport beyond the city boundary.

---

[111] Trip lengths measured by transportation studies are often expressed as straight-line ("airline" or "crow-fly") distances. In urban areas, these usually are about 60 to 70 percent of actual point-to-point distances on the ground.

[112] Tri-State Transportation Commission (1969).

[113] Beimborn (1969).

[114] National Capital Region Transportation Planning Board (1970).

Cab occupancy

In most cities, cab regulations specifically prohibit shared riding except occasionally to help service extraordinarily high demand levels. In fact, evidence from a number of cities suggests that the majority of trips are made with only one passenger. Single passenger trips account for 72 percent of all taxi fare trips in the New York City region, about 65 percent of Pittsburgh trips, and 81 percent of Washington, D.C., trips. The Washington percentage is particularly interesting in light of the fact that Washington regulations allow shared riding during the rush hours (and under certain other circumstances) at the discretion of the driver, and at other times at the discretion of existing passengers.[115] The proportion of single passenger trips is no lower in the morning and evening rush periods than during the rest of the daylight hours.

The 1970 Pittsburgh surveys suggested that women and non-whites tend to travel in taxis in larger groups than the rest of the riding public.[116]

The use of taxis in conjunction with other modes of transportation

One interesting analysis from the 1956 Chicago data, summarized in Table 16, shows how taxis were used in conjunction with other intraurban modes. For the great majority of journeys involving a cab ride, the taxi was the only vehicle used. For a much smaller proportion of journeys the taxi was used as a feeder or distributor at either or both ends of a rail rapid transit or commuter rail trip. In very few cases was a taxi used in conjunction with an automobile or bus.

Elasticity of demand

Not surprisingly in the light of the data problems which have been discussed, there have been very few attempts to develop quantitative behavioral models of the demand for taxi services, or to derive numerical estimates of demand elasticities. The limited evidence available suggests that fare elasticities are probably on the order of −1; that is to say, a 1 percent rise in fare would result in roughly a 1 percent drop in the number of taxi trips demanded.

In 1953 Sir Roy Allen made a broad estimate of the fare elasticity for London cab services as "around or rather below

---

[115] D.C. Government, Section 310 (1971).
[116] Rattien and Duckett (1971).

Table 16

Modes used in conjunction with taxis

	All journeys involving taxis	Journeys with destinations in	
		central area	noncentral area
	%	%	%
Taxicab used as:			
the only mode	86	88	84
the first mode of a linked trip	4	1	7
the last mode of a linked trip	8	8	7
both first and last modes	2	2	1
Main mode when taxi was first mode:			
suburban railroad	4	2	5
rail rapid transit	1	1	1
bus	1	*	2
automobile	*	*	*
Main mode when taxi was last mode:			
suburban railroad	5	7	3
rail rapid transit	2	1	3
bus	*	1	*
automobile	*	1	*

* denotes less than 0.5%

Source: Beimborn (1969).

unity."[117] A 1970 report on London taxicabs accepted this as still the best estimate available.[118]

In the United States, Wong (1971) has used taxi manifest-derived data for Washington, D.C., to test several cross-sectional taxi demand formulations. Of the three service aspects which Wong was able to consider, he concluded that the cab passenger in D.C. was most sensitive to the fare, next to the "availability" of cabs, and least sensitive to the in-vehicle time of the trip. The estimated fare elasticities were numerically slightly greater than unity (that is, less than -1), implying elastic demand.

Kitch et al. (1971) used two different methods to compute a fare elasticity for fleet cabs in Chicago. Examining gross revenues before and after a 1965 fare increase suggested a price elasticity

---

[117] Appendix to U.K. Ministry of Transport (1953).
[118] U.K. Home Office (1970).

of −0.8; however, on profit-maximizing grounds they argue for an elasticity on the order of −3 to −4.

Cross-elasticities between taxi and other modes represent the volume of traffic which is diverted to or from taxis by adjustment of the relative fares. In New York City, the newly formed Taxi and Limousine Commission argues, on the basis of fairly sketchy evidence provided by a 1970 citywide transit fare increase, that the cross-elasticity of taxi ridership with respect to transit fares is zero.[119] This is, however, not in accord with the findings of Maller who, following a 1948 subway fare increase (5 cents raised to 10 cents), estimated from circumstantial evidence that 7 percent of the traffic lost from the subway had diverted to taxi.[120]

INNOVATIVE USE OF TAXICABS

There are a number of ways in which taxicabs in various U.S. cities are providing innovative services to their passengers or to their communities, and we will mention some of these very briefly. Indeed, the International Taxicab Association includes among its activities a *Diversification Committee*.

One significant development has been the inauguration in April 1973 of *SkyCab*, a small-package delivery service via taxicab and plane. Associated cab fleets act as the local agents for the pickup and delivery of small parcels which are shipped intercity by air. By late 1973 the service had some 250 appointed agents, representing a total of about 14,000 taxicabs.

Twenty-four hour cab services may also act as Western Union agents, delivering telegrams by taxicab. In some cities radio-equipped cabs perform some police surveillance functions, report rush-hour traffic conditions to the local highway control center, or provide ambulance service for noncritical cases.

Some cab fleets are accepting payment by credit cards. In several communities—Richland (Washington) and Arlington (Virginia) for example—the local government is subsidizing cheap taxi service for the elderly.

---

[119] Glick (1971).
[120] New York City Mayor's Committee on Management Survey (1953).

Chapter 8

Kiran U. Bhatt
Michael A. Kemp

Dial-a-Ride
Services

INTRODUCTION

In recent years the term *dial-a-ride* has come to characterize transportation systems in which a shared vehicle provides door-to-door service on demand to a number of travelers with different origins and destinations. The name reflects the fact that the customary method of hailing such a vehicle is by telephone.

We have advisedly chosen to use the term *dial-a-ride* in preference to a number of other names which have been applied to this type of service. We prefer it to the terms *demand-responsive* and *demand-activated*, because the latter are more general and can be applied equally to taxicab and limousine service. We also prefer it to the name *dial-a-bus*, which implies a vehicle large enough to be called a "bus."

The conceptual and development work on dial-a-ride service was mostly carried out in the 1960s by staffs of the Ford Motor Company, General Motors Research Laboratories, Massachusetts Institute of Technology, and Northwestern University,[1] although demand-responsive shared-taxicab services, offering a form of dial-a-ride, have existed in some U.S. communities since at least

---

[1] See, for example, Wilson (1967); Massachusetts Institute of Technology (1969); and Highway Research Board (1971).

the 1930s. By late 1972 there were probably between 15 and 25 systems operating in North America.

These systems are providing service in a range of different operating environments, and they consequently vary somewhat in their operational details. Some are providing feeder services to other modes of travel, a situation which can be characterized as carrying passengers from many origins to one destination (or vice versa) and referred to in the dial-a-ride jargon as *many-to-one*. Other systems provide *few-to-few* intratown or intracity service between important activity centers in an area. Others operate a *many-to-many* service, providing each passenger with door-to-door transportation between any two points within the operating area.

The various systems do, however, share a number of features in common. Typically, the user desiring service must telephone the dispatching center and provide information about his origin address, destination address, and number in the party. The dispatcher then chooses, from the vehicles operating on the road, the one that is in the best position to serve the new request, and updates the scheduled stops of that particular vehicle to incorporate the new request. The caller is given the expected time of pickup based on the updated schedule. The vehicle operator is informed by radio about the revised future stop schedule, and amends the route accordingly.

Under the manual dispatching techniques currently in use by most systems, these operational decisions are all made heuristically. However, computer algorithms have been developed for the selection of the appropriate vehicle to respond to a particular demand and for routing and scheduling, and these seem likely to achieve greater efficiency.[2] Manual dispatching has been possible in the existing systems because of the relatively small scale of operations in terms of fleet size and service demands per hour. More extensive systems may need at least some level of computerization, though it is difficult to predict, at this stage, at what operating scale manual dispatching may become inefficient.

Existing dial-a-ride systems in North America

Table 17 lists the major dial-a-ride systems which were in existence (or in an advanced stage of planning) in North America as of late 1972. The operating experience and data summarized in this chapter are drawn from a number of these systems. However,

---

[2] Wilson (1967); Wilson et al. (1970b); Howson and Heathington (1970). Massachusetts Institute of Technology (1969) also foresees even the call-receiving chores being handled by computer.

it is necessary to emphasize that dial-a-ride is one para-transit mode for which the national picture is changing relatively rapidly. New systems are increasingly being planned, and since many of the existing systems are experimental they undergo frequent changes. The picture presented in this chapter therefore represents a snapshot of the situation at one point in time—late 1972 and early 1973—when most of this information was collated.

Table 17
Major North American dial-a-ride systems [3]

City	Year established	City
Bus- or van-based systems:		Taxicab-based systems:
Ann Arbor, Mich.	1971	Davenport, Iowa
Batavia, N.Y.	1971	Hicksville, N.Y.
Bay Ridges, Ont.	1970	Little Rock, Ark.
Buffalo, N.Y.*	1970	Lowell, Mass.
Columbia, Md.	1971	Madison, Wisc.
Columbus, Ohio	1971	Merced, Calif.
Ft. Walton Beach, Fla.	—	Richland, Wash.
Haddonfield, N.J.	1972	
Kingston, Ont.	—	
Regina, Sask.	1971	
Rochester, N.Y.	1973	
Toledo, Ohio	—	

Blanks (—) in the table denote information not at hand.
The Buffalo system (*) serves the elderly and physically handicapped only.

The operating experience of each of the most significant dial-a-ride systems has been documented in some detail in the literature.[4] In this chapter we first present very brief descriptions of four prototype systems which together exemplify a wide range of different types of dial-a-ride service. We then summarize various aspects of the operating experience accrued to date, drawing on information from a number of systems but particularly using the four prototypes as examples. Finally, we present a number of case studies which summarize the most salient details of each of the major North American systems.

[3] Table 17 is compiled from information in, inter alia, Highway Research Board (1971, 1973); Roos (1972); and *Transport Central* (1972). We strongly suspect that the list of cities where shared-cab services are provided is far from comprehensive.

[4] The interested reader is particularly recommended to consult Highway Research Board (1973).

FOUR PROTOTYPE DIAL-A-RIDE SYSTEMS

We will use four systems to exemplify the major variations in dial-a-ride service which are currently found in North America. These systems are:

- *Haddonfield, New Jersey—*
  The Haddonfield system operates the purest form of bus-based, 24-hour, many-to-many, dial-a-ride service currently in existence. By late 1972 it was serving an 8.1 square mile area with a population of 27,500, operating a total of twelve 17-passenger buses. The service functions primarily as a feeder to the PATCO high-speed line [5] to Philadelphia (7 miles away), and also as an all-day service for residents traveling to activity centers such as shopping plazas and entertainment facilities. The Haddonfield service is experimental, funded largely by an Urban Mass Transportation Administration demonstration grant.

- *Davenport, Iowa—*
  The Royal Cab Company of Davenport operates a 24-hour many-to-many service using (in February 1973) twenty-three standard 7-passenger Checker cabs. The primary service area is about 20 square miles with a population of 98,500. Although the city does have a privately owned bus company which is publicly subsidized, Royal Cab provides a significant proportion of the community's public transportation and is financially self-supporting.

- *Batavia, New York—*
  In Batavia, a city of 4.3 square miles with a population of roughly 18,000, the publicly owned transit undertaking operates four 19-passenger buses and one 10-passenger van to provide a variety of different types of service. In peak hours the system provides subscription service [6] for trips to and from work and school; in the off-peak hours it provides many-to-many dial-a-ride and small-package delivery service; on occasion a bus may operate essentially as a jitney along a fixed route with a comparatively high demand density; and vehicles are regularly chartered by local businesses to provide fare-free service to their customers.

- *Regina, Saskatchewan—*
  The municipally owned transit system in Regina operates a bus-

---

[5] The so-called Lindenwold Line.
[6] That is to say, dial-a-ride service provided on a prearranged, standing-order basis rather than in response to ad hoc requests.

based system with 6 vehicles, catering (in mid-1972) to a service area of roughly 2.75 square miles and a population of 18,000. The service functions primarily as a feeder to a fixed-route scheduled arterial bus line to downtown Regina. During the peak hours much of the ridership is on a subscription basis, and for the rest of the time the system caters basically to a many-to-few pattern of demand, carrying passengers to 6 major destinations within the service area. Many-to-many service is also offered, however.

THE LOCATION AND SCALE OF EXISTING SYSTEMS

The majority of the existing dial-a-ride systems are small operations with fleets of three to twelve vehicles serving primarily residential communities with populations of 12,000 to 20,000 spread over two to five square mile areas. Of the four prototype systems, only the Davenport shared-cab service caters to a population of over 30,000 or an area of more than 10 square miles. The residential densities in the service areas are generally low, on the order of 3,500 to 7,000 persons per square mile.

All of the bus-based systems are publicly owned and supported, whereas the taxi-based systems are privately owned. Dispatching is typically manual, although both Haddonfield and Davenport are moving towards computer-based dispatching. Royal Cab of Davenport experimented with computerized dispatching for 57 days in 1972, and a larger computer was due to be installed in mid-1973. The Haddonfield system also commenced part-day experimentation with computer-based dispatching in 1973.

Table 18 summarizes the scale of operation for six major systems. Most of these systems offer many-to-few or many-to-many dial-a-ride service in off-peak hours within their primary service areas. The systems in Batavia, Bay Ridges, and Regina offer peak hour subscription service to regional transport centers. The Batavia system is somewhat unique in that, along with many-to-many dial-a-ride and subscription services, it also offers a variety of other services such as subscription service to employment and educational centers, store charters, fixed-route jitney service, and package delivery service. It is no coincidence that, as we shall detail later in the chapter, Batavia with its many-faceted operation has been relatively more successful financially than the other bus-based systems.

The location and scale of existing systems

	System					
	Haddonfield	Davenport	Batavia	Regina	Bay Ridges	Ann Arbor
Date of information	Dec. '72	Apr. '73	July '72	June '72	June '72	Sept. '72
Ownership	Public	Private	Public	Public	Public	Public
Primary service area:						
population (thousands)	27.5	98.5	18.0	18.0	13.7	17.0
area (square miles)	8.1	20.0	4.3	2.8	1.3	2.4
population density (thousands per sq. mi.)	3.4	4.9	4.2	6.5	10.2	7.1
Service provided:						
weekday duration	24 hrs.	24 hrs.	12 hrs.	17 hrs.	19½ hrs.	11½ hrs.
nature in the peak	M - M	M - M	M - M sub	M - O sub	M - O sub	M - F
nature off-peak	M - M	M - M	M - M (and other services)	M - F	M - F	M - F
Equipment:						
fleet size (vehicles x seats)	12 x 17	23 x 7	4 x 23 1 x 10	2 x 14 2 x 23 2 x 42	5 x 11	3 x 10
peak vehicles in service	12	15-20	5	6	4	3
off-peak vehicles in service	4	12-16	3	3	2	3
Dispatching method	Manual	Manual	Manual	Manual	Manual	Manual
Transit competition	None	Bus	None	None (feeds scheduled bus)	None (feeds commuter rail)	Bus

KEY: M - M many-to-many service
M - F many-to-few and few-to-many
M - O many-to-one and one-to-many
sub subscription service offered

CHARACTERISTICS OF THE SERVICE PROVIDED

Dial-a-ride systems are designed to provide a guaranteed seat, door-to-door service at a reasonable fare, with reasonable waiting time and ride time—a service in the range between a fixed-route scheduled bus and a taxicab. The wide spectrum of possible dial-a-ride applications (from few-to-one through many-to-many) provides a correspondingly wide range of service characteristics. Obviously, the nature of the service will also depend on (among other variables) the fleet size and vehicle size relative to the population and extent of the service area.

Table 19 summarizes the major service attributes envisaged for the many-to-many dial-a-ride concept, relative to the service provided by the typical bus transit system or by the private automobile. The type of vehicle used to provide dial-a-ride would make some small differences in the service experienced by the passenger—in comparison with bus-based systems, for example, shared taxicabs would be less spacious, less private, and slightly more expensive.

How do the actual levels of service provided by the existing dial-a-ride systems compare with the original conception of this mode of travel? Some data are available on the average waiting times between the telephone request and the pickup for several systems, and these are presented in Table 20. Waits of between 10 minutes and half an hour appear to be typical. This is longer than might be expected from a telephone taxicab service operating in a central city area, but a 15-minute wait is probably comparable with suburban cab operations in areas with residential densities similar to those of the existing dial-a-ride service areas.

Table 20 also refers to the concept of *level of service*. This term is used extensively in the dial-a-ride literature to denote the ratio between the total time taken for the journey by dial-a-ride (that is to say, the time from telephone request to arrival at the destination) and the time it would have taken to travel directly by private automobile. The level of service ratios for three bus-based systems for which data are available appear to be on the order of two to three. The ratio is slightly higher for the Davenport shared-taxi operation, which is serving a larger area and a higher level of demand.

There are, of course, several other quantitative criteria against which the service provided to the public could be evaluated, but despite their experimental nature very few of the existing systems appear to have assembled the necessary data. In Haddonfield (see Table 21), estimates have been made of the *pickup time deviation*

—that is, the difference between the pickup time promised to the passenger (at the time of booking the journey) and the actual pickup time. The mean pickup time deviation appears to be just over -2.1 minutes, the negative sign indicating that, on the average, vehicles arrive slightly *earlier* than promised.

Table 19

Typical service characteristics envisaged for many-to-many dial-a-ride

Service attribute	Comparison with other modes
Start from and end at any location	Roughly the same as A and Ta, better than Tr
Availability at all times of day	Poorer than A, no better than Ta, at least as good as Tr
Waiting time before journey	Poorer than both A and Ta, at least as good as Tr
Overall average speed in vehicle	Poorer than both A and Ta, roughly the same as Tr
Perceived money price per passenger	Higher than both A and Tr, lower than Ta
Fare known before the trip?	Generally yes; at least as good as A and Ta, roughly the same as Tr
Privacy and general comfort	Poorer than both A and Ta, at least as good as Tr
Ability to do other things while traveling	Poorer than Ta, at least as good as A and Tr
Ability to carry luggage	Poorer than both A and Ta, at least as good as Tr
Convenience in coping with luggage	Poorer than both A and Ta, better than Tr
Need for parking space at destination	At least as good as A, roughly the same as Ta and Tr

KEY: A denotes a typical private or rental automobile
Ta denotes typical taxicab services
Tr denotes typical bus or rail transit services

Table 20
Average service by existing dial-a-ride systems

System	Date of information	Average for ad hoc on-demand service	
		waiting time	level of service ratio
Haddenfield	June 1972	12.6 mins.	2.5 - 3
Davenport	April 1973	10 - 20 mins.	3.5 - 6
Batavia	July 1972	10 - 15 mins.	2.5 - 3
Ann Arbor	Sept. 1972	10.8 mins.	2 - 2.5

Note: The assumptions adopted in calculating level of service ratios from the very scanty data available are such that this table probably *overstates* the service provided; that is to say, the ratios here are probably on the low side.

Table 21
Mean service parameters for ad hoc operation in Haddonfield

Time of day	Mean value of		
	waiting time	riding time	pickup deviation
	mins.	mins.	mins.
7 A.M. to 9 A.M.	9.9	7.3	−3.4
9 A.M. to 4 P.M.	13.0	10.2	−3.1
4 P.M. to 7 P.M.	14.3	11.4	−1.1
7 P.M. to 11 P.M.	16.3	10.9	+1.6
11 P.M. to 7 A.M.	15.8	8.0	−1.7

Source: Medville (1973)

THE LEVEL AND NATURE OF DEMAND

While most operating dial-a-ride systems have assembled aggregate ridership data, more detailed empirical information about the nature of the demand is difficult to come by. However, a number of systems have carried out survey research work to learn more about their markets—the socioeconomic characteristics of the riders, and the origins, destinations, and purposes of their trips—and fragmentary data of this nature are gradually becoming available. The development of good demand relationships will require such data for a wide range of service levels. In this section we attempt to draw together the empirical evidence from a number of systems.

Level of patronage

The low residential densities of the areas in which dial-a-ride is now typically operating have meant that the level of demand is quite low by scheduled bus transit standards. The present patronage levels of the major bus-based dial-a-ride systems range from roughly 200 to 1,200 rides per weekday, averaged over the year.[7] Davenport, the prototype cab-based system, carries between 1,250 and 1,600 riders on a typical working day.

Two measures of demand used extensively in the dial-a-ride literature are of value here. They are:

• the vehicle *productivity*, defined as the riders per vehicle-hour of operation

• the *demand density*, defined as riders per hour per square mile of the primary service area

The average productivities of the existing systems range from about 5 to 15 riders per vehicle-hour, although again the productivities for pure many-to-many operations do not rise above 10 passengers per vehicle-hour (see Table 22).

An important feature of dial-a-ride operations is the fact that the patronage has been highly seasonal. For example, in Bay Ridges, Regina, and Batavia the ridership in the winter months jumps to a level approximately 20 to 25 percent higher than the summer average (with peaks reaching as much as 100 percent higher). The door-to-door service feature of dial-a-ride becomes extremely attractive when the weather gets bad. Short work-trips and school-trips which are made on foot in summer are very likely responsible for this increase.

The patronage levels on most of the existing dial-a-ride systems (even the well-established shared-cab operations) continue to grow. Where a new dial-a-ride service has replaced a fixed-route scheduled bus service, the decline in ridership was typically arrested and the trend has been reversed. For example, after the introduction of dial-a-ride in Batavia, ridership increased by some 250 percent over the bus services which were replaced, and in Regina patronage grew by roughly 800 percent. It is difficult to say, however, to what extent these impressive increases are attributable to the many-to-many service, and to what extent they are due to subscription services.

---

[7] In fact, the high figure of 1,200 rides per day relates to Regina, where only some 10 percent of the riders are pure many-to-many dial-a-ride patrons, the rest being mostly many-to-few or many-to-one customers on a subscription basis.

Table 22

The level of patronage of existing systems

	Haddonfield	Davenport	Batavia	Regina	Bay Ridges	Ann Arbor
Date of information	Dec. '72	Apr. '73	July '72	June '72	June '72	Sept. '72
Rough year-round average:						
riders/weekday	750	1,250-1,600	300-400	1,200	530	200
demand density	3.9	2.5-3.5	5.8-7.7	26	21	7.2
market share (percent)	4-5	1-2	1-2	6-7	3	2
vehicle productivity	6-7	4-5	9*	19	10-11	6
Maximum productivity	9	5.5-6.0	12*	31	25	10

KEY: *demand density* is riders per hour per square mile
market share is a rough estimate of the proportion of area trips made by dial-a-ride
productivity is riders per vehicle-hour

* the productivity estimates for Batavia refer to many-to-many service only

Table 23 illustrates the patronage growth on a number of systems.

Table 23
Examples of growth in dial-a-ride patronage

	Approximate mean riders per working day		Approximate mean riders per working day
Haddonfield		*Davenport*	
May 1972	270	August 1967	500
June 1972	430	August 1968	550
July 1972	500	August 1969	600
August 1972	500	August 1970	700
September 1972	500	August 1971	1,000
October 1972*	660	August 1972	1,250
November 1972	730		
December 1972	790	*Bay Ridges*	
January 1973	720	July 1970	200
February 1973	800	January 1971	400
		July 1971	400
Ann Arbor		January 1972	600
October 1971	120	July 1972	530
January 1972*	220		
April 1972	190		
July 1972*	170		
September 1972	220		

KEY: * denotes the first listed month following an expansion of the primary service area.

Note: August is the least busy month of the year for the Davenport system.

The temporal pattern of demand

The theoretical analyses of dial-a-ride systems predicted that the demand would be unlikely to show as strong peaking characteristics as are normally observed for other modes of public transportation.[8] In fact many of the systems now operating do display strong peaking, but this is largely because the vehicles are being used in a many-to-one feeder role or for subscription services, and not purely for many-to-many dial-a-ride.

The theoretical research into many-to-many service predicted

---

[8] See Bauer (1971), and Golob and Gustafson (1971).

a flat peak spread between 2:00 P.M. and 8:00 P.M. Preliminary data from Haddonfield (Table 24) show roughly similar characteristics, with a fairly flat peak spread between 9:00 A.M. and 7:00 P.M. over which period nearly 70 percent of the riders are carried.

Table 24
Average weekday ridership in Haddonfield, June/July 1972

Time of day	Proportion of daily ridership	Mean hourly values		
		riders	vehicles in service	vehicle productivity
	%			trips/veh.-hr.
7 A.M. to 9 A.M.	10.0	23.0	6.3	3.6
9 A.M. to 4 P.M.	48.2	31.5	7.3	4.3
4 P.M. to 7 P.M.	21.4	32.7	7.8	4.2
7 P.M. to 11 P.M.	13.4	15.4	3.4	4.5
11 P.M. to 7 A.M.	6.9	4.0	1.4	2.9

Source: Medville (1973)

On the other hand, 64 percent of the trips in Bay Ridges are made during two peak morning hours and three peak evening hours, due to the extensive subscription feeder service. Similarly, the maximum hourly ridership in Haddonfield reaches almost 50 between 5 P.M. and 6 P.M., and is attributable to train arrivals at the Lindenwold Line station. Dial-a-ride vehicles are positioned at the station to meet trains, and since passengers do not have to wait for service many of them use the system on their evening return trip but not in the morning.

The characteristics of dial-a-ride users

There are some important questions regarding the composition of dial-a-ride patronage, the answers to which could help the analyst evaluate such systems and establish dial-a-ride's effectiveness in providing different types of service. For example, it is important to have answers to such questions as:

• What is the socioeconomic composition of the dial-a-ride patronage? Do a large majority of riders come from low- and middle-income households, or households with no cars? What fraction of limited mobility residents are using dial-a-ride?

• What types of trips does dial-a-ride currently serve? What is the fraction of work trips, of trips to line-haul terminals, of shopping trips, of hospital trips, and so on?

The data available up to now are generally too sketchy to provide definitive answers to questions like these.[9] Moreover, the systems now in existence vary somewhat in the types of service offered and the socioeconomic characteristics of the areas in which they operate, so it is difficult to abstract useful general consistencies from the sketchy data available. Some small degree of pattern does emerge, however, from the little that we do know.

The patronage of dial-a-ride systems appears to reflect the socioeconomic characteristics of the areas in which they are operating—by and large, no one group of the populace stands out as being heavier users than any other group. So, for example, in Haddonfield the dial-a-ride passengers reflect the middle- and low-income household profile for the area. And in Ann Arbor it is reported that

> There is no indication that any particular group within the service area population used dial-a-ride much more than proportionately, except that female riders greatly outnumbered males—a common condition on all public transit.[10]

The experience in Bay Ridges tells a very similar story:

> Little evidence was found to suggest that the socioeconomic characteristics of the trip maker were responsible for his choice of access mode.[11] In particular dial-a-ride users could not be distinguished from the total potential users by characteristics such as income, car ownership or age. It was found, however, that the proportions of persons not licensed to drive, females, and housewives were higher amongst the mini-bus users than the total market. Housewives accounted for 13% of users but only 1% of all Bay Ridges passengers. The figures for persons not licensed to drive were 30% and 23% respectively and for females they were 56% and 44% respectively.[12]

In areas with a relatively high-income profile, the comparatively wealthy appear to be riding the dial-a-ride system along with the middle- and lower-income groups. Thus in Regina, for example, about half of the riders are said to come from two and three car households, while the other half come from one car households. And in Ann Arbor it has been observed that the dial-a-ride system is carrying a higher proportion of "choice" as opposed to "captive" riders than do fixed-route buses. On the other hand, Davenport comprises mostly low- and middle-income households, and it is from this group that the ridership of the shared-cab

---

[9] However, more detailed descriptions of dial-a-ride users and their trips are gradually becoming available as the result of survey work carried out by the existing systems.

[10] Ann Arbor Transportation Authority (1973).

[11] That is, access to the rapid transit station fed by the dial-a-ride system.

[12] Bonsall (1971).

service is drawn—patronage is said to increase significantly at the time of the month when AFDC (Aid to Families with Dependent Children) checks are distributed.

So the lesson to be learned from the experience accrued to date is that dial-a-ride services *can* be tailored to attract riders of many different population subgroups—and in particular, the mode is capable of attracting the relatively affluent (with other transportation choices available to them) as well as lower income groups who may be more captive to public transportation services.

Turning next to the characteristics of the *journeys* made by dial-a-ride, again the available data are rather scanty. In Regina, 55 percent of the trips are to or from the central business district (many-to-one service); about 35 percent are to six other major activity centers—the government complex, two hospitals, and three shopping centers (many-to-few service); and about 10 percent of trips are many-to-many local trips. Similarly, in Bay Ridges about 80 percent of rides are many-to-one subscription trips, with the remaining 20 percent being local many-to-many trips. Much of the travel on these services, therefore, appears to be repeat traveling to and from work and school.

The many-to-many service, on the other hand, appears to cater more to nonwork journeys. This observation is supported by the many-to-many service in Haddonfield where almost 70 percent of all journeys are made outside of the peak hours for travel to and from work.[13] In Davenport, too, the many-to-many service is used heavily for nonwork journeys, particularly by housewives shopping in the downtown area.

Trip duration

There are some limited indications of the average duration of a dial-a-ride journey from a number of systems, and this information is summarized in Table 25. The average duration of a ride is likely to be influenced strongly by at least two factors—the nature of the service offered by the system, and the degree of route diversion which vehicles make.

Thus in Bay Ridges, where dial-a-ride is providing predominantly a feeder service on a subscription basis, the duration of trips to the transit station is said to be no more than two to three minutes on the average. The high proportion of subscription travelers presumably allows the operator to keep route deviation to a minimum.

For many-to-many service, however, trips are understandably

---

[13] See Table 24.

longer. Since many-to-many dial-a-ride fulfills a role similar to that of taxicabs, the trip lengths could be expected to be fairly similar. We would guess, however, that in a particular area the dial-a-ride journey lengths may be slightly greater than those for taxi since the dial-a-ride fare is typically a flat one, unrelated to the distance traveled.

Table 25

Average weekday journey durations

System	Date of information	Primary service area	Population density	Mean trip duration
		sq. mi.	'000/sq. mi.	
Haddonfield	Dec. '72	8.1	4.3	9.9 mins.
Davenport	April '73	20.0	4.9	10-12 mins.
Batavia	July '72	4.3	4.2	11.0 mins.
Bay Ridges	June '72	1.3	10.2	6.7 mins.
Ann Arbor	Sept. '72	2.4	7.1	12.6 mins.

The most detailed information about trip duration comes from the Haddonfield system, and these data have already been summarized in Table 21. The overall workday mean trip duration of 9.9 minutes is very close to the mean time by automobile for the same journeys (9 minutes), indicating that the level of route deviation in Haddonfield is small.

THE DETERMINANTS OF DIAL-A-RIDE DEMAND

The experience accrued with dial-a-ride services to date is still too limited for us to predict the demand changes that would be brought about by changes in the level of fare or service. Nor does this experience yet provide an adequate test of some of the theoretical models of demand which have been used to predict dial-a-ride patronage levels.[14]

A number of key questions remain to be answered in this regard. These include:

• How much *new* demand have dial-a-ride services induced, as against a *shift* from other modes? What is the real potential of dial-a-ride?

[14] See, for example, Stafford et al. (1971) and Golob and Gustafson (1971).

- To what extent is dial-a-ride likely to act as a substitute for other more common transit modes and to what extent would it be a complementary service?

- Are we likely to find strong cross-relationships between dial-a-ride and taxi or transit service and a weaker relationship between dial-a-ride and the private automobile (because the former modes are very close substitutes while the private car provides substantially superior service)?

Even though far from conclusive, some evidence from the existing dial-a-ride operations may provide a little more insight. The indications are that even though a substantial number of dial-a-ride passengers have been diverted from other transit modes, shifts from the private automobile and from taxis have also been significant.

Dial-a-ride's share of the market

Existing dial-a-ride systems have attracted between roughly 1 and 7 percent of their potential markets.[15] These figures, low as they are, still represent significant improvements over the fixed-route bus services which several of the existing systems replaced. For example, Table 26 illustrates that in seven months the dial-a-ride feeder service in Bay Ridges grew to become the most popular means of access to the transit station in Bay Ridges, in spite of free parking for private automobiles at the station.

Also, as mentioned in a later section, the shared-cab service in Davenport attracts roughly two-thirds as many riders as the fixed-route bus system even though the average fare is roughly three times the bus fare.

Shifts from other modes

In Bay Ridges, about half of the dial-a-ride patrons are former automobile riders. Of the other half, the proportions of former transit riders, taxi riders, and new patrons are not available. In Regina, out of 1,200 dial-a-ride patrons per working day, approximately 50 percent are former transit riders. The other half consists of riders shifting from private automobiles and of new trips. In Haddonfield, five surveys taken between August 1972 and January 1973 indicated that the shift to dial-a-ride was roughly as follows: 25 percent from automobiles, 25 percent from taxi, 11 percent from bus, 15 percent from walk trips, and the remaining 24 percent were new riders.

---

[15] See Table 22 for estimates of the market shares for individual systems.

Table 26
Means of access to the Bay Ridges transit station

Date of survey	Mode	Percentage by mode for trips of	
		1 mile	2 miles
Feb. 1968	walk	27	—
(prior to	private auto	64	65
dial-a-ride)	fixed route bus	9	35
		100	100
Oct. 1970	walk	43	—
	private auto	35	63
	dial-a-ride	22	37
		100	100
Feb. 1971	walk	14	—
	private auto	34	42
	dial-a-ride	52	58
		100	100

Source: derived from Bonsall (1971)

Evidence of demand elasticities

There have been few changes of fare since the existing bus-based dial-a-ride systems became operational. In Bay Ridges the dial-a-ride fare was increased from 25 to 30 cents per ride in May 1972,[16] and it is claimed that there was no discernible decrease in ridership in comparison with the preceding year. Evaluation is difficult, however, because of seasonal fluctuations in patronage and because ridership on the system has been growing continuously.

In Regina and Batavia, the fare was increased when fixed-route bus services were first replaced by dial-a-ride service—but the patronage increased also. This is, of course, in line with the well-known fact that the ridership levels of urban public transport services are more sensitive to the level of service than they are to the level of fare.[17] A low fare elasticity also appears to be substantiated by the fact that the Davenport system has been able to attract demand levels comparable to the bus-based systems in spite of a much higher fare and a competing, subsidized bus transit service.

---

[16] The price for a block of ten tickets also increased from 20 cents per ride to 25 cents.
[17] Kemp (1973).

THE COSTS AND REVENUES OF DIAL-A-RIDE SYSTEMS

Table 27 summarizes the available information about costs for existing dial-a-ride systems. The total costs of the bus-based operations have been in the range of $6 to $16 per vehicle-hour, of which approximately one-half to two-thirds is the vehicle operating cost. The figure at the lower end of the range is for low cost, low overhead, predominantly subscription systems, such as the one in Bay Ridges; while the highest figure is an approximate estimate for the many-to-many operation in Haddonfield, and includes the costs of intensive supervision and management which are exceptionally high due to the experimental nature of the project. Most other bus-based systems show costs in the range of $8 to $14 per vehicle-hour. With the existing fare levels of around 50 to 60 cents per trip and demand densities producing low vehicle productivities of 6 to 10 riders per vehicle-hour, bus-based operations seldom meet even the operating costs.[18]

In contrast to these bus-based systems, the Davenport shared-cab operation incurs costs in the range of $3.60 to $4.90 per vehicle-hour. The average fare of $1.00 along with an estimated productivity of between 4 and 5 passengers per vehicle-hour is sufficient to meet the full costs of the service. In other words, this is a profitable taxi-based operation under private ownership. There seem to be three major reasons for the success of this and other cab-based systems as against the dubious financial situation of bus-based services. First, the cab company owner has profited from his taxi management experience so that his managerial and dispatching costs are very low compared with the high overhead and costly administration typical of most bus-based operations, particularly the experimental ones. Second, the direct labor cost for taxi-based operations is generally much lower than for bus-based dial-a-ride operations because the taxi drivers are either nonunionized or belong to unions with weak bargaining powers, while the bus and van operators belong to unions with strong bargaining powers such as the Amalgamated Transit Union (ATU). Third, a reasonably high demand level has been sustained in spite of higher fare levels.

What can be said about the potential effect of vehicle-size and the nature of operation on dial-a-ride costs? Table 28 provides an approximate breakdown of various cost components, but these figures should be treated with great caution. For example, the ranges shown for amortization and other cost components in bus-

---

[18] Although in some cases they have produced better financial results than fixed-route bus services which they have replaced.

Table 27

Costs and revenues for existing dial-a-ride systems

	Haddonfield	Davenport	Batavia	Regina	Bay Ridges	Ann Arbor
Date of information	Dec. '72	Apr. '73	July '72	June '72	June '72	Sept. '72
Drivers:						
union status	U	NU	NU	U	U	U
average wage* ($/hour)	6.50- 7.00	2.30-3.50	3.60	5.50- 6.00	3.64	5.50
Vehicle operating costs:						
per vehicle hour ($)	8.00-10.00	3.20-4.50	4.00-5.00	11.40	4.15-4.60	8.20
per trip ($)	1.15- 1.65	0.70-1.30	0.35-0.45	0.60	0.40-0.45	1.45
Total costs:						
per vehicle hour ($)	15.00-16.00	3.60-4.90	7.00-8.00	12.25-13.25	5.50-6.00	14.55
per trip ($)	2.15- 2.65	0.80-1.40	0.60-0.75	0.65- 0.70	0.55	2.55
Mean revenue						
per vehicle hour ($)	3.20- 3.70	4.00-5.00	4.00-5.50	5.50	2.90	2.80
per trip ($)	0.53	1.00	0.45-0.50	0.29	0.265	0.47

KEY: U Union drivers; NU Nonunion drivers.
 * Estimates of average wage rates include fringe benefits where known.

based systems are mainly due to different vehicle types and sizes. The lower figures apply to vans for 8 to 12 passengers, while the higher figures relate to small buses. We believe, however, that the lower figures are somewhat underestimated by using exceptionally low maintenance costs and a long vehicle life over which the purchase cost is amortized. In fact, the real difference between vans and buses may be much smaller. In addition, one other major disparity between buses and taxicabs is in costs per vehicle-hour of communications, dispatching, and overhead (averaging $2.60 for buses, against $1.10 for cabs). The primary reason for this, as mentioned earlier, is that taxi-based systems have accrued considerable operational experience, whereas most of the bus-based systems are experimental in nature. This difference may be decreased or eliminated over time as bus operators learn from experience.

Table 28

Approximate cost breakdown for dial-a-ride operations [19]

Cost component	Estimated $ costs per vehicle-hour	
	bus-based systems	taxi-based systems
Direct operating costs:		
amortized vehicle purchase	0.50- 1.15	0.22
taxes and licenses	0.02	0.04
insurance	0.23	0.18
fuel, including tax	0.36- 0.65	0.44
maintenance and repair	0.30- 0.38	0.42
	1.40- 2.40	1.30
Direct labor costs	6.00	3.00
Total vehicle operating costs	7.40- 8.40	4.30
Communications and dispatch	1.50	0.50
Overhead	1.10	0.60
	10.00-11.00	5.40

A 1970 analysis, made prior to the accrual of any on-the-road experience with bus-based dial-a-ride systems, indicates the range of costs which might be expected for a bus-based or van-based operation under a wide variety of design and operating features.[20]

---

[19] Table 28 is compiled from information abstracted from Gramza et al. (1969), Stafford et al. (1971), and McLeod (1972), as well as the operating experience of the existing dial-a-ride systems.

[20] Stafford et al. (1971).

The basic dial-a-ride operating costs were estimated to be in the range of between \$5 and \$12 per vehicle-hour (Table 29). Such wide variation is attributable primarily to different driver wage rates which were assumed to vary from \$2.50 to \$7.00 per hour. In addition to the basic cost, the dispatching costs for an initial system were estimated to be between \$0.30 and \$0.50 per passenger, including costs of customer communications, vehicle communication, and computer processing. These figures indicate that productivities of 8 to 16 passengers per vehicle-hour would require break-even trip fares of \$0.61 to \$2.00. Lower break-even trip fares of \$0.40 to \$1.30 forecast for a production system reflect greater efficiency in dispatching and higher productivities of 12 to 20 passengers per vehicle-hour.

Table 29

Expected range of costs for bus-based systems

	Specification for	
	an initial system	a production system
Basic operating costs per bus-hour	\$5-\$12	\$5-\$12
Anticipated rides per vehicle-hour	8-16	12-20
Basic operating costs per passenger	\$0.31-\$ 1.50	\$0.25-\$ 1.00
Dispatching cost per passenger	\$0.30-\$ 0.50	\$0.15-\$ 0.30
Total costs per passenger	\$0.61-\$ 2.00	\$0.40-\$ 1.30

The "initial system" uses existing routing and scheduling algorithms and computer programs, with voice communication between dispatcher and vehicle; the "production system" would use improved algorithms and programs, with computerized communication.

Source: Stafford et al. (1971).

DIAL-A-BUS OR DIAL-A-CAB?

Given the sharp cost differential between the existing bus-based and taxicab-based dial-a-ride systems, it is relevant to ask whether the use of buses or vans to provide this service has any great operational advantages over the use of taxicabs.

Both from theoretical simulation studies of dial-a-ride and from the experience accrued by the existing systems it is apparent that, considering only many-to-many service, a van or even a taxi type of vehicle would not significantly constrain system operation. It is unusual to find more than five passengers on the same vehicle at the same time. However, with a significant proportion of many-to-one trips or when the vehicles will also be used for subscription or charter service, a larger bus type of vehicle is required, with a capacity of around twenty passengers.

It also appears that if the system is to operate as a bus type of operation (as opposed to shared-taxi) these non-dial-a-ride services are vital to the economic feasibility of the overall system. Given that a larger-than-necessary vehicle is used for many-to-many operations, there should be no adverse effect on the service or on system performance (as opposed to cost), since the mean vehicle speeds are virtually independent of vehicle size for short trip lengths, and the dispatching policy governs the number of passengers on a vehicle at any point in time.

THE LEGAL AND REGULATORY ASPECTS OF DIAL-A-RIDE

Dial-a-ride operations are typically regulated as a public utility and must also meet state-imposed motor carrier regulations. The initial indications are that new dial-a-ride systems will pass state restrictions because they are likely to be accepted as providing beneficial, distinctive, and different service when compared with other urban transport modes.

In Ann Arbor, an interesting legal situation developed.[21] Although the Ann Arbor Transportation Authority specifically designed its dial-a-ride program so that the city's taxicab companies could bid to become the operators of the system, no bids were received and the Authority proceeded with plans to operate the service with its own vehicles and employees. The two major cab companies then sued the city just prior to commencement of the service, complaining (among other things) that the dial-a-ride vehicles were really taxicabs and should be subject to taxicab licensing and regulation. The county court ruled[22] in favor of summary dismissal of the suit, and this ruling was upheld on

---

[21] Lax (1973).
[22] Kon et al. v. City of Ann Arbor et al., Washtenaw County Circuit Court 5967 (1971).

subsequent appeal by the plaintiffs to the Michigan Court of Appeals.

All existing bus-based and van-based dial-a-ride systems are owned and operated by local or state government agencies with a substantial promise to underwrite the losses. They have complete control over the selection of fleet size, vehicle size, operating policy, and level of comfort. Changes in fares usually require the approval of the state or local public utilities commission. All of the bus-based systems except Batavia are bound by agreements with local transit unions and are required to employ unionized transit operators as drivers. Batavia employs nonunion drivers who recently rejected a bid by the regional transit union body inviting them to become members.

The cab-based services, on the other hand, are privately owned, although at least one (in Richland, Washington) operates with a limited public subsidy. They typically employ nonunion drivers, but the fares are publicly regulated.

LABOR ASPECTS OF DIAL-A-RIDE

Dial-a-ride services are highly labor-intensive; that is, driver wages and benefits constitute a large percentage of operating costs. As a result, labor practices have a strong impact on the costs and financial viability of these systems.

We have already remarked on the fact that the financial success of shared cabs as compared with the dubious financial status of most of the bus-based systems can be partly attributed to the difference in driver wages which are approximately 50 to 100 percent greater for unionized bus drivers. It is worthwhile to speculate about the possible implications of labor conditions in the future. Dial-a-ride systems will become progressively more expensive to operate as wage rates go on increasing, and this increase will be relatively larger for the bus-based systems. The other major type of labor required is in dispatching, although the increase in labor costs for this function may be offset somewhat by the introduction of computerized routing and scheduling.

On the other hand, one must realize that if shared-cab dial-a-ride operations are actively promoted and supported by public agencies in the future, there is always a chance of cab drivers affiliating with unions with strong bargaining power. At the same time, the transit workers may realize that transit jobs will continue to decline, and successful dial-a-ride just may have the potential to arrest this trend if allowed to operate without such a heavy labor burden. This might induce them to ease their wage demands somewhat.

Batavia presents an example of this attitude. The drivers there sensed that their jobs depended on the success of dial-a-ride, which might collapse if driver wage demands were too high. They recently turned down an attempt to unionize, perhaps saving the system from extinction. They were rewarded with a 20 percent wage increase.

At present the posture of the Amalgamated Transit Union is somewhat ambiguous. It recognizes the woes of fixed-route bus systems and knows that spiraling wages have a strong detrimental effect on bus operations. The officials accept the need for new innovative services, such as dial-a-ride, which have a potential for stabilizing jobs in the transit industry and for realizing higher labor productivity by reducing idle time due to split shift rules. However, they are categorically opposed to any downward wage adjustments or any restriction in working conditions. In this context the President of the ATU has said:

> We are convinced that demand-responsive *transit* will provide the transit worker with better job security and the potential for greater earnings. Demand-responsive transit is, therefore, an attractive opportunity to the worker, can help stem the industry's economic decline, and can, at the same time, provide new job opportunities, better wages, and more adequate pensions, health and welfare, and other benefits and conditions of employment.
>
> Under no circumstances, however, should the city transit worker who provides dial-a-bus service, as distinguished from regular linehaul service, be asked to accept lower wages or more restrictive working conditions in order that dial-a-bus can be made to pay its way or that lower fares can be charged. . . . The suggestion that demand-responsive services be provided at substandard wages and working conditions, at least until they prove successful, is no less acceptable than any other request that the worker subsidize conventional transit operations whose true costs neither the employer nor the community as a whole is prepared to pay.
>
> As we see it, any special labor implications of demand-responsive service, which may require adjustments in wages, hours, and working conditions, are properly left to the local collective bargaining process.[23]

Understandably, the ATU sees dial-a-ride operations as within the exclusive prerogative of the transit industry, and union officials are on record as stating that they will oppose the provision of new dial-a-ride services by taxicab companies.

---

[23] Elliott (1973). Emphasis added.

CASE STUDIES OF EXISTING DIAL-A-RIDE SYSTEMS

In this section we present descriptions of the currently operating dial-a-ride systems in slightly more detail than hitherto. Again it must be stressed that many of these systems are evolving relatively quickly, and that data presented here relate primarily to the situation in middle and late 1972.

Haddonfield, New Jersey

The experimental 24-hour, many-to-many dial-a-ride service has been operating since early 1972.[24] This project is sponsored by the New Jersey Department of Transportation under a demonstration grant from the U.S. Urban Mass Transportation Administration. About 80 percent of the project's total funding is provided by the federal government. The primary functions planned for the system are to provide feeder service to the PATCO high speed line to Philadelphia, and all-day service for residents to local activity centers.

The demonstration is intended to study the operational feasibility and overall costs and benefits of the dial-a-ride concept. It has been designed in three stages:

- Study of the market reaction to determine whether there is a demand for such a service and whether efficiency can be obtained through manual dispatching. This phase ended in February 1973.

- The second phase involves computerization of the routing function and expansion of fleet from 12 to 18 vehicles. Computer operation has been under test since mid-1973.

- The third phase will explore a range of different operating policies and technological improvements (increased computerization, the adoption of computerized communications, and so on) to investigate the economic viability of the system.

By late 1972 the Haddonfield system was serving a population of roughly 27,500 in an 8.1 square mile area, using twelve 17-passenger air-conditioned buses. One of these vehicles is equipped with a special lift to cope with wheelchairs. The area is also served by taxis and some intercity buses.

The single trip fare is 60 cents, although the revenue averages about 55 cents per passenger because 50-cent tickets are available to people purchasing books of ten or forty, and 40-cent tickets

---

are available to senior citizens and group riders.[25] During the first eleven weeks of operation the wait times and riding times on weekdays averaged 12.6 minutes and 9.9 minutes respectively, leading to an overall mean level of service ratio of between 2.5 and 3.

Expansion of the original service area in September 1972 to include all of Lawnside—a predominantly black neighborhood—increased the initial levels of ridership significantly. The average weekday ridership in late 1972 was estimated to be around 750.

The vehicle productivity following the September 1972 expansion has been on the order of 6 to 7 passengers per vehicle-hour, resulting in total revenues of roughly $3.00 to $3.50 for each vehicle-hour of operation. The costs, on the other hand, have been around $15 to $16 per vehicle-hour, or approximately $2.15 to $2.65 per *passenger*. These exceptionally high costs are ascribable primarily to the high driver wage rates ($6 to $7 per hour, including benefits), to the presence of highly qualified managerial and monitoring staff, and to a control system designed for a much larger fleet size. In the subsequent phases of the demonstration, the costs per ride are expected to fall.

The dispatching for the Haddonfield system as of February 1973 was being performed manually with the help of two telephone operators, a scheduler, and a dispatcher.

In summary, this system provides safe, reserved-seat, comfortable, door-to-door service at a low fare, but at a very high cost—certainly more expensive (to the sponsors rather than the riders) than taxicab service. It is estimated that dial-a-ride has been successful in attracting approximately 4 to 5 percent of the potential trips.

Shared cab service in Davenport, Iowa

Shared taxicab service has been offered in Davenport for at least forty years. The Royal Cab Company (then the largest and now the only cab company in the city) was acquired in 1967 by its present owner, Robert Cherry.[26] Since that time this dynamic entrepreneur has managed to expand the operations of the company very significantly and is today providing an extremely successful and financially self-sufficient dial-a-ride service.

By early 1973 the company had 23 vehicles (standard 7-seat Checker cabs) providing door-to-door service on a 24-hour-a-day, 7-day-a-week basis. In direct competition with a publicly subsi-

---

[25] Group tickets may be used by parties of three or more traveling between the same origin and destination at off-peak hours.

[26] Cherry (1973) and Heathington et al. (1974).

dized bus transit system, Royal Cab has been able to attract some 1,250 to 1,600 riders per weekday[27] in spite of relatively high fares which average roughly $1.00 per passenger. The Royal Cab Company carries roughly two-thirds as many people in total as the bus company, even though the flat bus fare is only 35 cents.

The vehicle productivity is between 4 and 5 passengers per vehicle-hour of operation, implying revenues of about $4.00 to $5.00 per vehicle-hour. We estimate the total costs to be slightly less than this. Solid managerial know-how, low overhead, and efficient utilization of labor and equipment, along with relatively low driver wages, are primarily responsible for the low cost figures.

Passengers request service by telephone, or in person at the downtown waiting room. Empty cabs are not allowed to cruise: they wait for deployment by the dispatcher. The system is based on manual dispatching employing a total of three dispatchers. In 1972, however, the owner experimented with a small computer which helped the dispatching personnel to route the cabs and also indicated the expected fare. The caller requesting service would inform the control center about the origin, destination, and number in the party. These data were fed into the computer which located the appropriate cab and calculated the fare. This computerized dispatching was discontinued when it became clear that the hardware was inadequate to cope with the peak hour level of demands—the response time was too slow. A larger replacement computer was due to be brought into service in mid-1973.

The astute managerial and administrative skills of the owner are reflected in a variety of decisions and policies. For example, the cab charges passengers 10 cents per minute after waiting for three minutes outside their origin address, in order to reduce the wait time for other riders and to decrease the taxi idle time. On the other hand, there are methods of providing incentives for drivers and good service to customers: for example, after the first three bags of groceries, passengers are charged 25 cents for each additional package, and this fee goes to the driver. The drivers are also compensated for waiting for calls at various locations.

Royal Cab also provides a number of other services which are compatible with the operations of a cab company with vehicles on the road 24 hours a day. Thus, the company is the local Western Union agent, and cabs deliver the telegrams; during nine months of the year, cabs also service barges on the Mississippi with supplies at all times of day and night; Royal Cab is the local

---

[27] The company gets about 1,150 calls per day in summer and 1,550 per day in winter, with an estimated average of 1.1 riders per call.

agent for the *Skycab* air-taxicab freight service; and many local people call the company in preference to calling an ambulance when emergency service is needed.

The primary service area is somewhat larger than that of the bus-based dial-a-ride operations. The primary service area has a population (1970) of 98,500 in an area of 20.0 square miles, although Royal Cab will actually accept requests from anywhere in the home county. The fare system is on a zone basis, with the fare calculated per *call* regardless of the number of *passengers* wishing to travel between the same origin and destination. Passengers may obtain exclusive service by paying a $1.00 premium over the usual fare for the shared cab.

Demand continues to grow, and the owner claims that only financing problems inhibit the company from growing faster. One indication of the success of this operation is the fact that average revenues, which were only 18 cents per vehicle-mile in 1967, increased to 32 cents per vehicle-mile by early 1972, and still further to 44 cents while computerized dispatching was in operation.

Batavia, New York

In October 1971, a three-vehicle para-transit system began operation, replacing a fixed-route, two-vehicle system.[28] It is operated by Batavia Bus Service, a subsidiary of the Rochester-Genesee Regional Transportation Authority. The system offers a combination of services. In peak hours it provides subscription service for work and school trips, while in off-peak hours it provides many-to-many dial-a-ride and package delivery service. In addition, vehicles are occasionally chartered by stores to provide service to customers. Sometimes a bus is also operated as a jitney along a fixed route. The hours of operation are 6:00 A.M. to 6:00 P.M., Monday through Friday.

In mid-1972, a 4.3 square mile service area with a population of 18,000 was being served by four 23-passenger buses and one 10-passenger van, of which only three vehicles were normally used to provide off-peak dial-a-ride service. Weekday ridership averaged around 300 during the first year of operation, with a peak of around 400 in the winter. The ridership has been growing steadily since the start, and was expected to reach 500 by the winter of 1972/73. This patronage represents a 1 to 2 percent share of the potential market in an area with no other competitive transit service. Approximately 58 percent of the riders are subscription customers, 40 percent many-to-many customers, and the others are

---

[28] Aex (1973).

largely chartered service patrons. Dispatching is manually performed by a dispatcher with the help of a telephone operator.

The point-to-point dial-a-ride fare is 60 cents per ride. Weekly subscription rates are $4.00 for adults and $3.50 for school journeys; college students may buy twelve tickets for $4.00. The average fare is on the order of 45 to 50 cents per ride.

The vehicle productivity for many-to-many service has ranged from 7 to 12 passengers per vehicle-hour, and has averaged 9. For subscription services the productivity has ranged from 12 to 17, and averages 15 passengers per vehicle-hour. The total revenues from subscription, many-to-many and charter operations, from advertising, and from package delivery meet the vehicle operating costs (approximately $4 to $5 per vehicle-hour) and a part of the fixed costs (roughly an extra $3 per vehicle-hour). There appear to be two reasons for this relatively encouraging situation: first, the operating costs are exceptionally low for a bus-based system due to low driver wages ($3.60 per hour, including benefits), and second, the revenue from services other than many-to-many has been substantial.

In late 1972, an experiment was conducted with teleprinters in vehicles instead of voice communication.[29] This resulted in a 6 to 10 percent increase in vehicle productivity. The experiment was discontinued, however, because the cost increases of roughly 11 percent could not be tolerated.

It may be appropriate to point out how the dial-a-ride service has apparently helped in Batavia. The ridership and revenues had been declining on the Batavia fixed-route service which was in operation before the dial-a-ride system was started. The annual ridership was roughly 80,000 and the annual operating deficit had reached about $7,000 even though the vehicles were fully depreciated. The dial-a-ride service has reversed the declining trend and attracted roughly 105,000 riders during the first year of operation (30 percent higher than the fixed-route service) in spite of higher fares. The dial-a-ride system now meets all of the operating costs and a part of the fixed costs.

Regina, Saskatchewan

A many-to-many *Telebus* service sponsored by the Provincial Department of Highways and Transportation was started in Regina, a city of about 140,000 people, in September 1971.[30] It is being operated by Regina Transit System, a municipal department

[29] Guenther and Augustine (1972).
[30] Atkinson (1973).

of the city, and supported partly from the city's general funds. Telebus primarily serves as a feeder to a fixed route arterial bus line and to several other activity centers. It is in service from 6:45 A.M. to 11:35 P.M. on weekdays, and from 6:45 A.M. to 9:35 P.M. on Saturdays.

The service area for Telebus in mid-1972 covered 2.75 square miles with a population of roughly 18,000. Service was provided by two 14-passenger vans, two 23-passenger buses, and (when necessary) two conventional 42-passenger transit buses. All six vehicles were on the road in peak hours, and three to five vehicles operated during off-peak hours. Both the service area and the fleet size were scheduled for expansion before the winter of 1972/73.

The average weekday ridership in mid-1972 was around 1,200 passengers, with a wintertime peak of 2,200 riders per day. The implied vehicle productivity is relatively high for dial-a-ride, averaging about 19 passengers per vehicle-hour. This high productivity is due mainly to the large proportion of subscription patrons.

In fact, about 55 percent of the riders use Telebus as a feeder to and from the arterial bus-line stops, and another 35 percent use the service for access to a small number of local destinations. Pure many-to-many service accounts for only 10 percent of the patronage.

About 40 percent of the rides are made by regular subscribers as distinct from ad hoc telephone requests. The service area is in a relatively high-income residential district with up to 3-car families, and half of the Telebus ridership is said to come from families with 2 to 3 cars while the other half comes from 1-car families. The patronage, which was 5 to 6 rides per capita per year for a previous fixed-route transit system in the area, was by mid-1972 around 20 rides per capita per year for Telebus and was still increasing steadily.

Ad hoc users are required to call in at least 20 minutes before the desired pickup time. The average waiting time for service is therefore relatively long. The cash fare is 35 cents for adults, 25 cents for students, and 15 cents for children, with free transfer privileges to the line-haul buses going to downtown Regina. The resulting mean revenue per ride of about 29 cents falls far short of the operating costs which we assess to be around 60 cents per rider. All of the capital and administrative costs, together with the operating deficit, are borne by the city.

The dispatching is performed by one dispatcher who is assisted by a clerk in peak hours. The drivers are self-routed.

Finally it may be interesting to note that at least in one of the zones served now by the dial-a-ride service the ridership is roughly 400 passengers per weekday against 50 passengers per weekday on the fixed-route service which Telebus replaced, and this is in spite of a 10 cent fare increase. These figures reflect an increase in vehicle productivity from about 7 passengers per vehicle-hour for the fixed route to about 15 passengers per vehicle-hour for the Telebus. The total deficit appears to have decreased, since the costs of Telebus dial-a-ride service apparently are less than twice the costs of the earlier fixed-route service. In other words, a greater number of riders are served at a lower overall financial burden to the community.

Bay Ridges, Ontario

This dial-a-ride service, which began experimentally in July 1970, is operated by the GO Transit Branch of the Ontario Ministry of Transportation and Communications.[31] It was designed primarily to provide a feeder service to the Pickering station of the commuter rail service into downtown Toronto.

The service area in Bay Ridges covers roughly 1.3 square miles, with a population of 13,700. Service is available seven days a week between 5:30 A.M. and 1 A.M. the following morning, provided by five 11-passenger vans. In addition to the feeder service, the vehicles also operate an off-peak many-to-few service to local activity centers.

The weekday ridership on the system has been steadily increasing, so that by mid-1972 it averaged 530 passengers per day, representing a 3 to 4 percent share of all travel in the area. Since that time the ridership has continued growing, and the system was scheduled to expand greatly to cover North York in the fall and winter of 1973/74. Since dial-a-ride started in Bay Ridges, two local cab companies are said to have gone out of business.

Roughly 80 percent of riders use the feeder service, the other 20 percent being many-to-few patrons. Vehicle productivity is consequently high, averaging between 10 and 11 passengers per vehicle-hour. The cash fare is 30 cents per rider, although books of ten tickets purchased in advance cost $2.50. The mean revenue of about 26.5 cents per ride does not cover the vehicle operating costs which we assessed for mid-1972 as around 40 to 45 cents per ride. These cost and revenue estimates relate to both feeder and many-to-few service, so the many-to-few operation alone may

---

[31] Bonsall (1971); Bonsall (1973).

be even more unattractive financially. The deficit is met from provincial tax revenues.

Average waiting times are high, because the ad hoc users are required to call at least an hour before the feeder trip and a half hour before many-to-few trips. The average trip time is approximately 6.7 minutes. The dispatching is performed manually using, in mid-1972, a single dispatcher.

Ann Arbor, Michigan

A many-to-few service sponsored by the city of Ann Arbor has been operated by the Ann Arbor Transportation Authority since September 1971.[32] The system is operated from 6:30 A.M. to 6:00 P.M., Monday through Friday, and from 8:00 A.M. to 6:00 P.M. on Saturday. Its primary function is to provide door-to-door service for the southwest quadrant residents between the residential area and key downtown locations such as hospitals, government offices, the university campus, and shopping areas.

By September 1972, the service was being provided over a 2.4 square mile area to a population of roughly 17,000. Three 10-passenger vans were operated in both peak and off-peak periods, attracting an average of 200 riders on weekdays. These riders belong mainly to middle- and upper-income and student groups. One must also keep in mind that regular city bus transit was also operating 16 coaches on 6 fixed routes during mornings and evenings, in addition to providing some special services for schools and some charter service.

The cash fare is 60 cents per ride, with 50 cents for advance tickets and a monthly unlimited-use pass costing $15. The average revenue is about 47 cents per passenger, which compares with estimated operating costs of around $1.45 per ride. The average vehicle productivity over the first twelve months of operation was about 6 passengers per vehicle-hour.

Dispatching is performed by one person who answers the telephones and routes the vehicles.

Madison, Wisconsin

In Madison, a city of roughly 48.5 square miles and 173,000 people in 1970, the Badger Cab Company operates a shared-taxi dial-a-ride service in direct competition with a subsidized bus transit service (with a 25 cent fare), two other taxicab companies offering conventional cab service, and one other cab company

---

[32] Urbanik (1973); Berla (1973); Lax (1973); Ann Arbor Transportation Authority (1973).

offering shared-ride. The Badger company originated as a jitney service, but started the current dial-a-ride service in 1933/34 when a regulatory change made jitneys illegal in the city.

In September 1973 the company was operating 25 Chrysler, Plymouth, or Dodge vehicles, using one dispatcher and one telephonist. The fare structure is regulated by the city, which specifies separate fares for regular taxi, for shared-ride, and for the bus service. Currently the first passenger on a call is charged 55 cents, and additional passengers in the party are charged 15 cents—this is less than half of the fare for conventional cab service. About 95 percent of the company's business is in response to telephone requests.

The passengers are mostly middle- to low-income groups, school children, the elderly, and students at the University of Wisconsin. A number are regular passengers on a subscription basis. As in Davenport, the company management has been moving from an employee/commission relationship with the drivers to a system by which drivers lease their vehicles. This change is increasing productivity and otherwise working well.

Columbia, Maryland

A combination peak-hour subscription service and off-peak many-to-many service replaced a fixed-route bus service in January 1971 in Columbia, a new town in Maryland with a population of about 16,000 at that time.[33] The subscription service was operated from 7:30 A.M. to 8:30 A.M. and 5:00 P.M. to 5:30 P.M. between the residential areas and major employment locations. Between 8:30 A.M. and 11:00 P.M. many-to-many service was provided. This service was subsequently revised drastically in September 1971.

The service started with two minibuses, a third being introduced in February 1971. Vehicle dispatching was manually performed from a central facility. The fares were 35 cents per ride (or 10 rides for $3.00) for subscription service, and 25 cents per ride (or 10 rides for $2.25) for many-to-many service.

The subscription service attracted about 35 riders each day and the many-to-many patronage was between 250 and 300 per day, compared to a total of 50 riders per day for the discontinued fixed-route bus service. Waiting times were rather high: up to 15 minutes for 65 percent of the riders, between 15 and 30 minutes for 19 percent of the riders, and over 30 minutes for the remaining 16 percent.

---

[33] Stevens and Smith (1971); Roos (1972).

Average productivity was roughly 5 to 6 passengers per vehicle-hour, resulting in revenues of only $1.30 to $1.60 per vehicle-hour. On the other hand the system was very costly to operate—averaging about $10.50 to $12.60 per vehicle-hour during its final month of operation.

In September 1971, when a major shopping center was opened, the Columbia demand-responsive service was completely revised. In early 1972 a many-to-many service was offered from 6:30 A.M. to 8:30 A.M. and from 5:30 P.M. to 11:00 P.M. on weekdays, and all day on Saturdays. Fixed-route buses serve the shopping mall from 8:30 A.M. to 5:30 P.M. The primary function of the service (operated by the local government association) is to act as a feeder to commuter buses to Baltimore and Washington, D.C., and to provide intravillage transportation.

The equipment consists of five 10-passenger vans and four 23-passenger buses. Productivity for this reorganized service has averaged around 5 passengers per vehicle-hour. The adult fare is 50 cents per ride—not enough to meet the estimated costs of 80 cents per ride. Another interesting point is that the average trip is long, and hence takes a long time, because the new city is widely spread out.

DIAL-A-RIDE EXPERIENCE VERSUS EXPECTATIONS

Among the relatively novel modes of urban public transportation, dial-a-ride service (particularly bus-based many-to-many service) has the dubious distinction of being the one most thoroughly subjected to theoretical analysis *before* actual on-the-road implementation. How well does the *experience* which has accrued from the small number of dial-a-ride systems now operating actually agree with the *expectations* derived from the theoretical studies?

The answer, briefly, is that the services provided by existing systems generally fall short of the original many-to-many conception. The level of service has been poor and perceptibly worse than the taxicab equivalent, and the costs have been high —in many cases as high as taxi fares for comparable trips. How far is this due to erroneous prediction of dial-a-ride service and cost characteristics in general, and how far is it due to poorly conceived experimental systems and to the learning phenomenon?

Level of service and vehicle productivity

The key factors which influence the level of service provided by many-to-many dial-a-ride systems are the number of vehicles operating and the demand density (or requests per unit time per unit of service area). This relationship has been analyzed theoretically through simulation studies.[34] The following simple predictive model was calibrated from simulation experiments for a form of general demand combining both many-to-many and many-to-few requests:

$$LOS = 1 + \left[\frac{A}{N} (0.68 + 0.072D) \right]^2$$

where   N   is the number of vehicles operating

         A   is the service area (in square miles)

         D   is the demand density (in requests[35] per hour per square mile)

and   LOS is the level of service ratio, or the ratio between the request-to-arrival time by dial-a-ride and the door-to-door travel time directly by automobile

This relationship may be used to predict the level of service ratio for a number of the currently operating systems, given the numbers of vehicles used and the demand densities obtained in those areas. This has been done in Table 30 where the predicted level of service is compared with the level of service which has been actually achieved. However, the reader is strongly cautioned that these comparisons are extremely flimsy because information about the actual demand densities and level of service ratios for the existing systems is scanty.

Of the systems offering principally many-to-many service, the one in Ann Arbor has come closest to achieving the predicted level of service. But the table also highlights another important fact. By comparison with the range of values investigated in the theoretical analyses, the demand densities in the areas which currently have dial-a-ride systems are *very* low. For example, the simulations carried out at the Massachusetts Institute of Technology indicated that "dial-a-*bus can* operate with demand densities *as low as* 20 demands per square mile per hour."[36] It is significant that of the existing systems, only Regina and Bay

---

[34] Wilson et al. (1970b).

[35] It should be noted that this is a slightly different definition of demand density than that adopted earlier in the chapter—we specify here *requests* for service as distinct from the number of *passengers*. For example, the average number of passengers per request in Davenport appears to be about 1.1.

[36] Roos (1971). Emphasis added.

Table 30
Predicted and actual level of service ratios for several systems

System	Date of information	Service area	Daytime mean value		Predicted LOS ratio	Actual LOS ratio
			vehicles operating	demand density		
		sq. mi.		requests/ hr./sq. mi.		
Haddonfield	June '72	5.5	7.3	5.5	1.7	2.5
Davenport	Apr. '73	20.0	16.0	3.0	2.3	5.0
Batavia	July '72	4.3	3.8	6.8	2.7	3.0
Ann Arbor	Sept. '72	2.4	3.0	7.2	1.9	2.3

Ridges had achieved this level of demand on a regular basis by mid-1972. Their success in doing so may be ascribed to the fact that the residential densities in these two Canadian service areas are higher than in the other existing service areas and, more importantly, to the high proportion of many-to-one and subscription passengers in their patronage.

The MIT work also indicated that for the effective operation of group riding, residential density would have to be at least about 4,000 persons per square mile.[37] Most of the existing systems operate in service areas with densities higher than this, but we find it a little surprising that the most expensive and elaborate demonstration of the dial-a-ride concept to date is the one in Haddonfield where the service area residential density is only about 3,400 persons per square mile.

The low densities of demand on the existing systems have led to lower vehicle productivity values than those considered in the theoretical analysis. The MIT simulations showed that when the demand density falls below about 10 requests per square mile per hour, then vehicle productivity falls off sharply—as illustrated in Table 31. Given the low demand densities in most of the existing service areas, it is no surprise that vehicle productivities have been low—and that the decidedly more expensive bus-based systems are incurring substantial losses.

Of course, patronage is still growing on many of these new systems and it is not possible to determine whether the relatively low levels of demand can be ascribed to the wrong choice of service areas, to the fare levels chosen, to aspects of system operation (such as the amount of route deviation allowed), to the short time most of the systems have been in existence—or whether many-to-many dial-a-ride is inherently incapable of at-

[37] Roos (1971).

Table 31

The effect of demand density on vehicle productivity

| Demand density | Vehicle productivity under standardized conditions | |
	many-to-many service	many-to-one service
requests/sq. mi./hour	trips/vehicle-hour	trips/vehicle-hour
2.5	3.9	7.7
5.0	6.4	12.8
7.5	8.2	16.3
10.0	9.5	19.0
20.0	12.5	25.0
30.0	14.0	28.0

Source: derived from Wilson et al. (1970b).

tracting a greater patronage.

This discussion does highlight a major gap in the experience accrued to date with dial-a-ride. To our knowledge, no experience has yet been gained in operating a full-scale many-to-many service in areas where the demand densities are likely to exceed 20 requests per square mile per hour—in areas with residential densities greater than, say, 8,000 or 9,000 people per square mile.

SUMMARY OF DIAL-A-RIDE EXPERIENCE

The lessons from the existing dial-a-ride systems seem to be mixed. On the one hand, they have certainly demonstrated the operational feasibility of the concept. Many-to-many demand-responsive service can be provided efficiently. Manual dispatching has been successful for small fleet operations in areas with low request densities. It is not known, however, at what volume of demand computer dispatching becomes necessary, or even how successful computer operations can be, although the research at MIT and other places has suggested a high reliability for computer dispatching. In the meantime, there seems to be good potential for operations run by a manual dispatcher with a computer to perform the routing function—as exemplified by the experience of Royal Cab in Davenport.

On the other hand, serious doubts arise when one looks at the financial viability of dial-a-ride. So far, the demand attracted by *bus-based* systems, coupled with existing fare levels, has not been sufficient to cover the operating costs, with the single exception of the Batavia operation, where revenue meets all of the operating costs and a part of fixed costs. There is, however, considerable scope for reduction in costs, which have sometimes been exceptionally high due to inexperienced management and costly monitoring. Also, ridership on most of the systems has been growing steadily since inception, implying that the full potential has yet to be realized.

Privately-owned *cab-based* dial-a-ride services are financially self-supporting, even though they and the bus-based systems serve similar levels of demand. They have been financially successful partly because labor costs are lower than in the bus-based systems, and partly because they charge higher fares.[38]

Also, even though dial-a-ride systems have attracted only small fractions of the market and have been generally unprofitable, in some situations they appear to be superior to the fixed-route bus services which they replaced. Despite higher fare levels, they have been able to reverse the declining trend in ridership on the fixed-route services, and as a result, the deficits have decreased. For example, the dial-a-ride services which replaced the fixed-route buses in Batavia and Regina reversed the declining trend in ridership in spite of higher fares. Batavia dial-a-ride service meets all the operating costs and part of the fixed costs, while Regina Telebus appears to have reduced the operating deficits. In both cases greater patronage is served at lower overall financial liability.

In existing applications, dial-a-ride has filled a void between taxicab and conventional fixed-route services by providing a service that is generally better than fixed-route bus at a lower fare than the taxi. It should be emphasized, though, that in most cases these low fares have been made possible only by heavy subsidies, and that the actual costs of providing the service have often equalled or even exceeded the costs of taxicab service. The expectation that dial-a-ride would be able to provide both efficient feeder service to line-haul terminals and local door-to-door service at lower costs than could a taxi, has been primarily responsible for the introduction of seven or eight of these systems since 1970. Even now, several areas are in the process of establishing dial-a-ride systems and we are likely to see some 15 to 25 more in the next two or three years.

The experience of combination operations like the one in Batavia (which provides a wide variety of services as required) suggests that a close look should be given to the possibilities of de-

---

[38] Demand levels comparable to those for bus-based systems have been achieved by cab-based systems with more than double the average bus fares, indicating that the market is likely to accept such high fare levels.

veloping a variety of other services in conjunction with many-to-many dial-a-ride. Such operations may indeed be the only means of keeping bus-based many-to-many service financially viable. Subscription services to such places as line-haul terminals, sports arenas, entertainment sites, and employment centers need greater exploration. Dial-a-ride may also have promise as a package delivery system, a limited jitney operation, or a chartered service.

In summary, the existing systems have not yet provided conclusive evidence on the real potential of dial-a-ride. Some of the experiments have been conducted in a less than satisfactory manner. Perhaps the areas chosen were not suited to such operations, since they are all characterized by reasonably high auto-ownership levels, low population densities, and small proportions of limited-mobility residents.[39] Another significant feature of the experience to date is that the different systems provide substantially different types of service at different fare levels and there are few data that an analyst can use in comparative analysis. Also, there have been few experiments with fare and service levels; more experiments could provide the analyst with important information on the determinants of demand. Finally, data-gathering activities have been lacking in scope. If the progress of the existing systems were more carefully monitored (and this would include, for example, more careful separation of data relating to different types of service—many-to-many, feeder service, subscription passengers, and so on) the analyst would be helped significantly in drawing firmer conclusions about the potential of dial-a-ride.

---

[39] Areas with a significant proportion of limited-mobility groups (such as St. Petersburg, Florida, which has a large population of the elderly) may be more appropriate to study the dial-a-ride potential for such groups.

Chapter 9

Michael A. Kemp

Jitney
Service

INTRODUCTION

Jitney service is more difficult to define than taxicab service. The term was first applied generically to a type of transportation which spread rapidly through the urban areas of the United States in 1914 and 1915 but differed in many details from place to place.[1] Most commonly, jitneys provided a form of taxi service which was limited to relatively fixed routes (but allowing occasional slight variations from the main route) and was open to shared riding. The service was generally not formally scheduled, but headways were short. A potential passenger could hail a jitney with vacant capacity anywhere along its route or at designated stops and, usually for a flat nickel fare (although sometimes for a zone-rate fare), could dismount at any other point along the route. Jitney service is, therefore, somewhat intermediate between taxi service and bus transit service.

Principally because of political pressure from the street railways, the jitneys were regulated out of existence in most U.S. cities by the early 1920s. Today only two fully legal jitney operations of significant size remain in the United States—Pacific Avenue in Atlantic City and Mission Street in San Francisco—

---

[1] Eckert and Hilton (1972).

although there are systems operating without formal authority
in Chicago, Pittsburgh, Cleveland, Chattanooga, and almost certainly in other cities. Overseas, jitney services operate under a
variety of names in a number of countries in Latin America, the
Middle East, and the Far East. The vehicles used are small,
usually holding no more than twelve passengers.

The characteristics of jitney service

Table 32 briefly summarizes the typical service characteristics
of jitneys in comparison with those of the taxicab, the private
automobile, and traditional transit services. Particularly important
aspects of jitney service are short headways in comparison with
typical bus services (which implies a relatively short passenger
waiting time), and a flexibility of supply to meet changing
demand conditions.

A CASE STUDY: The Atlantic City jitney service

Since only two U.S. cities continue to maintain jitney operations
of a significant size on a fully legal basis, present-day operating
experience can probably best be documented by describing the
operation of the two services in some detail.[2] This description of
the Atlantic City (New Jersey) system is based heavily on interviews with the Atlantic City commissioner of revenue and finance, with the president of the Jitneymen's Association, and on
two unpublished reports.[3]

Origins of the service

The Atlantic City jitney service originated during a 1915 trolley
car strike. By the time the strike was settled in 1916 there were
approximately 400 jitneys operating along Atlantic Avenue, sufficient competition to force the trolley company into receivership.

Successive ordinances down the years have moved the jitneys
from Atlantic to Pacific Avenue (one block from the boardwalk),
regulated fares, and limited the jitneymen's freedom in a number
of ways—but unlike the situation in most other U.S. cities, the
jitneys were not completely eliminated. This is probably because

---

[2] Parenthetically one should note that Eckert and Hilton (1972) provide an
excellent and detailed review of U.S. jitney services during the years of the
jitney boom (1914 onwards), derived largely from a study of contemporary
trade journals.

[3] Urbanek and Guenther (1969); "Origin and History of Jitneys in Atlantic
City" (1967?).

Table 32
Typical service characteristics of jitneys

Service attribute	Comparison with other modes
Start from and end at any location	poorer than both A and Ta, at least as good as Tr
Availability at all times of day	poorer than A, no better than Ta, at least as good as Tr
Waiting time before journey	poorer than A, no better than Ta, at least as good as Tr
Overall average speed in vehicle	poorer than both A and Ta, at least as good as Tr
Perceived money price per passenger-mile	higher than A, lower than Ta, at least as high as Tr
Fare known before the trip?	generally yes; at least as good as A and Ta, roughly the same as Tr
Privacy and general comfort	poorer than both A and Ta, at least as good as Tr
Ability to do other things while traveling	poorer than Ta, at least as good as A and Tr
Ability to carry luggage	poorer than both A and Ta, roughly the same as Tr
Convenience in coping with luggage	poorer than both A and Ta, roughly the same as Tr
Need for parking space at destination	at least as good as A, roughly the same as Ta and Tr

KEY: A   denotes a typical private or rental automobile.
Ta denotes typical taxicab service.
Tr denotes typical bus or rail transit service.

their competition was relatively weak and fragmented, there was sufficient demand (based largely on the tourist trade) to permit economic survival, and because jitney interests had enough local political power to forestall crippling legislation. The Atlantic City service today is now the largest operation of its type in the country.

Public regulation of the service

Public utilities throughout the state of New Jersey (including transit companies) are regulated by the state department of public utilities, which levies a 5 percent gross receipts tax which is ultimately reapportioned to the local municipalities. The Atlantic City jitneys, however, are explicitly excluded from this provision. They are regulated by the city department of revenue and finance which prescribes the fare, the route, and the general operation by means of city ordinances.

The city issues licenses for jitneys at an annual fee of $85. These licenses are limited by ordinance to a maximum of 190 and are renewed each year to the previous owner provided he has no major traffic violations on his record, has not been a habitual violator of rules and regulations, and has not brought discredit to the jitney industry.

These franchises, like New York City cab medallions, can be traded privately, but this happens infrequently, the most common reason that a franchise changes hands being inheritance. The market price of a license has varied; a few years ago a license sold through the Jitneymen's Association would fetch $5,000, but the commissioner of revenue and finance informally estimated in late 1972 that the current price would be nearer $3,000. A franchise sold individually and in the off-season would change hands for substantially less. Not all of the 190 licenses are being actively used—a few are being held solely for their investment value.

In addition to the city license, a jitney owner must comply with state law as a public conveyor and must carry certain minimum levels of public liability insurance: $10,000 for injuries to one person, $100,000 for all injuries in one accident, and $5,000 for property damage. Evidence of this coverage must be on file with the city clerk.

Vehicles carry omnibus tags issued by the state of New Jersey ($24 per year), and are subject to an annual state safety inspection ($1). The city employs a taxi and jitney inspector whose function is to see that the city ordinances are observed.

Route and service provision

The jitneys operate in both directions along a basically linear route of 4.2 miles: from Caspian Avenue along New Hampshire Avenue, Pacific Avenue, Albany Avenue, and Ventnor Avenue to Jackson Avenue. Of this route, the greater segment (about 2.7 miles) is along Pacific Avenue, a central artery bounded on the seaward (southern) side by tourist accommodations, restaurants, night clubs, and other amusements, and on the northern side by shops, offices, schools, and theaters. Pacific Avenue is 40 feet wide (four ten-foot traffic lanes), with no on-street parking allowed. Jitney stops are designated by signs at all intersections along the route; in addition, some drivers will stop on hail.

There is no fixed schedule of service. The headways are controlled by fixing the maximum number of vehicles allowed in service at any particular time. The Jitneymen's Association assigns operators to one of three categories (A, B, C) which determines that man's rest and vacation days. Within each category there are four subdivisions (1, 2, 3, 4) which represent a work-shift classification. Each vehicle has its designation (C1, A4, for example) permanently and clearly painted on it, and at any one time only vehicles with certain designations are allowed to be operating.

The Jitneymen's Association produces a roster which allocates the vehicle designations to the different shifts in such a way that over time the less profitable and the more profitable shifts are shared equally. Table 33 illustrates how the roster works for a typical summer day.

Within his allotted time period a jitneyman is free to work or not, as he pleases. The roster system is policed by the jitneymen's association rather than by the city, whose sole concern is to see that the overall service does not fall below acceptable levels. Before the roster was introduced it is reported that there was oversupply at busy times and undersupply at other times.

Table 34 presents data from a very small number of sample observations of headways at points near the center of the route. The headways are not uniform, and vehicles tend to bunch. For this reason, the mean headway figures given in Table 34 may be misleading. The mean expected wait time for a potential passenger (assuming random arrivals at the jitney stop) depends not only on the average headway but also on the headway variance, and any bunching of vehicles will increase that variance. So, for example, for one set of observations when the average headway was 60 seconds, the mean expected wait time was 51 seconds, and when the mean headway was 78 seconds, the mean expected wait time was 60 seconds.

Further, a potential rider may have to wait longer at a stop than the calculated mean expected wait time, since vehicles which are fully occupied will pass him without stopping. However, observations suggest that for most of the daylight hours it is very unlikely that one would be required to wait more than five minutes near the center of the route. The bunching of vehicles appears in part to be an operating policy of some jitneymen who

Table 33

Atlantic City jitneys in service throughout the day

Shift	Time Period							
	5:30 A.M.- 7:30 A.M.	7:30 A.M.- 1:00 P.M.	1:00 P.M.- 2:45 P.M.	2:45 P.M.- 3:45 P.M.	3:45 P.M.- 4:00 P.M.	4:00 P.M.- 10:00 P.M.	10:00 P.M.- 2:00 A.M.	2:00 A.M.- 5:30 A.M.

Total jitneys in service	35	65	30	65	100*	70	35	6+

* A slight overlap of shifts between 3:45 P.M. and 4:00 P.M. ensures no lessening of service as shifts change over.

Source: Urbanek and Guenther (1969).

work in a leapfrog fashion so that, for example, each of two buses will stop at alternate stops. It is in part exacerbated by the traffic lights on Pacific Avenue. These are at every intersection, and they are operated on a platoon system, all changing simultaneously.

Demand and price

Atlantic City, with an indigenous population of roughly 48,000

Table 34

Sample observations of Atlantic City jitney headways near the center of the route

	Summer, 10:45 A.M.-11:00 A.M.	Summer, 2:15 P.M.-2:30 P.M.	Summer, 5:00 P.M.-5:15 P.M.	Winter, 5:00 P.M.-5:15 P.M.
Maximum possible vehicles in service (actual number unknown)	65	30	70	70
Mean vehicle occupancy	4.0	6.3	3.9	n.a.
Mean headways (minutes):				
eastbound	1.25	2.5	0.45	1.0
westbound	1.25	1.9	1.0	1.3

Source (in part): Urbanek and Guenther (1969).

within the incorporated city and 134,000 within the whole urbanized area,[4] is a city based almost completely on tourism and convention trade. Like most resort towns, large proportions of the resident population are retired people and seasonal service workers. We understand that some of the jitney operators work only in the tourist season (mid-June to mid-September), when the overnight population of the city can double or even triple the resident population.

During the summer months tourists are by far the greatest patrons of the jitney service, traveling to shop, to eat, or to convention centers during the day, and to entertainment and restaurants in the evening. Their journeys are usually short. Many visitors to Atlantic City bring their own automobiles, but because distances are short and parking is a problem, there is little incentive to use one's car once it has been garaged by one's hotel. It is reported that tourist patronage extends for nearly 20 hours a day, including Sundays. This is supplemented in the early morning and early evening by service and office workers traveling to and from work. In the winter, the jitneys transport conventioneers, (fewer) workers, and school children traveling to and from school.

The current fare is set by city ordinance at 30 cents per ride—15 cents for school children and school teachers traveling to and from school. The rider pays the fare on entering, and change is made where necessary. There is no tipping expected. Transit

---

[4] 1970 Census of Population.

buses do not operate along Pacific Avenue, but the flat transit fare in Atlantic City is also 30 cents or 10 rides for $2.50.

Ownership and organization

Each jitneyman is a private entrepreneur who owns his own vehicle, retains all of his own passenger receipts, and works whenever he likes within the constraints of the schedule roster. The nonprofit cooperative Jitneymen's Association, to which all franchise holders belong, was formed in 1934 to represent the collective jitney interests and to be responsible for setting work rules where it appears collectively advantageous to do so.

The association is governed by a 15-member elected executive board, and is administered by five paid part-time officers. The executive board can propose changes to the association's operating rules, but these must be approved by the membership at large before adoption.

We have been unable to obtain a copy of the operating rules and regulations (or even to ascertain whether a printed version of these exists), but some of the rules are reported [5] to be:

- Jitney A must not overtake jitney B unless jitney B has a full complement of 10 passengers or is stopped with its door open to allow passenger entrance or exit.

- When a jitneyman enters the system he must do so at one of the ends of the route; however, at the start of his shift period he may enter at the point nearest his home, thus avoiding a concentration of vehicles at the two ends of the line at the beginning of shifts.

- Operators are not supposed to converse with each other while in service.

There are no seniority advantages in operating procedures. Charges of infractions of the rules are heard by the association's seven-member traffic committee which can fine or suspend violators. Severe violations may on occasion be reported by the association to the city commissioner.

The association also operates a parts and repair shop, and sells oil and gasoline to the members. The profit realized on gasoline and oil is credited to the purchaser on a per gallon basis. From this credit is deducted the member's share of the association's costs (salaries, upkeep of facilities, benefits, and so on), and the surplus credit is distributed to the members annually. There is a limited death benefit and sickness benefit scheme

---

[5] Urbanek and Guenther (1969).

which is financed from the same general account. The executive board at one time proposed a group life insurance policy, but the idea was not accepted by the members. The association does give some legal assistance with vehicle insurance.

Interestingly, the association's president, a life-time jitneyman and the motivating force behind the association, claims to receive many inquiries each week about the Atlantic City system from all over the country. He suggests that there are many communities interested in establishing a similar service—but, impressed by the complexities of his own system and the great value of actual experience, he doubts whether others would be so successful without experienced assistance.

Vehicles

Eighty percent of the vehicles in use are International Harvester Metro buses; the remainder are Willis chassis with Brill-built bodies, General Motors Step Vans, Dodges, or Chevrolets. All have ten seats facing forward (no standees are allowed by state law), and most have automatic transmissions.

No new buses have been purchased since 1966; the 1972 price of a new vehicle was thought to be on the order of $7,000. A problem encountered with earlier models was a tendency for the body to break away from the chassis due to vibration.

By bus transit standards, the utilization of the vehicle is very low. A single-owner vehicle is used for about 100 shifts annually. The average vehicle is probably used for about 800 hours and 15,000 miles per year. The vehicles are usually amortized over six or seven years, but their useful life may be as high as ten to twelve years.

Between stops under uncongested conditions vehicles travel quite fast (30 to 40 mph). The passenger seats are upholstered, but the ride is bumpy.

Operating costs and income

We have been able to obtain only very uncertain information from which to estimate the current operating costs of an Atlantic City jitney. The figures cited here, therefore, must be regarded as largely unsubstantiated guesses.

We estimate that the 1972 average annual operating cost approached $1,800 per vehicle (see Table 35), excluding the annualized vehicle costs. Since all operating vehicles are now at least six years old and the amortization period is usually six or seven years, we may assume the capital costs of the vehicle to

Table 35
Estimated 1972 operating costs of an Atlantic City jitney

Cost item and estimation assumptions	1972 mean cost	
	per vehicle	per vehicle-mile
	$	¢
Fuel Assume an average of 15,000 miles per year at 9 mpg = 1,670 gals. @ 28¢ per gal. (net price, after profit rebate and state tax rebate)	470	3.1
Maintenance Estimated annual cost per vehicle from garage data (1969, inflated to 1972). Owner-maintenance would reduce this cost.	600	4.0
City and state licenses	110	0.7
Liability insurance	485	3.2
Share of Association costs	100	0.7
Total (excluding annualized vehicle costs)	1,765	11.8
Annualized vehicle cost $7,000 amortized over 7 years at 6 percent interest rate	1,255	8.4
Grand total	3,020	20.1

be fully discounted. However, these costs are relevant to the establishment of new systems and to the assessment of the financial performance of a jitney in an average year, so we can include a broad estimate of the annualized capital costs on the order of $1,250.

Our estimates of the aggregate level of demand must be regarded as even more tentative. Assuming an average annual mileage of 15,000 miles per vehicle implies 3,570 one-way runs along the 4.2 mile route per year. The mean number of fares received per run appears to be about 13 or 14 during summer daylight hours (from limited sample observations); assume that over the year the overall mean number of passengers per run is 10. Then at 30 cents per trip (ignoring school fares), the implied gross annual receipts are roughly $10,500 per vehicle.

So the surplus of income over current expenditure, which can be interpreted partly as labor costs and partly as return on capital, is on the order of $7,000 to $8,000 per vehicle per year. This seems to be an intuitively reasonable figure. The 1972 wage rate of New Jersey transit bus operators is equivalent to roughly $8,500 per year. The jitney operator works far fewer hours (say 800 to 900 per year, or less than half the hours worked by transit bus operators) but does have capital at risk. There is also the prospect of relatively large annual variations in income—in the short run, maintenance costs are very unpredictable, and tourist resorts are among the first places to experience the effects of national economic recessions.

A SECOND CASE STUDY:
The San Francisco Mission Street jitney

The second largest surviving jitney operation in the country is in San Francisco, where two lines dating back to the 1915 Panama-Pacific International Exposition are still in operation.[6] As in other cities, the survival of the service has been threatened in the years since its inception by political pressure from competitive public modes, and the San Francisco services have come under increasing regulatory constraint.

In 1916 the main jitney line was moved from Market Street, where the jitneys were in direct competition with the streetcars, to cobblestoned Mission Street. A referendum in the 1916 general election, which would have allowed the jitneys to return to Market Street but limited in number to 700 vehicles, was defeated by 56 percent to 44 percent. This referendum, incidentally, gives an interesting indication of the profitability of the service in 1916. Supported by the drivers, it called for the posting of an $11,000 bond by each driver and annual license fees of $10,000 per vehicle.

The early growth of the jitney in San Francisco parallels the story in most other U.S. cities. Despite the failure of the 1916 referendum, restraints on drivers were gradually relaxed (largely because of the need for public transport service during streetcar strikes) so that by 1917 there were approximately 1,400 vehicles operating over every major thoroughfare in the city. But by the 1920s the industry had fallen on hard times—there had been significant attrition in vehicle numbers due to cutthroat competition, rapidly escalating liability insurance rates, and strong political pressure from streetcar interests.

---

[6] This section draws heavily on Belknap (1973).

In 1939 the Market Street Railway managed to place on the November ballot a resolution to ban the jitneys; the resolution was defeated by 71 percent to 29 percent. Another attempt to kill the service was made in 1950. Although only 136 vehicles remained, the Municipal Railway complained that it was losing an annual $225,000 because of competition from the jitneys. The city public utilities commission was favorable to abolition, but the board of supervisors, the only body with the legal authority to ban jitney service, refused to do so.

Public regulation of the service

The jitney services operate entirely within the city boundaries so they are regulated not by the California public utilities commission but by the city board of supervisors operating through the San Francisco commissioner of police. The jitney regulations form Sections 1086 through 1111 of the city's police code and are enforced by the taxicab and jitney detail of the police department.

Each vehicle may have only one operator. Owner-drivers of the standard twelve-passenger vehicles pay an annual license fee to the city of $22.50 and must carry minimum levels of public liability insurance ($15,000 for injuries to one person, $30,000 for any one accident). They operate with regular California automobile tags. In addition, the regulations prescribe for the roadworthiness of the vehicle and for the fitness of the driver to operate a public service vehicle.

The police code limits the number of licenses permitted to no more than 700,[7] but in practice the number of vehicles has been limited to 120. As in Atlantic City, the rights to a license change hands by private treaty. A 1972 figure of approximately $2,000 to $2,500 was quoted to us for a Mission Street license. By comparison, taxicab licenses in San Francisco are currently being sold for prices in the range of $22,000 to $25,000. Jitney license transfer requires, in addition, a $1,500 fee to be paid to the city.[8]

Routes and service

The principal route remaining, on which 116 of the 120 jitneys operate, is along Mission Street, a major arterial running nearly eight miles from the Ferry Building in downtown San Francisco to the city border at Sickles Avenue near Daly City. This is a heavily congested street, passing through the city's major com-

---

[7] Section 1092.
[8] Curry and McGillivray (1971).

mercial and business areas downtown, and through the center of the low- and middle-income Mission District.

A jitney can traverse the approximately 9.5 mile length of the route in about 25 minutes at off-peak times and in 30 to 35 minutes during the peak hours. During the morning rush hour empty deadheading vehicles are allowed to divert from Mission Street onto the much faster freeway in order to avoid congestion delays.

Service is provided twenty-four hours a day, seven days a week. As in Atlantic City, the working rules have been developed by the voluntary association of the drivers, the Mission Street Jitney Owners' Association, to which roughly 90 percent of drivers belong. Each driver may work as and when he wishes up to ten hours per day, although this time limit is apparently not strictly enforced. He is, however, not allowed to work between 9 A.M. and 4 P.M. on one weekday each week, and a sticker displayed in his rear window shows the day on which he may not work. A number of drivers are reputed to work the morning and evening rush periods, occupying the interim time with another job. The city neither specifies nor enforces a minimum level of service provision, but any driver who does not work for a period of ten consecutive days should obtain permission from the commissioner of police to be absent.

During the peak hours each day headways are not regulated, but between 9 A.M. and 4 P.M. an association-employed starter dispatches the vehicles at 3.5 minute intervals.[9] Observations taken in February 1973 at the intersection of Mission Street with Van Ness Avenue revealed mean headways during the morning peak of roughly 57 seconds, and about 79 seconds during the evening peak. Bunching of vehicles was common.[10]

Jitneys are supposed to pick up and discharge passengers only at the far end of existing bus stops, but they will stop in midblock if requested.

There is also a system in the operating rules for shortening the route for some vehicles. On even-numbered days of the month even-numbered jitneys may make 29th Street their southern terminus instead of completing the extra 3.2 miles to Sickles Avenue; odd-numbered vehicles may do likewise on odd-numbered days.

A second, much shorter line (roughly four miles) is still in existence in San Francisco, but only four jitneys continue to work this route. It runs from Market Street near the Civic Center to the intersection of Third and Army Streets, with occasional extensions to the line's original terminus in the ghetto area near

---

[9] On slow days the headways are expanded to 4 minutes.

[10] Belknap (1973).

Hunter's Point Naval Shipyard. While these jitneys are said to be used by some commuters going to the Southern Pacific railroad depot at King Street, the general level of demand is reputed to be low. Consequently, we are told that Third Street licenses change hands for a much lower figure than the $2,000 to $2,500 attracted by Mission Street licenses.

Demand and price

The current jitney fares, set by the San Francisco board of supervisors, are 30 cents for rides approaching the total length of the Mission Street line, and 20 cents for shorter rides. Transit buses and trolleys also cover approximately the same route with a flat fare of 25 cents. In contrast to the transit vehicles, all jitney passengers get seats, the driver makes change, and smoking is permissible.

The great majority of the vehicles are now twelve-seat vans [11] with seating arranged either in rows or around the perimeter of the van. Observations taken in February 1973 at a point on the fringe of the downtown area revealed mean occupancies during the morning and evening peaks of about 11.2 passengers per vehicle.[12] The occupancy rate did not differ significantly between the two peaks, although fewer vehicles were working during the evening period.

It is very difficult to assess the aggregate number of passengers carried on the Mission Street line each working day, but it is probably in the range of 10,000 to 16,000 riders.

Financial aspects

The current cost of a jitney is thought to be between $3,000 and $4,000. Insurance costs are approximately $75 per month, and each driver contributes 50 cents to the association each day to pay for the off-peak dispatchers. As in Atlantic City, total operating costs are probably 20 to 25 cents per vehicle-mile, including depreciation and interest expense.

Revenues are more difficult to assess. Belknap (1973) cites one report of a gross revenue of $44 per ten-hour day, but this would appear to approach the maximum earning potential without working longer hours. It implies a gross revenue per vehicle-mile of just under 30 cents, and a net income to the driver (considering interest and depreciation expense) of roughly $14 per day. Even if these estimates are highly inaccurate, it seems clear that the level of re-

---

[11] Dodge, Ford, Chevrolet, or International.
[12] Belknap (1973).

muneration to the drivers must be very low. But the capital required to operate a jitney is small, and the financial prospects probably appear attractive to retired people and part-time drivers with other sources of income. In August 1970 when the Municipal Railway last raised fares, the jitney owners voted against filing an application for a similar raise.

OTHER U.S. JITNEY SERVICES

In addition to the Atlantic City and San Francisco systems, a number of smaller jitney services operate, either legally or illegally, in the United States. Chicago and Pittsburgh provide examples of semilegal and extralegal operations, and St. Louis provides an example of a relatively pervasive legal jitney network which has been regulated out of existence comparatively recently.

Chicago's King Drive

A small jitney service operates along King Drive (formerly South Parkway) in Chicago's south side between 28th and 63rd Streets, mostly a black ghetto area.[13] This service also dates back to the years of the jitney boom, but city ordinances have since made the service formally illegal. It is, however, well known to city officials. After World War II many of the jitneys were unlicensed taxis, but a high accident rate and complaints of excessive congestion have led to the exclusion of all but licensed cabs, which are informally required by the public vehicle commissioner to adopt a special blue and gray color scheme for jitney service.

The fare is 25 cents for any distance along King Drive, and an extra 25 cents for a deviation from the Drive to a passenger's destination if it is close by. The Chicago Transit Authority's flat fare is 45 cents.

Pittsburgh jitney service

An extensive jitney system exists in Pittsburgh, operating without formal authority between downtown and the black communities of Homewood, Northside, and the Hill District.[14] It is claimed, with good justification, that the jitneys exist primarily because of inadequate transit service and refusal by cab drivers to serve black areas. Persistent opposition by the public utility commis-

---

[13] Kitch et al. (1971).
[14] Marbury (1972).

sion, by Port Authority Transit, and by the cab fleets has failed to eliminate the jitneys, and the official attitude toward them appears to have mellowed somewhat in recent years.

Marbury (1972) documents the mode of operation in a first person narrative:

> We operate along bus routes. We just drive downtown to the busy streets. The people expect us, so they respond immediately when we toot our horns. Most of the drivers I know never take more than five passengers—unless it's real cold.
>
> A lot of the guys are retired. . . . A driver could make over 50 bucks a day if he gets a few long trips and has some steady customers.
>
> Some guys work out of jitney stations. How this works is, one guy will rent an old store front, install a phone in it, and we'll just hang around there until the community learns the number of the station. We give the guy who is renting the storefront a couple of dollars a week, and we operate just as if we were cabs.
>
> We're just men providing a service—a much needed service. If we pick up someone at a bus stop, we'll drive them to their block, sometimes to their doorstep, for the same price that PAT charges to take a person as much as three blocks away from their street. If a person calls a station for a car, we charge around the same prices that cabs do. Only we don't have a meter ticking away dimes. We don't pace the car to hit every red light, and we don't take the longest way imaginable to get to a person's destination. I get people just about every day who don't have enough money, but I don't worry. They usually pay me back as soon as they can. Wonder if PAT or Yellow Cab has a ride now–pay later plan?

St. Louis service cars

Until 1965, when the operating permits were bought out by the Bi-State Transit Authority, one of the most pervasive jitney systems in the country operated in St. Louis. Known as *service cars*, the jitneys were individually owned but the operating permits were all held by two associations, to which owners paid for the privilege of working under the permits.

The vehicles operated on fixed routes with unscheduled headways. In the 1930s the system was principally serving white, middle-class neighborhoods, but by the 1950s the service cars had a predominantly black patronage. About 85 vehicles operated a roughly circular route from ghetto areas into downtown St. Louis, in direct competition with the city's bus and streetcar transit services. A consultant's report in 1957 estimated that where transit and service cars were in direct competition the jitneys carried some 70 percent of the total public transport volumes at midday, and about 50 percent in the rush hours.[15] Both services

---

[15] Gilman (1957).

had a 20 cent fare, but service cars guaranteed seats to all riders, had shorter headways, and were usually able to make better time than the streetcars.[16]

Other U.S. cities

Rosenbloom (1972) documents the existence of legal jitney services in a number of other U.S. cities. A private service was started in Anaheim (California) in 1965, modelled on the Atlantic City system. Small jitney buses operate on six different fixed routes linking the baseball stadium, Disneyland, Knotts Berry Farm, and the commercial, hotel, and restaurant areas of Anaheim. Passengers may board only at prescribed stops, but may alight anywhere along the route. Fares are calculated on a zone basis.

In Miami a licensed all-black jitney service has operated between the downtown area and Liberty City, a largely black suburb, for over forty years. The service runs along three fixed routes with unscheduled headways, usually during the periods 5 A.M. to 9 A.M. and 3 P.M. to 7 P.M.

A similar black-operated service exists between downtown Baton Rouge (Louisiana) and the black suburb of Scotlandville. However, we understand that this service, which uses old school buses, has adopted fixed schedules, bringing it closer in service characteristics to transit or subscription bus than to jitney.

JITNEY SERVICES OUTSIDE THE U.S.

Jitney services flourish in a number of cities abroad, particularly in Latin America and the Middle and Far Eastern countries. Since much of this experience is in cities in less-developed countries with markedly different urban transportation demand and supply situations, it is doubtful whether it has very much relevance for the United States. Table 36 attempts to summarize very briefly the characteristics of some of the better-known foreign jitney systems. The interested reader will find more detailed information from the references cited in that table, and some of the major systems are described briefly below:

- *Caracas—*

  The *carros por puesto* system of Caracas, Venezuela, is very pervasive, with more than 6,000 registered vehicles. In addition, it is estimated that about half of the 6,000 taxicabs in the city also operate as "pirate" *por puestos* during peak periods.

---

[16] Solomon and Saltzman (1971).

Table 36

Major jitney systems outside the United States

Place	Name of jitney service	Persons per auto	Competitive public modes	Jitney entry restriction	Type of vehicle	Capsule description of service	Reference
Caracas, Venezuela	Por puestos	11	bus, taxi	Restricted	6-seat sedans	6,000 vehicles operating 60 fixed routes through all medium- and high-density areas. During peak, effective headways are 36 seconds to 3 minutes over most of the system. Jitneys carry 17 percent of the city's daily trips.	Kudlick (1969)
Mexico City, Mexico	Peseros	—	bus, taxi, subway	—	6-seat sedans	3 fixed routes along arterials. Flat fare.	—
Buenos Aires, Argentina	Colectivos	—	bus, taxi	—	22-seat buses	Zone fare.	—
Puerto Rico	Públicos	9	bus, taxi	Restricted	6-seat sedans	13,000 vehicles operating fixed routes (urban and interurban) all over the island.	University of Puerto Rico (1972)
Paris, France	Collectifs	4	bus, taxi, subway	Restricted	—	Only two fixed routes remain. Unscheduled service at flat fare. Some preferential traffic lanes.	U.K. Home Office (1970)
Beirut, Lebanon	Service	27	bus, taxi	Free, but requires bribes	6-seat sedans	3,000 vehicles operating a very pervasive system of fixed routes at flat fare with short headways.	Farmer (1967) Khleif (1972)
Israel	Sherut	22	bus, taxi	—	8-seat autos	Jitneys normally follow bus routes.	Harel (1965)
Istanbul, Turkey	Dolmus	—	bus, taxi	Restricted	—	16,000 vehicles providing over 40 percent of all passenger trips in the city.	Ozdirim (1973)
Manila, Philippines	Jeepneys	11(?)	bus, taxi	Free	6-seat jeeps	14,900 jeepneys in a pervasive network of fixed routes provide principal public transport service.	Grava (1972)

Jitney systems are also known to exist in other South American, Middle Eastern, African, and Asian cities. A blank (—) in the table signifies that the information is not at hand.

Although in direct competition with a cheaper but poor bus service and with ordinary cabs, the *por puestos* carried over a third of all the public transport trips in the city in 1966.[17] Obviously substantial numbers of residents are prepared to pay the incremental price for a service which is better than the bus but much cheaper than the regular taxi.

- *Buenos Aires—*
  Colectivos, or minibuses holding about twenty passengers, are used extensively in this city. Tickets which are color coded by destination are dispensed to passengers as they board. When passengers leave, their tickets are checked to see that they have paid the proper fare for the zone where they disembark.

- *Puerto Rico—*
  Jitneys known as *públicos* serve a giant share of the public transport market on the island, both within and between cities. Table 37 illustrates the modal shares in three major cities in 1964.

Table 37

1964 mode split of weekday person trips (Puerto Rico)

| City | Mode share (percentage) | | | | Total |
	auto	bus	público	other	
Mayagüez	66.5%	0.5%	31.9%	1.1%	100.0%
Ponce	63.6	5.9	26.4	4.1	100.0
San Juan	62.3	26.4	8.7	2.6	100.0

Source: Wilbur Smith and Associates/Padilla and Gracia (1968).

- *Bogotá—*
  High auto taxes coupled with low incomes create an enormous captive market for public transportation in Colombia. This demand is served by buses, microbuses, *colectivos* (multiple passenger taxis), and taxis. With the exception of one of the twenty-three bus companies serving the city, all of these modes function essentially as jitneys. There are no bus stops; all vehicles are hailed at curbside. Buses are the cheapest and slowest mode; 20 passenger microbuses charge twice as much as buses and are a little faster; taxis charge by distance and are generally the fastest and most expensive mode.[18]

- *Istanbul—*
  Dolmus comprise 13 percent of the vehicles on Istanbul's streets,

---

[17] Kudlick (1969).
[18] Kulash (1971).

and provide 41 percent of the city's passenger trips.[19] By comparison, buses and trolley-buses carry 27 percent of all trips, and private automobiles 10 percent. However, a study by the directorate of highways has shown that the *dolmus* drivers refuse to obey traffic rules and drive so negligently that they are a significant hindrance to traffic flow and safety. The authorities would like to prohibit the *dolmus*, but this is very difficult politically.

One point of significance drawn from the foreign experience is that, whereas the jitney largely disappeared in the U.S. because of political opposition from transit interests, in most cities of the world where jitneys flourish today they do so in conjunction with (and often in competition with) both bus transit and taxi services. In other words, buses and jitneys *do* coexist in these cities.

SUMMARY OF THE JITNEY OPERATING EXPERIENCE

Current operating experience in the United States demonstrates that jitney services can operate profitably (in both a financial and a social sense) in at least two sorts of demand environments: low-income areas inadequately served by bus and taxi (San Francisco, Pittsburgh, Miami), and tourist resorts (Atlantic City, Anaheim). While these existing services appear to be operating at a fairly low level of profitability, the financial rewards are sufficiently attractive to potential suppliers of the service that, under restricted entry conditions, the rights to operate are changing hands at a premium price, and in some cities service is being supplied outside of the law. Experience from overseas, albeit largely from countries with markedly different economic conditions from those in the United States, suggests that jitneys might usefully play a still wider role in urban transportation.

By and large, since the accrued operating experience in major U.S. cities under the socioeconomic conditions of the 1970s is so small, the value of promoting expanded jitney service must be largely conjectural. But, given that jitneys can provide a service superior in many respects to that of the transit bus for only a small increment in fare, we believe that jitney service is in line with the currently evidenced patterns of demand for urban transportation services, and that the continued suppression of jitney operations by local regulation probably acts against the public

---

[19] Ozdirim (1973).

interest. Consequently, expanded jitney services appear at the very least to be worthy of public attention, consideration, and experimentation.

Chapter 10

Robert G. McGillivray
Michael A. Kemp

Daily and Short-Term Rental Cars

INTRODUCTION

This chapter is concerned with two distinct car rental concepts. On the one hand, it documents some of the salient operating features of the *existing* rental car industry in the United States. This industry rents automobiles to members of the general public on a daily basis as a relatively short-term proposition, or on an annual lease as a longer-term proposition. For the sake of distinction we will refer to the concept of hiring automobiles by rental agreement for a period of less than a year as the *daily rental car*.

On the other hand, we are also concerned with a concept which we will refer to as the *short-term rental car*. The principal distinguishing feature of this type of rental is that drive-it-yourself vehicles (probably small and low polluting) would be made available for renting by the trip or by the hour—certainly for periods shorter than one day. Short-term rentals by the trip are not now available in the United States, but the concept has been formulated and discussed as a possible solution to several urban transportation problems. We will summarize the important points in the development of the idea in the United States and the theoretical analysis which has been made of the idea. There has been an actual on-the-road experiment in France, and serious plans are being developed for a trial in the Netherlands. These developments are presented as case studies.

Of course, the two concepts have a great deal in common. There is, for example, little to stop the daily car rental industry from providing short-term car rentals at the present time. Why they do not has to do with several factors which we will discuss in some detail—the current patterns of demand for rental cars, certain financial aspects of the rental car industry, the lack of restraints on the use of private automobiles in urban areas, and so on. However, since short-term rentals have not been seriously tried in the United States, it will be useful to treat them as a distinct rental category.

This chapter will first summarize existing operating experience with daily rentals and will then present the salient features of the short-term rental concept, paying particular attention to the economic and social aspects of the idea rather than technological requirements.

THE SIZE AND ORGANIZATION OF THE DAILY RENTAL CAR INDUSTRY

Unfortunately, even reasonably precise data are not publicly available on the number, type, and location of rental cars in the United States. Although the industry is dominated by a small number of major suppliers, data concerning their operations and markets are usually treated as highly confidential. Even the aggregate size of the domestic industry is difficult to assess: the leading firms operate internationally and their published financial reports typically do not distinguish between domestic and overseas revenues. Nor do the two industry trade associations, the Car and Truck Renting and Leasing Association and the American Automobile Leasing Association, play any significant role in the collection of industry statistics.

But it is possible, using a variety of sources, to approximate very roughly the number of vehicles involved. The research staff of one major automobile manufacturing company indicated to us in 1972 that they assessed the current size of the daily rental industry as between 270,000 and 300,000 automobiles. Some corroboration appears in an independent estimate made by the trade journal *Automotive Fleet* (see Table 38) which cites a figure of 341,000 daily rental cars for 1972.[1] This represents an average annual growth rate in vehicle numbers of 12.6 percent since 1964. In addition, *Automotive Fleet* estimates that there were roughly 2.4 million leased automobiles in the United States in 1972, of which about 38 percent were individually leased.

Table 38
Estimates of vehicles rented and leased

	1967	1972
	thousands	thousands
Automobiles:		
daily rentals	204	341
leased business fleets, 10 or more cars	895	1,483
leased individually	487	925
Trucks:		
daily rentals	79	147
leased	353	639

Source: *Automotive Fleet* (1973).

There are also some data obtained from General Motors Corporation which describe new registrations of rented and leased automobiles (see Table 39). Unfortunately the data are not entirely complete in their coverage, but they do show that the majority of leased and rented automobiles are full-sized American cars. Very few foreign makes appear in the rental and leasing market. There are about as many Volkswagens as there are all other foreign makes combined, but even these are a small proportion of the number of American-made subcompacts, which in turn is but a small fraction of the full-sized automobiles.

The size of firm in the daily rental industry varies widely from large organizations operating internationally to small fleets of a few cars run in conjunction with other businesses such as gasoline stations, or automobile dealerships and service departments. Most of the largest companies are controlled by conglomerates which have seen the fast-growing automobile rental industry as a profitable investment. The leading U.S. firms, in order of sales volumes, are:

---

[1] *Automotive Fleet* (1973). It is not clear how complete a coverage of relatively small enterprises in the industry these estimates provide.

Table 39

New registrations of rental and leasing fleet automobiles, 1971

	Proportion of new registrations, 1971
	percent
Price class of automobile:	
low	14.8
intermediate	22.2
regular	53.7
high	9.3
Some selected automobile models:	
Chevrolet Impala, Caprice	14.8
Ford Galaxy, LTD	10.3
Ford Pinto	2.3
Chevrolet Vega	1.8
Volkswagen	0.7

The table is based on new registrations by rental or leasing companies buying ten or more new units in the year. The base for the table is new registrations for the U.S. domestic market, which excludes the states of Oklahoma and Connecticut after April 1971. The data do not distinguish between daily rental cars and cars for leasing.

Source: R. L. Polk and Company statistics, obtained from General Motors.

- *The Hertz Corporation—*
  Hertz is a wholly-owned subsidiary of the RCA Corporation and has car rental outlets in over 2,000 U.S. cities offering mainly Ford or Mercury automobiles. The company is also strong in short-term truck renting, and in car and truck leasing. Worldwide, Hertz claims a 1972 total of roughly 160,000 automobiles in over 100 countries.

- *Avis Rent A Car System—*
  Avis Rent A Car is the car and truck rental and leasing subsidiary of Avis, Inc., controlled by the International Telephone and Telegraph Corporation. In 1972 business outside the U.S. accounted for 21 percent of the company's revenues, and daily car rentals produced almost 74 percent of Avis' worldwide sales volume. In the United States Avis offers mainly Plymouth vehicles; since 1965, in fact, Avis has been leasing a sizable proportion of its U.S. fleet from Chrysler Leasing Corporation.

- *National Car Rental System—*
  National, controlled by the Household Finance Corporation,

operates out of approximately 1,900 locations in the United States.

- *Budget Rent-A-Car Corporation of America*—
Budget is controlled by the Transamerica Corporation.

- Other major companies operating on a national scale include Airways, American International, Econo-Car, Dollar-a-Day, Kinney, and Thrifty.

The revenues of the largest firms have been growing by about 15 percent to 20 percent per year since the middle of the 1960s, and those of their "economy" competitors have been growing at an even faster rate. The outlets of most of the nationally represented companies are usually either directly owned by the company or are independent licensees. Generally speaking, the larger the firm the greater is the proportion of directly controlled outlets: in 1969, Hertz owned roughly 90 percent of its local offices, Avis about 60 percent, and National about 40 percent. Budget is largely a franchise operation.[2]

THE DEMAND FOR DAILY RENTAL CARS

The bulk of rental cars in the United States are new, full-sized American automobiles rented at an airport or downtown location by a private company to out-of-town air travellers on business. The period of rental is usually a day or several days, the typical rental being about three days and costing the customer about $40. Hourly and half-day rentals are not very common, but they are available at punitive rates.

It has been estimated that up to 85 percent of the U.S. car rental business is conducted from airport locations,[3] and in fact most of this revenue can be ascribed to the nation's eleven largest airports. The marketing staff of General Motors has estimated that 95 percent of the business is transient as opposed to hometown or local rentals. The same staff also believes that about 90 percent of the revenue is *generated* by the airport, in the sense that rental cars provide feeder transportation for roughly 10 percent of all intercity air travel, presumably mostly for transients.[4] Estimates of the proportions of rental car hires which are transient air-related, or nontransient, or non-air-related are not available

---

[2] *Business Week* (1969).

[3] Car and Truck Renting and Leasing Association (1973).

[4] Reflection and casual observation suggest that both of these estimates may be too high.

for more than selected airports. Roughly 80 percent of the revenue from renting cars is for business-related travel which is estimated to be less price elastic than the rest. Business travellers generally want a current year's, well-equipped, full-sized car.[5] Frequently they also want the added convenience of an airport location for pickup and dropoff, and they appear to be quite willing to pay for these features.

There are exceptions to these generalizations. In New York City, the costs of owning an automobile are higher than in most other cities of the country. Parking and insurance are more expensive than anywhere else. The marketing staff of General Motors believes that weekend rentals are important in Manhattan to enable the higher-income urbanite to escape to the country. One indication of this is that about 40 percent of the business in New York is from local residents as opposed to the national average of roughly 5 percent from local residents. Another manifestation of the relatively unique New York City rental car market is the growing popularity in the summer of the 60 to 90 day lease options in Manhattan.

Other important exceptions to the national demand pattern are resort areas, principally Florida and California. The rental car season in Florida is from the week before Christmas to Easter Sunday. Package vacation plans offered in conjunction with airlines and hotels (under which a certain period of rental car usage is included with air fare and hotel accommodations at a single quoted price) are becoming an increasingly important source of revenue for the major companies. In Florida, New York City, and California only about 60 percent of the revenue is estimated to be business-related, as opposed to 80 percent for the country as a whole.

OPERATING METHODS OF DAILY RENTAL SERVICES

In renting an automobile, the rental agent must make two judgments, both of which are crucial to the car rental company's financial viability. First, the agent must assess the credibility of the prospective client's ability to pay and the likelihood of his skipping out with the car or leaving claims against the car, such as parking tickets. This assessment is easier to make if the pros-

---

[5] Some firms and government agencies require their employees to rent compacts or cheaper cars. This has been fairly successfully blocked by the rental companies through their willingness to accept advance reservations only for higher priced cars, and by their purchasing strategy which is influenced by their maintenance and resale policies.

pective customer has a valid national credit card; consequently, the screening is often made on this basis. Second, the expected loss due to accidents or other problems is heavily reflected in the rental car company's insurance premium, which accounts for almost a quarter of the total operating costs. Therefore, the agent's ability to choose honest and safe drivers as clients is crucial for a successful enterprise.

In addition to establishing financial credibility, there are other screening stipulations, such as requiring the customer to present a valid driver's license and to be older than a critical age (often twenty-five). The rest of the procedure involves checking the vehicle out, including checking its condition; upon return, checking it in, including checking for any new damage; and preparing the invoice for the customer. The customer must ordinarily return the car in the same city, and sometimes at the same location where it was rented. The one-way option exists for some operators (for example, Hertz, Avis and National), but it is frequently a higher-cost service than the more typical rental. It appears to be used mostly for ground connection between neighboring airports, and in resort regions like California. During the rental period the renter enjoys the attractive service characteristics of the private automobile, except that no one else may drive the car without obtaining the agent's permission.

The vehicles are owned or leased by the rental car company and financed privately by them. Chrysler Leasing Corporation has a six-month leasing option which Avis, in particular, uses extensively. Most of the fleets of the car rental companies are owned vehicles, usually being held for a period of six to eighteen months (or 20 to 25 thousand miles) and then sold. This highlights two important facts about the business. First, the rental car business deals almost entirely with new cars, avoiding, as much as possible, the maintenance business. Not only does maintenance become financially unattractive after about 25,000 miles, but there also appears to be a strong marketing advantage in offering an "all-new" fleet of vehicles. Second, the rental companies hold a large stock of futures in year-old cars. As a result, they obviously seek to invest in cars that have good resale value.

OPERATING COSTS AND REVENUES

In 1972 it was estimated that major rental car operations required an average daily rate of $15 with a minimum utilization rate of two-thirds, thus yielding an average revenue of $10 per day per vehicle operated.[6]

Table 40 indicates the average operating costs per month of rental cars. It should be pointed out that the user might incur additional parking and toll costs, but fuel and parking at the operator's lot are included. Depreciation and insurance are ob-

Table 40
Average monthly operating costs and revenues for rental cars

| | Major operator | | Economy operator | |
	Standard Ford sedan		Volkswagen Beetle	
	dollars	percent	dollars	percent
Depreciation	48	19	34	19
Insurance	54	22	41	23
Administration	60	24	40	23
Parking	35	14	25	14
Fuel and service	38	15	26	15
Washing	12	5	10	6
Total cost	247	100	176	100
Average revenue	325		225	

Source: Friedman (1972).

viously important components of total costs. When a major rental operation buys rather than leases cars, depreciation is minimized by buying in volume and consequently obtaining discounts of about 17 percent to 25 percent below list price. Cars are often resold to the delivery dealers within a year at higher-than-wholesale prices and without marketing costs. Insurance is considerably higher than the average for private automobiles; about $650 against $225 was reported by Friedman for a full-sized car. As noted previously, insurance is the main barrier to the small operator.

The savings to be gained from the use of smaller vehicles do not appear to be worthwhile to the major car rental companies, particularly considering the high proportion of business-related hiring in their market, the relative price inelasticity of that business demand, and the market's predilection for large, new auto-

---

[6] All data quoted in this section were taken or derived from Friedman (1972). Other unpublished sources tend to corroborate them.

mobiles. Full-sized cars predominate. Rental car companies are moving into intermediate vehicles more than into subcompacts. Resale prices of one- and two-year-old used cars of this type are consistently above those of full-sized cars. Therefore, the relative depreciation for this size of vehicle is quite favorable in comparison with full-sized and even compact and subcompact cars.

Administration expenses also comprise an important element of total costs, largely because the check-out and check-in procedures are relatively labor-intensive and are often carried out at high-value locations. Hertz, Avis, and National maintain rental desks in all major airline terminals, where competition for space is often intense. The economy operations often maintain sites near but not on the airport territory, thus achieving cost savings; on the other hand, this arrangement adds an additional half-hour or so of inconvenience to the traveler at both check-out and check-in.

Away from the airports, it is customary for the major companies to maintain rental locations in the downtown areas of cities, close to or inside leading hotels. In recent years, Hertz, in particular, has been making agreements with hotel chains and (experimentally) department store chains in order to enlarge the number of rental outlets.

The major companies have also been trying to reduce labor costs by investing in the development of computerized central reservation systems and inventory control. Computerized reservation also offers benefits to the traveler, particularly in reduced check-out and check-in time. Hertz and Avis have recently established computerized files of information on repeat users (trade-named the *Hertz Number One Club* and the *Wizard of Avis*) which not only facilitates speedy preparation of the rental agreement but should also reduce car thefts, credit losses, rentals to accident-prone drivers, and sloppy arithmetic in calculating charges.

LEGAL AND REGULATORY ASPECTS OF RENTAL CARS

So far as we can determine, rental cars have been regulated only as a business, not as a public utility. For example, in Pennsylvania

> both the legislature and the courts distinguished the rent-a-car operation from common and contract carriage. . . . The Court of Common Pleas found that "(Hertz) is not acting either as a common or a contract carrier and does not compete substantially with common or contract carriers by motor vehicles." . . . The Pennsylvania Supreme

Court agreed, frequently describing Hertz's activity as a private business.[7]

The reason given was that Hertz *selects* its customers. The same author also reports that in other states the lessors of vehicles who do not retain control (by providing a driver, for example) are excluded from regulation.

One major legal problem associated with the rental car industry is negligent entrustment. The usual doctrine is that an owner who entrusts his car to another is not liable per se for loss and injuries caused by the negligent or wanton acts of the borrower, unless the decision to make that entrustment is itself an act of negligence. This has traditionally involved a face-to-face meeting between borrower and lender, including rental companies as lenders. A similar procedure applies regarding potential criminal acts. Typically the penalties for permitting intoxicated persons, minors, or unlicensed drivers to operate a vehicle are incurred by the person in control of the vehicle at the time.

The hirer of a rental vehicle is responsible in the normal way for any penalties personally incurred for infractions of the law in connection with the vehicle. This presents a particular problem with parking offenses, for nonpayment of parking fines incurred by rental cars is common. In 1972 the controller of New York City claimed that automobile rental companies in that city owed almost $3.6 million for over 186,000 unpaid parking tickets.[8] A similar claim in the courts by the City of Chicago, attempting to recoup unpaid parking fines for 1966, has been dismissed. However, local ordinances imposing liability for parking violations upon the vehicle rental companies have been enacted in several communities, and such ordinances appear likely to become increasingly common.

THE ROLE OF DAILY RENTAL CARS IN URBAN TRANSPORTATION

The services performed by rental cars are similar to those performed by owned or leased cars. We have noted previously that rental cars are usually employed by the relatively more affluent members of society, often by out-of-town air passengers traveling on business. A few inferences can be made on this basis.

Except as a temporary replacement for an out-of-service owned car (often but not always rented from the service department of a

---

[7] Krasnowiecki (1970).
[8] *New York Times*, March 12, 1972, p. 70.

car dealer), rental cars are not used for the home-to-work trip. Therefore, their use as a commuting or feeder mode of travel is essentially negligible. Except on roads to airports, their contribution to peak-hour traffic congestion should be small. Indeed, since daily rental cars comprise only between 0.3 and 0.5 percent of the nation's stock of private automobiles, doubling or tripling the number of rental cars, or even eliminating rental cars altogether would be likely to have only minimal impact on traffic congestion.

Similarly, the effects of rental car usage on the environment are individually about the same as those for the private automobile, although collectively they form but a very small fragment of the total picture. To the extent that the average rented automobile is used in a different way from the average privately owned (or leased) car, so one might expect the impacts to differ slightly. Speaking very broadly, most of the travel by rental car is in urban environments, and on the average the vehicles are used a little more than a comparable privately owned vehicle. Therefore, a rental car would contribute more than an owned car to the congestion of roads and parking areas and to the noise and air pollution effects on the surrounding community.

It is also to be expected that, except for the persons living in very dense parts of urbanized areas (Manhattan, for example), the impact of rental car availability on automobile ownership levels is slight. Moreover, since such a high proportion of rental car usage is business-related—for trips where a much higher value is placed on time, on personal comfort, and on convenience than on the money price—there appears to be only a low possibility of substituting any other public mode of transport (except perhaps taxi) for rental car travel. Rental cars generate a relatively high cost per mile, although for those trips or groups of trips which end near rental car terminals they provide maximum convenience. The business executive in a hurry frequently cannot depend on buses or cabs. Once acquired, the rental car is generally a dependable travel mode.

THE SHORT-TERM RENTAL CAR CONCEPT

The short-term rental car concept has been discussed in certain developed countries as a possible way to mitigate several urban transportation problems, particularly the reduction of congestion, pollution, and parking space requirements in densely developed areas in the metropolitan core. Basically, the idea is to divert travelers in these areas from their private automobiles to readily-available, small, low-polluting vehicles which can be rented by the hour or by the trip. The concept is sometimes discussed in conjunction with the imposition of various forms of traffic restraint on private automobiles in central city areas—for example, physical restraints, parking taxes, outright banning, or various forms of congestion pricing.

To our knowledge, short-term rentals are not currently a mode of travel anywhere in the world, although a limited experiment has been carried out in southern France and there are serious plans for a trial in the Netherlands. We will summarize this experience later in the chapter. In the United States, research has concentrated on the technological feasibility of the concept and on its environmental implications.

Our perspective here differs somewhat from previous American research on short-term automobile rentals in that we are not particularly concerned with the size or the relative pollutive effects of different types of automobile. Nor will we focus on the feasibility of electric or improved internal combustion engines in reducing pollution or energy requirements, even though these are worthy topics. Instead, we attempt to evaluate short-term car rental with regard to its economic and social desirability (including, of course, its ability to improve urban transportation) and with regard to its financial feasibility.

Other theoretical examinations of the concept have been made in the United Kingdom[9] and in Japan,[10] although there again the emphasis has been on the design both of the vehicle and of the system.

THE DEVELOPMENT OF THE CONCEPT
IN THE UNITED STATES

American research in this area has concentrated on so-called *minicars.* These are small, low performance and low-polluting automobiles which use less space and have lower emissions than standard cars. Some vehicles of this type already exist and are available today. There is a small U.S. market in electric vehicles which are used mainly as golf carts and as industrial fork lifts in confined areas. There are also several quite small internal combustion automobiles being marketed. For example, both Honda and Subaru manufacture vehicles which are about ten or eleven

---

[9] U.K. Ministry of Transport (1967).
[10] Toyota Motor Sales Company Ltd. (1972).

feet in length compared to about fourteen feet for subcompacts and eighteen or more feet for full-sized cars.

There have been two families of research study relating to short-term rentals in the United States. The first comprises a series of studies carried out in the late 1960s by the University of Pennsylvania,[11] from which the name *minicar* has been taken. The second derives from a Stanford Research Institute (SRI) study of the so-called *public automobile system* (PAS),[12] which has been used subsequently as the basis for the design of a system for a particular area—as a feeder service to the Bay Area Rapid Transit in Contra Costa County (California).[13]

The various studies have had different emphases, particularly with regard to the areas where the proposed concept would be viable. The Pennsylvania work considered demonstrating the concept in the downtown area and in a low-income area of Philadelphia. Those who were studying a public automobile system considered setting up a demonstration in a more affluent suburban setting, as a feeder to line-haul transit. In both cases a small, utilitarian, low performance vehicle was suggested, to be rented for short periods using an automated check-in and check-out procedure, a network of terminals or stands, and a procedure for redistributing vehicles to points where they are needed. Both systems were thought of as being publicly owned, though the level or form of government involvement was not developed very far in either case. Financing was not considered in any detail either; in both cases it was felt that there was some chance that the operation could ultimately be at least self-supporting, if not profitable. However, it was expected that, initially, state or local subsidies would probably be necessary, supplemented by a federal demonstration grant or technical studies support. Management arrangements would presumably be part of such a demonstration program.

In both cases, the following procedure for renting a vehicle was suggested. The customer would obtain a credit card and a key which, together, would allow access to and use of the vehicle, and would identify the user for billing and liability. The user would drive the vehicle to the destination and there park it at a stand, or would reserve the vehicle and use it later for another trip, finally returning it to a stand. Billing would be on the basis of time and mileage, possibly in addition to a subscription or club membership fee to obtain the right to the service.

---

[11] University of Pennsylvania (1968, 1970, 1972a, 1972b).

[12] Stanford Research Institute (1968).

[13] DeLeuw, Cather and Company (1971); Schmidt et al. (1972).

The club idea appears to be necessary to allow screening of drivers for financial, driving, and lending responsibility. The procedure involves behind-the-scenes work: billing and other administrative duties, maintenance and cleaning, and redistribution. The last of these deserves particular mention since it is not currently an important consideration in the daily car rental industry. The ability to redistribute vehicles at a reasonable cost is the most questionable part of the operation.[14] If the costs are too high, the viability of the system is severely limited. Redistribution has been thought best achieved by linking the vehicles together in a train, which would require special vehicle design. Another possible solution is to use trucks similar to those presently used for transporting automobiles.

Two types of location have been considered for stands or terminals: at curbside and in standard parking lots. In the latter case, economies in parking would be achieved due to the reduced need for reshuffling vehicles within the lots, since the cars would be interchangeable and not individually owned. In addition, if the cars were small they would use less space than standard models.

Short-term rentals in different operating environments

Obviously the level of demand for short-term rentals and the level of service supplied by the system are highly interdependent. They are also both influenced by the type of service area in which the system operates, so one must specify the service area before evaluating the transportation, economic, social, and environmental impacts of the concept. We will summarize briefly the analysis to date relating to implementation of the idea for *three* different types of service area.

The use of short-term rentals in a *downtown area* has been examined specifically in two studies—the Pennsylvania work considered the central business district of Philadelphia, and the Japanese work related to Tokyo's Marunouchi business area. As mentioned previously, the chief aim of a downtown short-term rental system would be to improve downtown circulation by diversion from the private automobile. Because of their physical characteristics, minicars would be expected to produce less congestion, improve parking efficiency, and lower the pollution and fuel consumption levels. Since the system is flexible and can easily evolve incrementally, it requires a relatively small capital investment compared to travel modes which require construction

---

[14] There is a close runner-up—the question of the expected losses of not being able to assign liability for theft or damage to, or caused by, the vehicle.

of their own guideway. Moreover, the system is easily maintained, and it offers levels of service (in terms of privacy, comfort, convenience, and flexibility) which approach those of the private car.

Both the Pennsylvania and Japanese research included simulation studies which examined the minicar rental system in the context of the real-life conditions holding in the particular downtown areas under consideration. The Pennsylvania analysis predicted the levels of diversion to minicars from private automobiles, from conventional transit, and from taxis. But no evaluation was made of the desirability of the minicar relative to the other paratransit modes. Our own preliminary opinion is that a somewhat expanded notion of what is currently the taxi would probably be more efficient in high density areas. Taxis, jitneys, and dial-a-ride vehicles do not need to be parked and, since the driver is present, do not offer such an easy target to potential thieves and vandals. On the other hand, it is true that the absence of a driver is likely to give short-term rentals a strong labor cost advantage over other forms of para-transit.

We have similar but even stronger reservations about the applicability of short-term rental cars to *low-income areas*, the second type of environment considered in the Pennsylvania research. Public facilities are frequently abused in such areas.[15] A related but quite distinct welfare problem is how to provide mobility to the poor as one way of improving access to employment. A short-term rental car system is one possible way, but other options should be compared with it in a comprehensive cost-benefit framework. One other option is to provide subsidized taxi, dial-a-ride, or scheduled transit at a reduced fare, or even free. Still another is to assist the poor person or family to have access to a private automobile. The central concern is not to justify short-term rental cars but to find the best or most cost-effective way to meet the problem.

The PAS research also considered short-term rentals in a third type of operating environment—providing service in an affluent suburb as a *feeder* to fixed-rail rapid transit service from the suburbs to the downtown. Such a feeder system depends heavily on the ability to reshuffle the cars to achieve maximum utilization. In the PAS work it was assumed that the vehicle would be prohibited from freeways and therefore would not be able to compete effectively with line-haul transit. The vehicle would be most useful for short trips because of its low speed (25 mph maximum), a characteristic of currently feasible electric vehicles. It was en-

---

[15] The interested reader is directed to the literature on public housing. See, for example, Rainwater (1970).

visaged that it would be used most heavily by persons making other local trips on personal business or for visits. It was felt that in low density areas these services would be performed most effectively by a form of dial-a-ride for those not able to drive or without access to a PAS car, while PAS cars were considered a more attractive alternative for most persons. It was also felt that a driver's license for a PAS car would be easier to authorize than the one currently required for standard automobiles. The PAS studies unfortunately did not deal with the concept of taxis, whether conventional or shared, or with jitneys; consequently, no case was made for choosing the PAS and dial-a-ride mixture over one comprising taxis or jitneys.[16]

A computer simulation was carried out by Stanford Research Institute to test a redistribution procedure which they devised. The analysis indicated that, under their assumptions, redistribution of cars could be completed within a few minutes. Simulation indicated that, for the area in Minneapolis studied, 20-car stands seemed appropriate. Further, reasonable lengths for redistribution trains were found by simulation to be five cars long. The SRI simulation proved encouraging.

Under a wide variety of conditions, it was found that few passengers had to wait longer than five minutes, redistribution mileage was low, and relatively few redistribution drivers were needed.[17] It was estimated that, in the service area described, a stand with a capacity of 18-20 cars could serve an area expected to generate 54 trips during the peak morning hour. Such an area might consist of one city block in a high density area, and four blocks in a low density area. With a mixture of these it was felt possible to achieve as many as 40 revenue trips per redistribution driver hour.

Estimates of costs for short-term rental systems

Costs for minicars have been estimated under some assumptions about maintenance policy and economic life which are considerably different from assumptions for standard rental cars.[18] The first column of Table 41 represents costs under the assumption of using a Volkswagen with a single overhaul at the end of four years, yielding an assumed life of eight years. The second column gives costs for minicars using an assumed life of twelve

---

[16] This is also true of the Pennsylvania work, although University of Pennsylvania (1970) indicates that high cross-elasticities of demand between taxis and minicars were suggested by their simulation.

[17] However, part time and split shift work were assumed feasible; this may be overoptimistic with respect to U.S. labor.

[18] Friedman (1972).

years, again with a single overhaul at the half-way point. Development costs were assumed to be amortized over 7,500 units and the lifetime of the vehicles. These figures can be compared with those for existing rental car companies shown in Table 40.

Table 41

Estimated average monthly costs for the minicar system

	Vehicle type			
	Volkswagen Beetle		Minicar	
	dollars	percent	dollars	percent
Depreciation	30	21	23	19
Insurance	41	29	25	21
Administration	25	17	25	21
Parking	15	10	10	8
Fuel and service	26	18	21	18
Washing	6	4	6	5
Development	—	—	9	8
Total cost	143	100	119	100

Source: Friedman (1972).

At first glance, on a cost basis the short-term rental car system envisaged seems like a much better scheme than the current daily rental operations. Comparison of Table 40 with Table 41 shows that, for all components of the cost, the Volkswagen operated under the minicar system was cheaper than the Volkswagen currently operated by an economy daily rental company. Furthermore, in Table 41 the only category in which the costs for the minicar vehicle exceed those for the minicar system Volkswagen is in the expense of development. Why then do we not presently have the check-in and check-out system and other terminal components of the minicar system at least for some rental car applications? The answer partly lies in the caveat that accompanied these cost estimates in their original source:

> Some drastic innovations would be required in administrating the system so as to reduce the very high administrative costs which are represented by Hertz and discount systems.
> This was particularly true in view of the fact that the system as envisioned in the operating concept involves substantially more terminals, a very much larger number of *check-ins and check-outs* per day per car and primary operation in central business districts where high *costs of space* are likely. Furthermore, insurance costs which are a high percentage of the total cost were likely to be higher

in view of the *less selective* approach to be taken on subscribers to the system and the *large number of subscribers* using each car each day.[19]

It appears then that the costs of owning and operating terminals and of recirculating vehicles included in the estimates in Table 41 are probably understated.

As already mentioned, short-term rental vehicles are usually thought of as relatively low polluting, low performance, small automobiles, with carefully specified safety, reliability, and space-saving features. The concepts emphasize safety and reliability more and performance less than the current norms for auto manufacture; such norms may, of course, be changed by recent legislation on safety and environmental standards. In any case, we find it curious that in this earlier research both the vehicle and the rental system were considered necessary candidates for change. A more natural approach would be to consider the system using presently available vehicles without major changes.

The frequency of service with short-term rental cars more nearly corresponds to that of a transit mode that must be walked to but not waited for, than it does to the private automobile. If it were possible for a potential user to find out (or otherwise be sure) that a functional vehicle was available at the nearest stand, an important element of this service would be guaranteed. This has been discussed in the minicar-PAS literature, but the costs of surveillance and redistribution are uncertain, at best.

A CASE STUDY: The Montpellier Experience

Historic Montpellier is the chief city of the Languedoc region of southern France and lies six miles north of the Mediterranean. The resident population of the city approaches 150,000. Montpellier is predominantly a regional center rather than an industrial town. Situated in one of the richest wine-growing regions of the country, it is an important market for wine, fruit, and vegetables. The city houses an historic university and school of medicine and is the medical, legal, and religious center for a wide region. Its manufacturing industry includes textiles, chemicals, electronic equipment (IBM is the major employer), and licorice.

The central area of the city is compact and not of a particularly high density. The center comprises a mixture of residential and business property and, relatively speaking, could not be described as a very busy central area. However, old and narrow streets

---

[19] Friedman (1972). Emphasis added.

create very difficult traffic conditions and low vehicle speeds; during peak hours it is faster to walk than to use a vehicle. Parking, in particular, is a severe problem.

The enterprise

The private concern which designed and operates the Montpellier short-term car rental system is the Société Procotip, and the acronym TIP *(transport individuel public)* is used extensively in connection with it. This company was formed by an engineer who designed the mechanical aspects of the system, and his partner, a man with insurance company interests who was able to obtain financial backing. In addition to private financing, the French Ministry of Transport has given some financial and legal aid to the company, and it is for this reason that the experiment has been monitored by the Institut de Recherche des Transports (IRT), a governmental nonprofit organization sponsored partly by the ministry.

Société Procotip investigated the possibilities of implementing its system in a number of southern French cities and finally decided on Montpellier. The municipality provided 17 very small parking lots for the firm's exclusive use. All of these are situated in the compact central area, in a circle with a radius no larger than one kilometer (1,100 yards).

The equipment

The company leased 35 new Simca 1000 cars [20] with automatic shifts, painted them a distinctive bright blue, and installed the patented payment equipment, the *TIPmètre.* This is a form of slot machine designed to allow prepayment with security against theft —there are no coins in the system. After unlocking the equipment with his personal key, the user inserts a plastic token which rotates slowly within the meter at a rate determined by the engine speed. As it rotates, the edge of the token is physically mutilated, thus cancelling its value. A token is good for approximately 18 kilometers (around 11 miles). If the driver reaches the destination without using up the token, it can be withdrawn and the residual value used on a subsequent occasion.

There are several refinements. When a key is first inserted in the equipment a small camera photographs the number on it as a precaution in case of accident or theft. The driver does not have to buy gasoline—a red light on the outside of the vehicle shows when the tank is almost empty, and a cruising tanker operated by

---

[20] Simca is a subsidiary of the Chrysler Corporation.

the Société fills up parked *TIPtaxis* displaying the warning light.

Since the charging mechanism responds solely to engine speed, long-term retention of the vehicle presents a problem to both the individual user and the company—and these problems have not been solved by the present equipment. A user who parks a TIP-taxi and wishes to use it subsequently cannot reserve it in any way. When parked in the central area, it is possible that another user will remove the vehicle, and the original driver will have to rely on finding another car. However, if it is parked outside the central area (the vehicles may be driven anywhere within the city boundaries of Montpellier), there is a much greater chance of being able to retain the car. So a central area worker who lives at the city boundary might, for example, drive home in a TIPtaxi, park it overnight at home, and use it to drive to work the following morning. The charge would not reflect the fact that the vehicle had been held relatively inaccessible to other users for a long period.

The Société has tried to lessen this problem by discouraging (orally rather than financially) the retention of vehicles outside the central area. On the other hand, they recognize that a user would like to make short stops without the fear of losing the car, and so they have tried to discourage people from taking TIPtaxis not parked on one of the designated lots.

The demand

The Société Procotip is a cooperative. Originally, a prospective TIPtaxi user first had to become a member of the cooperative for a lifetime membership fee of 420 francs ($8.40). However, some legal objections were raised to the fact that publicly owned parking facilities were being reserved for what, with membership, would be a private group. This matter was taken as high as the Conseil d'Etat, which ruled that the membership fee was, in fact, illegal. The Société apparently overcame these objections by introducing a new class of membership—*abonnés* (season ticket holders) who buy subscription membership for one, three, or six months at a time. This arrangement somehow appears to overcome the legal objections.

For the initial membership fee, the user receives a numbered key and, hence, access to the system. In addition, tokens are sold for 10 francs each ($2.00), so that the variable price to the user is about 56 centimes per kilometer (18 cents per mile). By comparison, Hertz and Avis rent Simca 1000s in Montpellier for roughly 26.50 francs per day plus 20 centimes per kilometer. Thus a potential user would need to drive about 75 kilometers (47 miles) per day before the rate per unit distance of a car hired from the major rental agencies falls as low as that of the TIPtaxi. However, one should note here that the Procotip rates are failing to cover costs, as will be discussed later. In early 1973 the average vehicle was being driven almost 20 kilometers (12.5 miles) per day, which is about 11.25 francs ($2.25) in gross revenue.

Montpellier has a bus system, but the routes do not penetrate the historic center of the city. There are taxis also, but not many of them, and these mostly serve the interurban transportation terminals.

The Société has issued 80 keys, and claims to have identified a further 180 "potential members," although it is not entirely clear what this latter term means. One gets the strong impression that membership has largely been sold on a "good old boy" network basis. Most members of the cooperative know one another socially (which may mean that there is a stronger disincentive to antisocial use, negligence, or vandalism than would be the case in a larger city). Membership does not cost a particularly large amount, and it seems probable that the number of "potential members" means very little in terms of potential usage of an expanded system.

The users are, in fact, drawn predominantly from the high-income upper- and upper-middle classes. The main interest is from shopkeepers, business and insurance executives, traveling salesmen, and the medical profession—and some university students, although their interest waned as possibilities for fraudulent usage were discovered and eliminated.

Almost all members own their own automobiles, but it is doubtful whether they are using TIPtaxis for travel which they previously made in their private cars. No significant reduction of congestion in the central area has been detected, and it seems likely, bearing in mind the compactness of the center and the parking problems, that TIP journeys are replacing walking rather than any vehicular mode.

The outcome of the experiment

By January 1973, informed observers who had followed the Montpellier experiment appeared to agree that it should be judged a "failure," although a detailed analysis of the accumulated experience had yet to be performed. No operating costs for the system are available to us, although the consensus is that the mode is costly. In the first year of operation (ending August 1972) the Société incurred a loss of roughly $200,000 even after the French government subsidy. To break even under the current pricing policy the average daily mileage per vehicle would need to triple. This loss has been privately borne, but it is possible that the public sector may ultimately accept a share of it.

Our French informants in January 1973 were forecasting a probable termination of the government subsidy and closing of the Montpellier system. It was thought that the company would probably survive, however, switching its attention to further research and development work. The city of Orléans (and possibly Rouen also) has shown some interest in adopting a Procotip system. None of the large car rental agencies have displayed much interest in the Montpellier experiment, although SNCF (the French nationalized railroad system, which owns a car hire subsidiary) has inspected the Procotip system.

The principal problems encountered in Montpellier appear to be, in order of importance:

- The compactness of the city center, and the consequent limited extent of the system. Most of the parking lots are within walking distance of each other, and we would guess that more TIPtaxi demand derives from diverted walk trips than from diversion from any other type of transport. The limited geographic extent of the system's principal area of operation has also led to the low average utilization (in mileage) of the vehicles.

- Parking space in the historic center of Montpellier is at a distinct premium, and while the city has reserved 17 small lots for TIPtaxis, these are unsupervised and there has apparently been significant poaching of the space by other vehicles. The city authorities have been somewhat ambiguous in their attitude towards this, and it has probably been reflected in a lack of enthusiasm by the police for ticketing offenders. It is rumored that the high-income profile of Procotip subscribers is a matter of some political embarrassment to the authorities.

- There have been some small mechanical problems with the TIPmètres, but these have been successfully overcome in the course of the experiment. The hardware appears to work well, given that engine speed is taken as the only criterion for usage charges. After 17 months of the system's life the automobiles were still in good condition; there was very little evidence of negligence or vandalism.

What are the lessons to be drawn from the Montpellier experience? Two obvious conclusions are that the short-term car rental idea ought to be tested in an area of much larger geographical extent than Montpellier (which implies a correspondingly greater number of vehicles to ensure that users have a good chance of locating one when they need it), and that it is important to provide the user with a reasonable assurance of being able to park conveniently. It seems wise, also, to open up the users' cooperative to corporate memberships, since the Montpellier demand experience suggests that this type of system is partly in competition with daily car rentals. Businesses, hotels, airlines, and travel agencies, for example, could be allowed to lease a batch of keys to give or hire out to whom they please. Introduction of wider, more complete coverage of the market and the incorporation of a time-related component in the pricing mechanism would increase the system's chances for becoming financially feasible.

Interestingly, before the Montpellier experiment began, IRT built a simple simulation model of the system. The demand assumptions, of course, had to be very simplistic because of the lack of any empirical evidence about demand levels, but the simulation appears to have turned out quite well after the fact. One problem highlighted by the simulation work is that of geographically asymmetric demand patterns. If the vehicle usage turns out to be highly asymmetric in this way, the system will run into a ferrying problem with empty vehicles. This has not been serious in Montpellier because of the compact geographical nature of the system, but the problem could prove important in any larger implementation.

A SECOND CASE STUDY:
Plan for Short-Term Rentals in Amsterdam

Serious planning for a short-term car rental system in Amsterdam, capital of the Netherlands, has reached an advanced stage.[21] A cooperative called Witkar CVUA ("Whitecar Cooperative Union") has been established to develop the system. Negotiations have been in progress with the General Bank of Holland for a loan which may be guaranteed by some of the city's principal stores. Further financing is envisaged from equipment suppliers and cooperative members. A total of 1.5 million guilders ($462,-000) is needed to finance an initial system of 100 cars and 15 parking stations serving 3,000 members. Negotiations have also been going on with the city's public works department over loca-

---

[21] This section draws heavily on Mikofsky (1973), Bendixson (1973a), and on *New York Times*, August 5, 1973, p. V10.

tions for the 15 parking places. The city council has approved funds for the construction of the first station.

The promoters aim to develop Witkar in three stages: first 100 vehicles, then 500, and finally 1,000 or 1,200. In the third stage, this system (representing a total capital outlay of 15 million guilders or $4.6 million) envisages 150 parking stations serving the entire central area of Amsterdam—roughly 3 square kilometers (1.2 square miles) bounded by the Singel Canal. The resident population of this area is about 75,000; between a third and a quarter of the households now own cars. There is an influx of about 30,000 private cars into the area each day.

The motivating force behind the project is Ludd Schimmelpennink, a mechanical engineer and former city council member. The principal aim of the proposed system, as the promoters express it, is the reduction of pollution and traffic congestion in the center of the city.

The equipment

In December 1972 two prototype vehicles were in existence, designed by Schimmelpennink and built by a company called Cock (specialists in electric delivery vans) at Assen in northern Holland. The cars are small, weighing about 500 kilos (1,100 pounds), with room for two persons and with a luggage rack on the roof. They are over six feet tall, less than six feet long, and about four feet wide. The body is made of polyester and fiberglass on a steel chassis. Thus, although the wheelbase is smaller than the height, the center of gravity is low and the vehicle is stable. The cars also have sliding doors and electrically heated windows.

The vehicles are electrically powered. At the current state of the technology, the design of an electrically powered automobile must represent a trade-off between the amount of time the vehicle is in use, the time needed to recharge its batteries, and the energy storage characteristics of the batteries. One prototype has been fitted with a 130-to-140-kilo lead/acid battery, and the other with a 70-kilo nickel/cadmium battery. Both allow a driving time of between 40 and 65 minutes. The lead battery requires a longer charge time but has a higher energy density. The two are roughly comparable in cost.

The total energy required to recharge after a one mile ride is about 400 watt-hours, which Schimmelpennink likes to equate to the energy used per passenger mile by a typical electric train, or to 27 electric toaster minutes. The recharge time for such a journey is two minutes.

Day-long tests of driving, stopping, and charging have been carried out to provide data for simulation exercises, but which kind of battery most suits the Witkar system will remain uncertain until more is known about the patterns of use under real conditions. Present thinking is that the maximum use made of the cars is likely to be about 40 percent of the time, or some five or six hours a day.

The maximum speed is about 28 kilometers per hour (17.5 miles per hour). The promoters believe that the slowness and apparent fragility of the vehicles will permit their use in streets reserved for pedestrians and cyclists.

The system will be operated under the control of a small computer built by N.V. Nederland at Haarlem. As of December 1972 considerable development work remained to be done on the control system. Computer programs had yet to be written, and the computer-controlled monitoring device at parking stations required further development.

The method of operation

The system would operate as follows. Witkars would be used only for travel between the network of parking stations which would be either within buildings or at curbside. A curbside parking stand, for example, would be 18 meters (60 ft.) in length, the equivalent of three normal parking spaces, and would be able to accommodate ten Witkars in a queue. Vehicles would be taken from the front of the queue and returned at the tail. Overhead contacts would supply DC current to recharge the batteries as the Witkars stood in the stand. As each car was taken from the front of the file, those behind would be automatically moved up to create an additional parking space at the rear.

Beside each stand there would be a customer monitoring device (or *kiespaal*) linked to the central computer. The intending user inserts a machine-readable membership card into this device, and the identification information is checked to ensure that the card is not a stolen one and that the user's account is in credit. If the card is acceptable, the intending customer indicates to the computer the proposed destination stand, and whether this will be a *direct* (up to 15 minutes) or *indirect* (up to 60 minutes) journey.

Only if parking space is available at the destination stand will the customer be allowed to proceed. If no space is available, the user is advised to look for an adjacent stand. The ultimate aim is to provide parking stations no more than 300 meters (330 yards) apart. If parking space is available at an acceptable destination, the *kiespaal* issues a key for the Witkar at the head of the queue, and the issue of this key marks the beginning of the period of hire.

The user then drives to the destination. Since the key fits only that vehicle, short stops may be made en route without fear that the Witkar may be taken by another user. At the destination station, the car is driven to the rear end of the queue, and the key is deposited in the monitoring device, thus terminating the chargeable hire period.

As the batteries in a vehicle begin to get low in charge, a warning light or buzzer will indicate that the driver should change to a recharged Witkar. The central computer could also be programmed not to release vehicles unless they have an adequate charge to reach the specified destination.

Anticipated demand and pricing

Persons wishing to use the Witkar system will first have to join the cooperative for an initial fee of 25 guilders ($7.50) and an additional security deposit of 25 guilders for each membership card issued to the member. By August 1973 it was reported that the cooperative had some 1,200 members.[22] In addition, short-term membership will be available to out-of-town visitors from counters at Schipol airport and the main railroad station. It has also been proposed to the cooperative that hotels should be allowed to include short-term membership in the Witkar cooperative as an automatic part of booking a room.

It is envisaged that rental charges will be computed on an elapsed time basis, although the option for including a rank-to-rank distance element in the charge obviously also exists. A figure of about three U.S. cents a minute has been mentioned. Charging on an elapsed-time basis is likely to mean that peak-hour travel will be more highly priced than off-peak travel. Billing and payment will be made through the municipal banking system.

For the first 15 parking stands, there are 105 possible origin-destination pairs. For 34 of these pairs the direct distance is less than one kilometer; for 31 pairs the distance is 1 to 1.5 kilometers; and for 27 pairs the distance is 1.5 to 2 kilometers. Only 13 origin-destination pairs are over 2 kilometers apart. The mean trip length is expected to be about 1.5 kilometers (1 mile), to take about 6 minutes, and to be charged at about 20 to 30 U.S. cents. The maximum trip length envisaged would be 4 to 5 kilometers, around 3 miles.

The promoters expect the service to be particularly popular

---

[22] *New York Times*, 5 August 1973, p. V10.

with the employees of large firms who travel to workplaces in the central area by public transport. Witkar stations will be located in prominent positions near the premises of such firms—preferably where employees can look out of a window to check on the availability of vehicles so that queueing for Witkars is minimized. In addition to the street stands, companies will be invited to finance stations convenient for their visitors and employees at a cost of 100,000 guilders ($30,000)—this fee will include some advertising rights at stations. Additional cars might be financed in the same way.

There are a number of ideas for coping with the problem of geographically asymmetrical demand patterns. To a certain extent the requirement of an assured parking space at the destination stand will lessen the problem. In addition, ferry crews can be employed to move the vehicles around. However, the promoters hope they can persuade members of the cooperative to help solve the problem by offering the user a reduced charge to ferry vehicles in a short train when driving directly to an appropriate destination station. Ferrying in this way will not be obligatory. When a driver indicates willingness to the computer to ferry additional vehicles, the hooking-up of the cars is automatic. A third possibility for correcting flow imbalances is to limit trips to oversubscribed destination areas. This solves the problem, but only by significantly lowering the service offered by the system.

The political situation

There is considerable support in Amsterdam for physically restraining private automobiles in the central city, and for the proposed Witkar system. In December 1972 the city council considered and rejected a proposal to ban cars from entering the central area between 7 A.M. and 9 A.M., but agreed that some less drastic measures were necessary.

Support for Witkars has come from the central area stores, which are feeling competition from a huge new shopping center at Amstelveen, a new suburban extension to the south of the city. The first thought was to build multistory parking garages, but these have generally been expensive and unprofitable. Four street committees of shopkeepers have been formed to support the Witkar project. One is based at Dam Square, and includes De-Bijenkorf, the well-known quality department store.

The Amsterdam public transit company also has shown interest in the project, regarding Witkars as complementary to the Amsterdam streetcars. However, strong opposition has predictably come from taxi operators. They are especially concerned that

Witkar stands might be granted locations which have been denied to taxi drivers for years. Hire-car firms such as Hertz and Avis are said to see no competition from the Witkars. However, the police have also voiced doubts. They fear that the low maximum speed of the Witkars will slow down other traffic, possibly presenting a safety hazard.

THE FUTURE FOR SHORT-TERM RENTAL CARS IN THE UNITED STATES

On the basis of the analysis carried out to date and the very limited foreign operating experience, we believe that the concept of short-term public automobiles deserves further study and possibly, in some yet to be determined form, development and demonstration. While it is clear that short-term car rental is not currently a self-supporting business proposition, the potential of the daily rental car industry expanding into this area is one of a few promising solutions to the problem of restricted mobility in low-to-middle-density, middle-to-high-income residential areas, particularly where feeder service to rapid transit could be the chief function of the system. At this time we are much less enthusiastic about applying the idea to low-income areas, since this form of para-transit is most susceptible to heavy losses due to damage, theft, and vandalism. And it is still far from clear whether short-term car rentals would be significantly better than other para-transit modes in improving the circulation in high-density downtown areas, particularly in the absence of restraints on private automobile use.

An experiment may well be feasible with currently available vehicles, perhaps slightly modified to allow assembly into trains for redistribution purposes. First, however, simulations for specific locations seem necessary to justify such an experiment. The major hardware problems yet to be fully solved appear to be the equipment for surveillance, checking in and out, and billing. One possible way to conduct the experiment without this hardware would be to contract with gasoline stations or other small businesses to provide check-in and check-out facilities. Screening for financial and driving competence should probably be left to financial institutions—the automobile insurance companies might be a logical answer, since joining a public auto club might require screening similar to that now required for buying car insurance.

Chapter 11

Kiran U. Bhatt

Subscription Buses and Car Pools

INTRODUCTION

This chapter describes services in which a number of travelers make an agreement to travel together on a regular basis. A number of modes are used to provide these prearranged ride-sharing services, ranging from informal pooling by car or van for small numbers of travelers to formal subscription bus services with routes and schedules carefully tailored to meet the travel needs of the subscribers. (Generally, we use the term *pool* to refer to prearranged ride-sharing services for which the driver does not receive a fee, and the term *subscription* to refer to services with paid drivers.) Most of the operations provide service between a residential neighborhood and a particular employment area, involving some route deviation for minor collection and distribution patterns at either end of the trip.

New riders generally sign up for the service in advance and then travel with one group of people on essentially the same schedule each day. Inflexibility of schedule is perhaps the major shortcoming of typical prearranged ride-sharing services, and in this respect such services are more restrictive than conventional transit modes.[1] However, for many trips this problem is of little concern because the travelers are already tied to fixed schedules connected with their trip purposes (work or entertainment schedules). Also, back-up alternatives can often be organized for days when the regular arrangements are inconvenient.

In most other respects the service is generally superior to conventional bus transit: easier access, fewer stops en route, shorter trip time, and greater comfort. Service is often provided in a congenial and club-like atmosphere (some operations even organize "happy hours" on afternoon trips with drinks, music, and so on). Also, since there is usually a high level of vehicle occupancy, the per passenger trip costs for this service are usually quite low.

Operations in the U.S.

Informal car and van pools exist all over the country and are used mainly by people from the same neighborhood for commuting to a common place of employment. To a lesser extent, informal car pools are used to transport school children between home and school. In this chapter we will describe some notable examples of car pool, van pool, and subscription bus operations occurring at one time or another over the last ten years. Brief case studies for these operations are presented in a later section of the chapter. For the discussion in the earlier sections of the chapter, however, the operations have been listed in Table 42 and their important operating characteristics have been summarized in Tables 43, 44, and 45. Tables 46 through 52 provide additional data on the service characteristics, costs, patronage, and growth of the services.

The car pools described in this report are organized on a fairly large scale, with several hundred employees of one institution participating in the program. The van pools are all relatively small operations with 1-25 vehicles providing 25-1,200 person trips per day. The subscription bus operations are also small, each operating with less than 50 buses, and serving less than 3,000 person trips per day.

All the car pools discussed here use private automobiles. The employers of the car pool riders are involved only to the extent that they help match riders by furnishing match boards at the

---

[1] This problem has been circumvented by some of the larger subscription bus services, which permit riders to choose between buses, and provide a daily fare for infrequent riders.

Table 42

Notable car pool and subscription bus operations [2]

	Metropolitan location	Year estab-lished	Year dis-con-tinued
Car Pools			
NASA	Washington, D.C.	1964	OG
FHWA	Washington, D.C.	—	OG
McDonnell Douglas	St. Louis, Mo.	—	OG
Burroughs Corp.	Los Angeles, Calif.	—	OG
Bay Bridge	San Francisco, Calif.	—	OG
Van Pools			
Monarch	New York-New Jersey	—	—
B&B Minibus	Long Island, N.Y.	—	—
Little House	Palo Alto, Calif.	—	—
3M	Minneapolis-St. Paul	1973	OG
Subscription Bus			
Specialty Transit	St. Louis, Mo.	1958	OG
Premium Special	Peoria, Ill	1964	1970
Reston Express	Washington, D.C.	1968	OG
Maxicab	Flint, Mich.	1968	1971
GGBHTD "Commute Clubs"	San Francisco, Calif.	1971	OG
National Geographic	Washington, D.C.	1968	OG
COM-BUS	Los Angeles, Calif.	—	OG

KEY: OG On-going as of mid-1973.
          —   Denotes information not at hand

place of work and providing special incentives such as inexpensive and close-in parking spaces. For most van pools, however, the employers that are served play a major role in organizing the service, providing vehicles at reduced rates, or contracting with outside operators to perform the service. Monarch [3] is the only van pool operation we discuss which was organized entirely by a private entrepreneur in the business of leasing vehicles to commuter groups. The subscription bus services show the greatest amount of diversity in organization and

[2] Table 42 is compiled from information in Golden Gate Bridge, Highway, and Transportation District (1973), Bain (1970), Blurton (1968), Curry and McGillivray (1971), Pratsch (1971), and Solomon and Saltzman (1971).

[3] Hines and Sloan (1971).

Table 43
Characteristics of car pools

	McDonnell Douglas	Burroughs	FHWA	NASA
Date of information	1972	1972	1972	1972
Service provided				
Type of trip	H-W	H-W	H-W	H-W
Nature	F-O	F-O	F-O	F-O
Schedule flexibility	No	No	No	No
Access	D-D	D-D	D-D	D-D
Matching	Boards	Boards	Computer	Boards
Special incentives	Parking	Parking	Parking	Parking
Transit competition	——	——	Bus	Bus

KEY: H-W Home-to-work or work-to-home   D-D Door-to-door
F-O Few-to-one or one-to-few   —— No data available

ownership. Peoria Premium Special[4] was operated by the City Transit Company; Specialty Transit[5] is operated by a private operator; while most others[6] are operated by a group of travelers who organized to lease buses from public or private bus operators.

SERVICE CHARACTERISTICS

The services provided by car and van pools and subscription buses are, generally, substantially better than bus transit in terms of access, door-to-door trip times, and comfort, and trip times are often not much in excess of auto trip time. The extra time spent collecting riders at the neighborhood origin is often partly made up at the work destination by close-in, priority parking provided for

---

[4] Blurton (1968).
[5] Pratsch (1971).
[6] See, for example, Golden Gate Bridge, Highway and Transportation District (GGBHTD) (1973), Curry and McGillivray (1971), and Bain (1970).

Table 44
Characteristics of van pools

	Monarch	B&B Minibus	Little House	3M
Date of information	1971	1971	1971	1973
Ownership	Private company leased limousines to groups	Private	Private	Private
Service provided				
Type of trip	H-W	H-W	H-W	H-W
Nature	F-O	F-O	F-O	F-O
Schedule flexibility	No	No	No	No
Number of routes	——	20-25	——	6
Route length	——	up to 60 miles	——	——
Access	D-D	D-D	D-D	D-D
Equipment				
Fleet size	——	20-25	1	6
Seats/vehicle	9	10-12	12	12
Type	Limousine	Ford Econoline	Ford Econoline	Van
Special incentives	None	Subsidized costs	Subsidized costs	Parking
Transit competition	Bus	——	Bus	——

KEY: H-W Home-to-work trips   D-D Door-to-door
      F-O Few-to-one   —— No information

high occupancy vehicles. In fact, the total door-to-door times have been estimated to be only about 25 percent greater than automobile time for many of the services reported in this chapter. (For shorter trips this difference is likely to be greater.) These operations generally provide comfortable, reliable service with guaranteed seating, and offer the travelers relief from the burden of driving through congested streets. Conventional bus transit and the private automobile have the distinct advantage of greater schedule flexibility, however.

Table 45

Characteristics of subscription bus operations

	Specialty Transit	Peoria Premium Special	Reston Express	Flint Maxicab	GGHBTD "Commute Clubs"	National Geographic
Date of information	12/72	2/66	6/73	6/71	12/73	12/71
Ownership	Private	Public	Reston Association (leases buses from WMATA)	Public	Public (leases buses)	D.C. Transit runs the buses in contract w/NG
Service						
Type of trip						
Nature	H-W F-O	H-W M-O	H-W M-F	H-W M-F	H-W M-O	H-W M-O
Access	Line-haul—must be accessed via other means	D-D	D-D	D-D	Almost D-D	Almost D-D
Access at origin	By car	From door	Within a block	½ block	1 or 2 blocks	1 or 2 blocks
Access at destination	To door	To door	1 or 2 blocks	To door	To door	To door
Schedule flexibility	No	No	Yes	No	No	Yes
Number of routes	21	21	5	26	11	10
Average route length (miles)	45	8	25	3	35-40	20-25
Equipment						
Fleet size	21	21	22	26	11	10
Vehicle capacity	41	40	50	45	45	50
Nature of equipment	Remodeled school buses	Transit buses	Some city transit; some suburban coaches	New transit buses	Suburban coaches	Standard transit bus
Transit competition	None	Bus	Bus	Bus	None	——

KEY: H-W Home-to-work; D-D Door-to-door; F-O Few-to-one; M-O Many-to-one; M-F Many-to-few; —— No information.

As mentioned earlier, the services provided by different sub-scription bus operations vary considerably. Table 46 summarizes the service characteristics of the selected operations. It is neces-sary to emphasize at this point that the comparative trip time advantage that subscription buses enjoy over conventional buses is due primarily to nonstop line-haul express operations. As a result, subscription bus operations are more attractive for long trips.

Table 46

Service characteristics of subscription buses

	Specialty Transit	Peoria Premium Special	Reston Express	Flint Maxicab	GGBHTD "Commute Clubs"	National Geo-graphic
Average speed (mph)	30	16	15	N.A.	N.A.	N.A.
Average LOS	1.25-1.50	1.00-1.25	1.00-1.30	N.A.	N.A.	N.A.
Average fare (¢/pass. trip-mile)*	1.2-1.7	3.0	5.0-6.0	9.0-10.0	2.0-4.0	1.3-1.5

KEY: N.A. Information not available

LOS Level of service, defined as the ratio of total door-to-door time by subscription bus to that by automobile

* The number of passenger trip miles produced is given by the sum of the trip lengths for the passenger trips served, where trip length is defined as the direct over-the-road distance be-tween the trip origin and the trip destination.

The service characteristics of typical car pools and subscription buses are summarized in Table 47 and compared with those of the single occupancy automobile and conventional bus transit.

COSTS AND REVENUES OF CAR POOLS AND SUBSCRIPTION BUSES

The costs of car pools vary with the type of equipment used (size of automobile or van), parking charges at the destination, and toll payments en route. Since toll payments and parking charges vary with the location, we shall not discuss them in de-tail. Although actual cost data were unavailable for the services studied, estimates can be obtained from a report on automobile

Table 47
Relative service characteristics

	Subscription bus	Car pool	Fixed route bus transit	Auto
1. Average waiting time	(a)	(a)	(a)	0
2. Schedule reliability	G	G	F-P	VG
3. Average door-to-door LOS (b)	1.5-3.0	1.0-2.0	>3.0	1.0
4. Privacy	P	F	P	VG
5. Social compatibility	F	G	P	VG
6. Ability to do other things while traveling	G	G	F	VP
7. Areawide door-to-door service?	N	N	N	Y
8. Change in O/D possible?	N	N	Y(?)	Y
9. Guaranteed seat?	Y	Y	N	Y
10. Safety from seat crimes?	H	H	L	M
11. Safety in vehicle	H	M-L	H	M-L
12. Feeling of spaciousness	G	F-G	F-P	G
13. General comfort	F-G	G	F-P	VG
14. Need for parking at destination?	Y(?)	Y	N	Y
15. Flexibility of departure	P	P	G	VG
16. Cost known before trip?	Y	Y	Y	N(?)
17. All day availability	N	N	N	Y
18. Ability to carry luggage	F	F-G	F-P	VG

KEY: (a) Scheduled service
    (b) LOS level of service = door-to-door trip time including wait/ door-to-door auto trip time
    (?) Some question

P = poor, F = fair, G = good, VG = very good, N = No, Y = yes, H = high, VP = very poor, M = medium, L = low, O = origin, D = destination operating costs prepared by the U.S. Department of Transportation (1972a). This report estimates automobile operating costs at between 10 and 18 cents per mile, depending on the size of the vehicle. For vehicles with five to six seats, car pool costs are likely to be in the range of 2 to 3 cents per seat-mile. Van operating costs (excluding driver wages) were estimated in Chapter 8 to be roughly 20 cents per vehicle-mile, so that, with ten to twelve seats per van, costs would be 1.6-2.0 cents per seat-mile. Needless to say, costs per passenger trip-mile[7] will depend on the occupancy figure for vehicles and the amount of route deviation, as well as on the total per vehicle-mile cost. With reasonably high occupancy, the costs per passenger trip-mile will be well below the costs of single occupancy automobiles.

The costs of subscription bus operations are likely to vary even more dramatically depending on the equipment, any labor agreements, the nature of the operations, and so on. At one extreme we have Specialty Transit in the St. Louis area, which is privately owned and is operated much in the manner of a large car pool by a private entrepreneur at a cost of just over one cent per productive seat-mile.[8] Low costs have been possible for a number of reasons: a passenger serves as the driver and is paid only for actual operating time, deadheading is avoided by parking the bus at the place of employment, and the vehicles (austere school buses without air-conditioning) are inexpensive to maintain. At the other extreme we have the Reston Express and GGBHTD "Commute Clubs" which lease comfortable air-conditioned buses with operators and must pay for costs associated with deadheading. The costs of these operations are high—on the order of 2 to 4.5 cents per productive seat-mile. Table 48 summarizes the costs of the selected systems described earlier.

As the above discussion indicates, the costs of subscription bus operations are a function of vehicle size and age, labor conditions, and organizational structure. American Transit Association data[9] for conventional bus systems provide some useful guidance for those components of vehicle operating costs which probably do not vary a great deal between different operations:

Equipment maintenance and repair	15¢/vehicle-mile
Fuel and oil	3¢/vehicle-mile
Insurance, taxes, etc.	9¢/vehicle-mile
TOTAL	27¢/vehicle-mile

[7] See Table 46 for the definition of "passenger trip-mile."
[8] Productive seat-miles for a service are defined as the product of the vehicle seating capacity and the length of the route served.
[9] Wells & Thomas (1972).

Table 48
Costs of subscription buses

	Specialty Transit	Premium Special	Reston Express	GGBHTD "Commute Clubs"	National Geographic	Flint Maxicab
Equipment	Remodeled school buses	Transit buses	Air-conditioned city & suburban buses	Suburban coaches	Air-conditioned city buses	New transit buses
Ownership	Own	Own	Lease	Lease	Lease	Own
Operator	Part-time	Full-time	Full-time	Full-time	Full-time	Full-time
Deadheading	No	Yes	Yes	Yes	Yes	Yes
Cost/productive seat-mile (in cents)	1.0	1.8	3.5-4.5	2.0-4.0	2.9-3.2	8.0-10.0

Other cost components will vary significantly with type of service provided, however:

- *Administrative and general—*
  American Transit Association data for small conventional bus systems show an average figure of 8 cents per vehicle-mile. This could be reduced substantially where the operation is relatively small and simple, possibly to as low as 1 or 2 cents per vehicle-mile.

- *Vehicle acquisition cost—*
  This can be calculated directly from the purchase price, which must be converted to annual costs by assuming a discounting rate and average life. Per vehicle-mile costs can then be obtained if annual miles per bus are known.

- *Driver costs—*
  This item will vary a great deal depending on labor agreements, driver utilization, and wage levels. In the worst case, full daily wages of drivers must be borne entirely by the two trips each driver provides; this occurs when drivers cannot be used at other times and labor agreements insist on their being hired for eight hours. In some other situations very high split-shift penalties may have to be paid.

Existing operations show that the costs per productive seat-mile can be as low as 1 cent and as high as 4.5 cents. A recent analysis done for the Reston service [10] has projected 1974 costs

[10] Washington Metropolitan Area Transit Authority (1973).

for that service at over 5 cents per productive seat-mile, with driver costs accounting for over 50 percent of this total.

THE LEVEL AND NATURE OF DEMAND

The information available on ridership for these services is generally very sketchy. Only a few of the systems have carried out detailed surveys of their riders, and while these surveys provide some general characteristics of the market for the services, the information is too fragmentary to draw firm conclusions about demand elasticities with respect to fare or service levels, or about cross elasticities with respect to alternative services, such as the private automobile and conventional transit. Most of the systems started out on a small scale with only a few vehicles (just one bus in many of the subscription bus operations) and have grown gradually over a period of time. Tables 49, 50, and 51 provide an overview of the selected operations at the dates shown.

Growth in service

The patronage and service offered have grown steadily for most of the systems reported, and many are expected to grow still further. The 3M Company planned to expand its van operation

Table 49
Patronage of car pools

	McDon-nell Douglas	Burroughs	FHWA	NASA
Date of information	12/72	12/71	12/72	12/72
Competitive modes	A, T	A	A, T	A, T
Riders/weekday*	——	260	——	——
Auto occupancy after initiation of pooling	2.8	1.5 times the prior occupancy	——	——
Auto occupancy prior to pooling	<2.8	——	——	——
Market share	——	30%	——	——

KEY: —— No information
    A   Auto
    T   Transit
    *   Each rider makes 2 trips per day.

Table 50
Patronage of van pools

	Monarch	B&B Minibus	Little House	3M
Date of information	1971	1971	1971	mid-1973
Competitive modes	A, T	A	A, T	A, T
Riders/weekday*	——	300	25	55

KEY: —— No information
   A   Auto
   T   Transit
   *   Each rider makes 2 trips per day.

from six to sixteen vehicles by the winter of 1973, and to 30 by the spring of 1974. These projections indicate that the subscriptions will go up to about 140 by the winter of 1973 and to 250 by the spring of 1974, resulting in a reduction in parking needs of as many as 200 spaces.

Table 52 summarizes the growth patterns in subscription bus

Table 51
Subscription bus patronage

	Specialty Transit	Premium Special	Reston Express	Flint Maxicab	GGBHTD "Commute Clubs"	National Geographic
Date of information	12/72	12/67	8/73	12/70	12/73	12/71
Competitive modes	A	A, T	A, T	A, T	A	A
Subscribers*	650-800	500-540	850	300-330	470	540-580
Market share (per cent)	50-70	9	19	——	——	50
Average load factor (pass./seat)	0.75	0.60	0.65-0.75	0.25	0.60-0.70	——
Total employment per destination	30,000	19,000	Large	——	——	1,150

KEY: —— No information
   A   Auto
   T   Transit
   *   Each subscriber makes two one-way trips daily on an average, except for the "Commute Clubs" where the average is 1.5 one-way trips per day per subscriber.

operations, and shows that the growth in some of these operations has been quite substantial. In fact, the Reston Express service might have expanded even further in 1973 had it not been
for the reluctance of the Washington Metropolitan Area Transit
Authority to lease more buses to the operation.

Table 52

Growth in subscription bus services

	Date	Number of buses +	Average number of subscribers
Specialty Transit	1958	1	30
	1972	22	650 in summer
			800 in winter
Premium Special	Jan. '65	3	30
	June '65	11	220
	Dec. '65	20	410
	Feb. '66	21	500
	*		
	June '66	17	400
	Nov. '66	17	400
Reston Express	Mar. '68	1	24
	Dec. '68	3	100
	Oct. '70	12	350
	Oct. '71	17	515
	x mid-1973	22	850
Maxicab	Sept. '68	26	—
	Mar. '69	—	300
	Dec. '69	—	330
GGBHTD "Commute Clubs"	Mar. '71	1	30
	Mar. '72	3	110
	Mar. '73	4	130
	May '73	7	240
	Aug. '73	9	350
	Dec. '73	11	470

KEY: + Each bus makes two trips per day.
   * Service was curtailed when the demonstration project came to
     an end.
   x Estimated
   — No information

Characteristics of users

Subscription bus services have typically been tailored to respond to certain specific types of travel demand, and have been able to attract ridership ranging from blue-collar, low-income riders (as with Specialty Transit and the National Geographic service) to white-collar, upper-income riders (as with the Reston Express and the GGBHTD "Commute Clubs"). On the one hand some services provided at low cost have been attractive to low-income groups; while on the other hand, more specialized operations have been provided, at a higher cost, to meet the travel desires of upper-income groups who greatly value the comfortable, relaxed, and club-like atmosphere.

The data from Peoria seem to indicate that the subscription bus patronage is rather different from that for conventional bus transit. The typical subscription bus rider was found to be male. He was younger and more affluent, and came from a household with more autos than did the typical rider of the transit bus, who was female (Table 53). User surveys indicate that riders value the following service features highly: reasonable travel time, low cost, door-to-door service, the comfort and convenience of a regular and reliable schedule, a guaranteed seat in a familiar environment, and no driving effort. The bus systems described earlier have been able to provide such features and to attract substantial numbers of former and potential auto users.

Table 53
Socioeconomic characteristics of Peoria riders

	Subscription bus	Conventional bus (peak)	Conventional bus (off-peak)
Average family income	$9,167	$7,460	$6,387
Average auto per household	1.30	0.83	0.69
Percent male	69	31	21
Average age	38	45	51

Source: Blurton (1968)

Type and length of trips

One would normally expect prearranged ride-sharing services to be most successful for peak-hour trips made on a regular basis. And this has been the case for almost all the operations discussed earlier. However, a study team recently reported that in the Shaw Urban Renewal Area in Washington, D.C., 28 percent of those not owning automobiles (54 percent of the sample) used car pools for their weekly grocery shopping. Also, informal car pools are fairly common for school trips.

The limited amount of data available on trip lengths for pre-arranged ride-sharing operations suggests that they generally serve long trips. Even though we do not have any specific trip length information on the car and van pools described in this chapter, a look at the areas where they operate indicates that they also serve fairly long trips. Monarch van pools served trips of up to 20 miles between northern New Jersey and Manhattan. B&B Minibus provides commuting for trainees living up to 60 miles from the destination plant on Long Island. The subscription bus services, with the exception of the Premium Special and Maxicab (both now discontinued), all served trips of between 20 and 50 miles in length. As mentioned earlier, the buses enjoy a significant travel time advantage over conventional transit only when the nonstop, line-haul part of the trip is quite long. It is hardly surprising then that both of the operations which have been discontinued served relatively short trips.[11]

Market share

The market share of subscription bus services appears to be quite large in the corridors they serve. Specialty Transit claims to have attracted 90 percent of the market at terminal points, and 50 percent at the intermediate points along its routes in the St. Louis area. Bain (1970) established that about 16 percent of the Reston workers employed in Washington, D.C., ride the Express, and Morin et al. (1972) give a more recent figure of 17 percent. Peoria Premium attracted 9 percent of the potential market at its peak. The data relating to market shares for car pools and van pools are virtually nonexistent; the only indication we have is that the Burroughs car pool system is attracting up to 30 percent of the potential market.

Available data indicate that the majority of subscription bus, van pool, and car pool users are former auto drivers. For example, in Peoria 72 percent of the Premium riders were former auto drivers, auto passengers, or members of car pools. In operations such as Specialty Transit and B&B Minibus the shift is entirely from autos and car pools since conventional transit does not serve those markets. The overall indications are that car pools and subscription buses have, indeed, attracted substantial num-

---

[11] In Peoria, the average trip length for the Premium Special was 8 miles; the Flint Maxicab served even shorter trips.

bers of riders from other lower-occupancy modes, thus reducing the number of vehicles on the roads.

Demand elasticity

While ridership surveys indicate that a range of service variables have been important in attracting riders to prearranged ride-sharing, the relative importance of these factors is difficult to assess. We have little data upon which estimates of elasticities can be based. However, the Peoria user-survey indicated that 70.9 percent of the riders considered convenience, reliability, and low trip time as the most important aspects of the service, while only 6.8 percent considered lower cost the most important factor. Freedom from the burden of driving was selected by 17.5 percent as the most important factor. Recent data[12] from Reston indicate that 55.8 percent of the riders feel that reduced travel time should have first priority, while 23.5 percent feel that lower fares are more important. A general observation that holds for many of the operations is that trip time and service reliability appear to be more important than fare levels.

Data from Peoria indicate that demand elasticity with respect to fare could be approximately 1.0. That is to say, as the fare increases, there is a proportionate decrease in ridership, and vice versa. In 1966, a 20 percent fare increase resulted in a 21 percent decrease in ridership over four months. (However, the service level also declined during this period, so the demand response may really be fare inelastic.) On the other hand, ridership on the Reston Express has increased steadily despite a gradual upward trend in fares.

Impact on auto ownership and residential location

Information on causal relationships between these operations and trends in auto ownership and residential location is provided by only two of the services reported. A survey of the Reston Express riders conducted by Morin et al. (1972) in November 1971 indicated that of roughly 510 riders answering the questionnaire, 21 percent had actually reduced the number of automobiles they owned as a direct result of the subscription bus service. Another 8.4 percent said that they would probably reduce the number in the future, and 43.4 percent said that they would probably not increase the number. In addition, 49.4 percent mentioned that they would own more automobiles if the bus were not available. Also, 43.6 percent said that they would not have moved to Reston

---

[12] Morin et al. (1972).

if the bus service had not been available. A recent report on 3M van pools suggests that about 9 percent of the subscribers have sold their second cars, another 5 percent are seriously contemplating it, and 9 percent have been able to postpone purchase of another car.

LEGAL AND REGULATORY ASPECTS[13]

Passenger carrier services generally fall under one of two kinds of regulatory environments: interstate carriers are governed by Interstate Commerce Commission (ICC) regulations while services which are strictly intrastate are subject to regulation by public utilities commissions.

Share-the-expense car pools using the private automobile do not come under federal, state, or local regulations, and are covered by standard automobile insurance policies. Interstate subscription bus services and van pools operated for a profit would be subject to ICC certification. Intrastate van pools may or may not be regulated, depending on the statutes of different states, while intrastate subscription bus services are likely to require certification by public utilities commissions.

Interstate operations

Van pools and subscription buses providing interstate service are classified as either common or contract carriers, regulations for the former being somewhat more strict than for the latter. Car pools with leased limousines such as Monarch Associates are also classified as common carriers. Subscription bus operations are required to obtain a permit from the ICC and must comply with economic and service regulations, including regulation of fare levels. In litigations to date, the ICC has generally concluded that these operations provide distinct and beneficial services. The Monarch Associates service was found to be "materially different" from other services and a request from a competing carrier that the service be prohibited was denied, though some restrictions were placed on the route structure.[14]

Intrastate operations

Most of the existing operations provide service within one particular state and are subject to state public utilities commission

---

[13] This section draws heavily on Hines and Sloan (1971).
[14] Hines and Sloan (1971).

regulations. Classifications and regulations for these services vary from state to state. No state appears to exempt any carrier from maintaining safety and equipment standards, proper licensing, and financial responsibility, however. Variations in the level of regulation are confined to economic and service standards, including the control of fares, schedules, routes, and general service levels.

In some states only "common carriers" need certification, while in others "contract carriers" also need some kind of permit. In general the contract carriers have less onerous regulations than common carriers. Also, as mentioned earlier, the classification schemes vary from state to state. For example, in some states, car pools operated on a profit basis (as opposed to a share-the-cost basis) come under limited regulation. Van pools operating on a share-the-cost basis need certificates in some states (e.g. Washington) but not in others.[15] Generally vans which are leased for pooled service are classified as contract carriers and need a permit. The van pools provided by Little House in Menlo Park (California) and by B&B Minibus in Long Island (New York) are, however, considered specialized services and are not regulated.

Transport clubs which provide subscription service by vans or buses to "sufficiently" limited membership and use monthly or weekly passes are not considered public utilities and are exempt from regulation in some states. This is the case with the Reston Express and GGBHTD "Commute Clubs" which have the freedom to set and change fares, routes, and schedules. However, in other cases such as Specialty Transit and COM-BUS, the public utilities commission monitors services, and any changes in fares, routes, or schedules must meet their approval.

The regulatory environment appears to be reasonably favorable as far as prearranged ride-sharing operations are concerned. The existing operations have generally prevailed in suits of unfair competition filed by other competing modes: the Wayward Bus in San Francisco successfully fought off a challenge in court by Greyhound, and Monarch Associates was permitted to continue operation despite protests by an established carrier.

LABOR ASPECTS

In car pools and van pools the driving burden is generally shared on a rotating basis by the members, and, as a result, they avoid labor problems. Subscription bus operations and some van pools

---

[15] Ibid.

use specially assigned operators to provide the service. They fall into two categories:

- For some operations, vehicles are chartered or leased from transit companies along with the operators (e.g., Reston Express, GGBHTD "Commute Clubs," Wayward Bus in San Francisco, National Geographic Society, B&B Minibus Company, and Peoria Premium Special). In such operations, labor rules play an important role. The transit companies are required to use full-time union drivers whose wage rates and associated benefit packages are usually fully allocated to the subscription bus service, along with prorated overhead costs. Such operations are generally relatively expensive to operate, and charter rates have been increasing rapidly because of rising driver wages and other operating costs (the Reston Express charter rates increased from $27 per bus trip in 1968 to $30 in 1969, $40 in early 1973, and are expected to rise to almost $60 in 1974).

- The second category includes operations which use part-time drivers who are actually making the trip along with other passengers. For example, the drivers for Specialty Transit are paid only for the time spent driving, and the resulting cost savings are passed on to the passengers in lower fares.

It is evident that driver cost is a crucial item in the total cost picture, and that improved driver utilization could reduce costs substantially for operations in the first of the above categories. Use of drivers for off-peak services, reduced deadheading, higher speeds that would permit more runs to be made by each driver, and reverse commute services using deadheading vehicles are all important strategies for improving driver utilization. The Wayward Bus in San Francisco is a good example of the last strategy; deadheading vehicles are chartered at low rates to provide relatively inexpensive commuter service.

CASE STUDIES OF SELECTED CAR POOLS, VAN POOLS, AND SUBSCRIPTION BUS SERVICES

In this section we describe some of the more notable car pool, van pool, and subscription bus operations in greater detail. While these operations comprise only a small and not necessarily representative subset of such services, we feel that they indicate the range of services provided. It must also be stressed that a few of the systems may no longer be operating, while others may have expanded and evolved substantially in recent months. For these reasons we have provided the date of the information presented in the tables throughout this chapter.

Car pools [16]

(a) The *National Aeronautics and Space Administration* (NASA) in Washington, D.C., has maintained an auto occupancy rate of 3.3 persons per car since 1964 (more than twice the national average). This has been achieved through special incentives to use car pools, including priority parking, and a match-board scheme to provide car pool information to the employees.

(b) *The Federal Highway Administration* (FHWA) of the U.S. Department of Transportation has a parking incentive and match-board program in Washington, D.C.

(c) *McDonnell Douglas Aircraft Corporation* of St. Louis has been able to raise the car occupancy rate of the workers' cars to 2.8 with the help of parking incentives and a match-board.

(d) At *Burroughs Corporation* in Los Angeles, intensive information and advertising efforts organized by "Operation Oxygen" [17] reduced the number of cars requiring parking by 35 percent (from 659 to 427) by attracting many auto drivers to car pools. This implies a 53 percent increase in the auto occupancy rate.

(e) The *Oakland Bay Bridge* provided car pooling incentives by eliminating the 50-cent toll for cars with three or more occupants and giving them access to priority lanes. The preliminary reports suggest a two-fold increase in cars with three or more occupants. It is not clear, however, whether the increase is a result of a shift from low occupancy autos or from buses.

Van pools

(a) *Monarch Associates*,[18] a private concern, used to lease 9-passenger limousines to groups of residents of northern New Jersey for travel to Manhattan. Until recently, when some financial problems resulted in its liquidation, the company helped form car pools and provided and maintained the vehicles used, operating successfully in this manner for several years. No data are available on costs or ridership. This service was recognized as "materially different" by regulatory authorities because it provided a service superior to other common carriers in the area. As

---

[16] Information based on Pratsch (1973).

[17] A volunteer, nonprofit organization located in Pasadena (California) dedicated to reducing the number of autos on the roads.

[18] Hines and Sloan (1971).

a result, Monarch Associates successfully fought off most of the charges of unfair competition, although it was not permitted to use the routes that were used by the conventional transit alternative.

(b) *B&B Minibus Company*,[19] a minority-owned enterprise, uses 20 to 25 12-passenger vans to provide free service to approximately 300 black trainees from their homes to the Grumman Aircraft plant in Nassau County on Long Island, New York. The service is provided under contract with Grumman and is funded by a U.S. Department of Labor, Manpower Administration training grant. The trainees live in low-income residential areas up to 60 miles from the plant. The cost of this door-to-door service to Grumman is approximately $2.10 per person per day, or approximately 3.5 cents per passenger trip-mile. The system provides good service to low-income residents at a very low cost.

(c) *Little House*,[20] a multipurpose center for senior citizens located in Menlo Park (California) provides Ford Econoline (12-passenger) service to its members for trips between their homes and the center. The vans are driven on a rotating basis by 10 members and make morning, afternoon, and lunch time runs. They carry about 25 riders per day out of 1,800 members. The cost of approximately 60 cents per ride is covered by a philanthropic organization. This service has been successful in providing good service to senior citizens at costs which are lower than taxicab fares.

(d) *3M Van Pools:*[21] The 3M Company center is located east of St. Paul, Minnesota. In March 1973 the company began an experiment by purchasing six 12-passenger vans and starting van pools for the employees. Each van is driven to and from work by an employee who pays nothing for the trip to work and is given use of the van in the evenings and weekends at 7 cents per mile. Also, the driver receives the fares of any passengers in excess of eight (including himself). The vans get free, close-in parking as an added incentive. There are approximately 55 subscribers (an average of nine subscribers per van), and fares range from $19.50 to $29.50 a month (depending on the distance). The introduction of this service immediately reduced parking requirements by 30 spaces.

The program has been so successful that as of August 1973, the company was planning to purchase ten additional vans by the winter of 1973 and 20 more by the spring of 1974. It is reported

---

[19] Soloman and Saltzman (1971).

[20] Curry and McGillivray (1971).

[21] *Citizen League News*, August 28, 1973, p. 2.

that of the 55 subscribers, five have sold their second cars, three are considering such a move, and five more have postponed the purchase of another car.

Subscription bus operations

(a) *Specialty Transit Company, Inc.*, as described by Pratsch (1972), is a privately owned system which provides subscription bus service between the rural communities outside the greater St. Louis urban area and the McDonnell Douglas Corporation plant located in a northwestern suburb of St. Louis. Started in the late 1950s by its present owner, Thomas V. Jourdan, who was a land developer in the area, this service initially consisted of just one bus operating over a fixed route to the plant with approximately 30 subscribers. In 14 years, it has grown into a 22-bus operation which, each weekday, carries approximately 650 subscribers in summer and 800 in winter between their homes and the McDonnell plant. The equipment consists of 41-passenger used and remodeled school buses and one used rear-engine 50-passenger coach. (Additional leg room is provided in the school buses by removing two seats on each side.) The operation is regulated as a common carrier by the Missouri Public Service Commission which must approve any changes in fares or routes.

The service area consists of 14 communities with a total population of 20,000 (the largest has 7,200), together with an additional scattered rural population of 20,000. This very low-density region extends from 20 to 100 miles from the plant. Since the longest bus route is 52 miles one way, some riders have to reach the bus routes by private automobile. The owner estimates that about a third of the patronage is kiss-and-ride. Much of the remainder is park-and-ride, so quite a lot of fringe parking is required. Most of the riders are blue-collar workers at the plant, which in 1971 employed a total of 30,000 workers, in three shifts.

The service is maintained at a level high enough to be competitive with car pools and, to an extent, the private automobile. On most routes, buses make only three stops to pick up passengers and then travel express to the plant. (Since the bus must get off and on the expressway for a stop, about 10-15 minutes of travel time are wasted each time a stop is made.) The operator also arranges to provide free and plentiful parking at carefully located boarding points.

The service at the destination is particularly good, because the owner has arranged with the plant management to have close-in parking and special priority at traffic junctions within the plant property, resulting in minimal delays once the bus enters the plant property. Consequently, access to the service at the destination is very quick and convenient, and substantially better than access to the automobile. The overall door-to-door time is only 25 percent greater than by auto and is comparable to that of car pools.

Fares are very reasonable, ranging from $3.00 per week for the shortest run of 17 miles one way (1.76 cents per passenger trip-mile), to a maximum of $6.50 per week (1.25 cents per passenger trip-mile) for the longest run of 52 miles. Costs per passenger trip-mile are thus lower than for private automobile travel and lower also than for car pooling in most instances.

The high overall level of service has resulted in sustained patronage. It is estimated that about 95 percent of those who have tried the service have continued to ride. Also, the owner estimates that the service has attracted approximately 50 percent of the market at intermediate points and 90 percent of it at the end points. As a result of this high level of patronage, 75 percent of the overall seating capacity of the system is filled, with some runs being 100 percent full.

Astute management, which is sensitive to user needs, has resulted in extremely good and reliable service at low fares, and the service is fully paid for through the fare box. The following actions taken by the owner illustrate the importance of good management to the success of such services:

- The owner decided to remove air-conditioning and install a smaller fuel tank on the buses to bring down the road weight to a point where the Internal Revenue Service road tax could be avoided.

- Free and plentiful parking is provided at boarding points through negotiations with local fire stations, jails, bowling alleys, etc. Sometimes, certain gas stations agree to provide free parking in return for gasoline or diesel purchase.

- Negotiations with plant management have resulted in privileged parking and free movement through restricted areas and traffic junctions on the plant property.

- The owner does meticulous pre-route analysis through dry runs along the proposed route to check road conditions, sight distance, speed, and delay potential. A new stop is generally introduced if more than four passengers request it, provided the route deviation is not more than one mile. On the average, 10 passengers board the buses per stop.

- Buses are kept in top mechanical condition by two highly skilled, full-time mechanics. Bus drivers are required to report any deficiency in the vehicles, however minor. The owner has found that reliability of service is of utmost importance to his riders.

- Level of service is always maintained. Buses do not wait for late passengers, and each bus is assigned a back-up driver.

- The costs are kept low by employing part-time drivers who are also workers at the plant. They are paid only for the actual driving time to and from the plant.

(b) The *Peoria Premium Special*, described by Blurton (1968), was set up in Peoria (Illinois) along with a similar service in Decatur (Illinois) [22] with the help of UMTA grants in the mid-1960s. The demonstration was planned and monitored by the University of Illinois.

Between December 1964 and February 1966, subscription service was provided as a demonstration project. Peak hour service was provided to the workers at the Caterpillar Tractor plant located in Peoria, and off-peak service was provided between residential areas and downtown. In 13 months the service grew from 3 to 21 routes. The ridership growth was quite encouraging—from 30 to 500 subscribers in 13 months. In February 1966, the City Transit Company took over the operation and tried to cut costs by reducing the routes to 17 and discarding special service features (hostess, telephone service, and emergency cab service). Five weeks later, the fare was increased 20 percent. This arrested the growth trend, and by July 1966 patronage had declined by 21 percent and had leveled off at around 400 subscribers. The transit company, a private firm, went out of business in 1970 and the Premium Special service was discontinued.

Peoria is an industrial center with a population of 125,000. The one large employer, the Caterpillar Tractor plant in East Peoria, employs 19,000, of whom 9,000 live in Peoria proper. Prior to the Premium Special, a privately owned transit company operated seven routes with 39 buses in peak hours and 24 in off-peak hours, with peak headways of 12 to 15 minutes. The fare was 25 cents for adults and 10 cents for children. There was a progressive decline in ridership and revenue of 14 percent per year.

---

[22] This service functioned from January 1966 to June 1966. Decatur is a city of 90,000 with several medium-sized employers (approximately 1,000 to 4,000 employees). The subscription service was much less successful than in Peoria, and failed to attract sufficient patronage to meet even the operating costs. The service was discontinued at the end of the demonstration, even though the users petitioned for continuation.

Peoria is primarily a blue-collar city and the Premium service was aimed at these workers. A household survey indicated that the median income was approximately $7,000 per year and auto ownership was about 1.3 vehicles per household. Transit usage was low: 9 percent used transit daily, 10 percent rarely, and 81 percent never rode. Transit service was criticized on the basis of trip time, noise, access problems, transfer problems, and cost. The transit user survey indicated that the users were, to a large extent, poor, older, and with low car ownership.[23] Eleven percent worked at the Caterpillar plant and 40 percent were without drivers' licenses.

The Premium Special subscription service was planned and promoted by the demonstration contractors. Pre-experiment home interviews and fixed-route bus user surveys provided travel and socioeconomic characteristics. Work shifts and home locations of the plant workers were analyzed, and results were used to set up routes and fares. Peak hour routes to the plant were aimed at only those workers who had regular schedules (71 percent of 19,000). The routes were selected to attract patronage from 4,870 workers who lived in Peoria and worked certain convenient shifts. The route structure and operation were maintained with the help of ride boards which indicated the route, stops, timings, and names of riders. The routes and scheduled pickup times were updated every week to reflect changes in the subscriber list, and a high level of service was maintained, including low fares, low door-to-door time, and hostess service.

Ridership on the Premium Special grew rapidly (Table 54) until the service was taken over by the City Transit Company in February 1966, when the number of routes was reduced, the service level was cut back, and the fares were increased. At its peak of 500 subscribers, the ridership represented about 9 percent of the potential market of 4,870. (One group of routes captured 28 percent of those who lived within an eighth of a mile of routes and worked on fixed shifts.) This accounted for a total increase of 13 percent in the overall transit ridership for the city.

It is interesting to note that while on the conventional transit system the typical rider was female, from a lower-income household, without access to car and elderly, the Premium rider was typically male, had a car, and was in the middle-income bracket (Table 53). Also, before the Premium Special was organized, 43 percent of the subscribers were car drivers, 28 percent were bus

---

[23] Income $5,000 to $7,500; age 40 to 60; auto ownership 1.0; 60 percent female.

Table 54
Growth of service of Premium Special

Date	No. of routes	No. sub-scribing	Subscribers per route	Growth rate Jan. '65-Jan. '66
January '65	3	30	10	
March '65	7	110	16	1.7
June '65	11	220	20	passengers per
Sept. '65	13	270	21	weekday
Dec. '65	20	410	21	
January '66	21	500	24	
June '66	17	400	24	
Nov. '67	17	400	24	

riders, 20 percent were car passengers, and 9 percent were members of car pools.

An average speed of 16 miles per hour resulted in low door-to-door trip times. Thirty-three percent of the subscribers said they left for work later than before, and 33 percent left at the same time. The cost of providing the service was estimated to be approximately 50 cents per vehicle-mile [24] or about 1.8 cents per productive seat-mile (where the productive seat-miles are given by the product of route length and the number of seats).

The Premium Special route lengths varied from 5.7 to 13.5 miles, and were served by 15-year-old, remodeled buses with 36 to 45 seats. Of the 21 routes, eight served manufacturing workers, eight served office workers, three served the downtown area, one served an evening shift, and one was a high mileage route for domestic workers. High utilization was achieved because each bus served two routes. This was possible because work-starting time was staggered 45 minutes between blue- and white-collar workers.

The fare varied with distance, with an average of $9.90 per month for an average distance of about 8 miles (23 cents per one-way trip of 8 miles or 3 cents per passenger trip-mile, compared with a regular bus fare of 25 cents). The monthly flash pass cost from $9.25 to $15.25. The fare was lower than regular bus fare, and service was much superior. The Special provided door-to-door service from home to the plant with little walking required at either end. The trip was in a club-like atmosphere with the same riders and a hostess every day.

[24] Driver wages of $2.60 per hour, plus benefits, accounted for 34.5 cents of this total.

Reasonably high productivities were achieved due to high ridership levels. On one group of nine routes, the average ridership
was 2.17 riders per bus-mile, while on the other six the figure was
1.61 riders per bus-mile. Overall, at peak performance, the average
revenue of 39.2 cents per vehicle-mile more than met the variable
costs, but not the total costs. We should also note that the first
group of nine routes met all variable costs in six months and total
costs in 11 months, while the other group of routes met variable
costs in four months.

In summary, the routes to the employment location were a
success because comfortable and reliable service was provided
to workers at a reasonable fare, and because there was a single
destination with large employment. On the other hand, Premium
service to the central business district was a failure and did
not attract sufficient ridership to meet more than 25 percent
of the costs. The key reasons for the failure of these latter routes
were:

• Low employment density in the business district

• Widely dispersed origins and destinations

• Staggered work hours

• Good fixed-route regular service to the business district was
  available

• Parking was nearby, plentiful, and inexpensive, so the bus could
  not match the door-to-door time by auto

(c) *Flint (Michigan) Maxicab:*[25] In September 1968 a subscription bus service (termed "Maxicab"), similar to that in Peoria, was
started as a demonstration in Flint. This UMTA demonstration
was run by the American Academy of Transportation, a research
firm in Ann Arbor (Michigan). The Flint Transportation Authority
was the local agency responsible for most of the operational aspects, and drivers and vehicles were provided by City Coach
Lines, the former transit operator. Maxicab service was provided
to factory workers for work trips along 26 routes. Flint is a city
of 196,000 in southeast Michigan, and the major employer is
General Motors Corporation. Eight different factories, each with
several entrances, were served by the Maxicab.

Despite the assistance of a $125,000 promotional campaign, the
ridership was a disappointment. The growth of ridership was extremely slow and the service never came close to financial viability—it did not even meet the operating costs. The ridership

---

[25] American Academy of Transportation (1972).

reached 600 trips per day (300 subscribers) in March 1969, and a maximum 660 trips per day (330 subscribers) in December 1969. Fares varied with distance and the number subscribing on a route. For a round trip of six miles, the monthly fare was $13.

Even though this service was almost identical to that in Peoria and a substantial sum was initially spent on promotion, it was never successful. There seem to be a wide variety of reasons for this relatively poor performance:

- The routes, service level, and fares were not as well preplanned as in Peoria. There was no preservice survey conducted as in Peoria. So, the planners had little indication of what kind of service and fares people would consider acceptable.

- Even though the economic characteristics of the population are very similar to those of Peoria, there may be very subtle differences in social values. Since General Motors is the major employer in Flint, one would expect the population to be much more attached to the automobile. The previous regular bus service had served a very small market (average 3,000 per day out of the total population of 196,000 as against 11,200 per day in Peoria out of 125,000). Also, it had a reputation for bad service which probably was carried over to the subscription service.

- A substantial number of people did not have a sufficiently regular schedule, and overtime policies were a problem. In Peoria the employees generally knew about overtime the previous day, but in Flint they were informed during the day in question. On these days they would get off late and would need an automobile. So there was greater uncertainty involved.

- There was much greater scatter in destinations in Flint, with eight plants, each with several entrances.

- The fare ($13 per month for an average round-trip distance of about 6 miles) was much higher than Peoria ($9.90 per month for a 16 mile round trip).

All these factors resulted in smaller total ridership in Flint (where the growth rate was only 33 percent of that of Peoria) and in average route subscriptions of only 10 to 12, against 26 in Peoria. The cost of the service was also higher—roughly 8 to 10 cents per productive seat-mile.

(d) *Reston Express:* The Reston Community Association, a group of local residents, provides subscription bus service between this northern Virginia suburb and Washington, D.C., some

22 miles away. The service was started in 1968 and has been successful in attracting an increasing number of riders ever since. By late 1971, there were 17 inbound runs to Washington in the morning and 17 outbound runs in the afternoon. By mid-1973, there were 22 trips in each direction each day. The areas served at the destination are: downtown and U.S. federal government complexes in the District, Rosslyn in Arlington County, and the Pentagon.

Reston in 1973 was a residential community of 23,000. It is predominantly an upper-income suburb with a median income of $20,000 and high auto ownership per household. About 50 percent of the work force in Reston is employed in the Washington area. Auto travel via county roads is reasonably slow (perhaps an average speed of 20 miles an hour), and parking in the downtown area is very expensive and often requires long walks. Also, a majority of residents belong to the highly-educated, socially-conscious class who may prefer to spend their commuting time reading or writing rather than drive their own cars in stop-and-go traffic on congested streets.

These factors indicated that a comfortable, easily accessible, and reliable alternative service could be successful. The experience since 1968, when the first bus was introduced, has vindicated the predictions. The use of subscription bus service has grown continuously and is fully paid for from the fare box.

The basic data about population, labor force, and bus ridership are summarized in Table 55. In five years the operation grew from one bus trip each way every weekday to 22 bus trips. The association first leased buses from the W. V. and M. Transit Company of Virginia and now leases them from the Washington Metropolitan Area Transit Authority (WMATA). WMATA provides drivers and charges the association a flat rate of approximately $40 per bus-trip (about $1.80 per productive vehicle-mile or roughly 3.6 cents per productive seat-mile), which is expected to be raised to about $60 per trip shortly (5.5 cents per productive seat-mile).

The fare was $1.60 per round trip in March 1968 and $2.00 per round trip in March 1969. Since the fall of 1971 it has been $2.40 per round trip (approximately 5.5 cents per passenger trip-mile). If the charter rates are increased to $60 per bus trip, at the current level of ridership, the fares will have to be raised to $3.60 per round trip (or just over 8 cents per passenger trip-mile).

The daily ridership increased from 48 passenger trips per day to 1,700 passenger trips per day in five years. These 850 sub-

Table 55

Reston Express Data

Date	Population	Labor force	Workers going to Washington	Bus subscribers	Percent of potential market	Number of buses	Subscribers per bus	Average fare per one-way passenger trip ($)	Cost per one-way bus trip	Bus subscriber per 100 residents
3/68	3,000	1,200	600	24	4.0	1	24.0	0.80	27.00	0.8
12/68	5,000	2,000	1,000	100	10.0	3	33.3	0.80	27.00	2.0
6/69	6,000	2,400	1,200	157	13.1	5	31.4	1.00	30.00	2.6
4/70	8,000	3,200	1,600	260	16.2	8	32.5	1.00	30.00	3.2
10/70	10,500	4,200	2,100	350	16.6	12	31.8	1.00	30.00	3.3
10/71	15,000	6,000	3,000	515	17.1	17	30.3	1.20	38.50	3.4
* 6/73	23,000	9,200	4,500	770	18.9	22	35.0	1.20	40.00	3.4

* =estimates
Source: Bain (1970) and Morin et al. (1972)

scribers in mid-1973 represent 18.9 percent of the potential market (those residing in Reston and working in Washington).

The buses pass through residential areas to pick up riders and then travel express to Washington. There they make pre-planned loops and drop off people at predesignated stops within two or three blocks of their destination. The service in Reston is practically to the front step, resulting in an overall door-to-door speed of about 15 miles an hour (85-90 minutes for the 22-mile trip). Another exclusive feature of the Reston Express is that the subscribers are not tied to one particular bus and have considerable schedule flexibility. The ride is comfortable and allows passengers to read, write, or sleep. There is no driving worry, and the atmosphere is like a country club. All these factors have helped to keep the ridership above 30 per bus, sufficient to meet all the costs of providing the service (see Table 55).

A recent study by Morin et al. (1972) indicated that the Reston Express has not only been financially successful, but has gone a long way toward reducing auto ownership, as mentioned earlier in this chapter. In addition, there are indications that the availability of the subscription service played an important role in the decision of many riders to move to Reston to live.

(e) *The Golden Gate Bridge, Highway and Transportation Authority (GGBHTD) "Commute Clubs"*: Since February 1971,[26] several commuter clubs in the San Francisco Bay area have organized subscription bus service for their members. White-collar, middle- and upper-income residents of communities in Marin and Sonoma counties (from 20 to 55 miles from San Francisco) use these buses to commute to and from San Francisco.

The system grew from a one-club, one-bus operation in early 1971 to a five-club, eleven-bus operation in December 1973. Subscriptions increased from about 110 to 470 in the same period, and subscribers make, on an average, 1.5 one-way bus trips per working day. (Many subscribers work only two or three days a week at the University of California Medical Center.)

The "Commute Club" leases buses from the GGBHTD which in turn acquires them through a bidding process from charter and sightseeing bus companies. The clubs determine the best routes and schedules in cooperation with GGBHTD, solicit their own members, collect dues, and make monthly payments to GGBHTD. The fares are set between $30 and $50 (depending on the route length) by GGBHTD, which also allows free passage over the bridge and use of the exclusive bus lane. The District also has

---

[26] See, for example, U.S. Department of Transportation (1974).

the authority to subsidize the operations up to $500 per bus per month if necessary. Subsidies so far have averaged around $350 per bus per month, since the average passenger loads of 60 to 65 percent are a little below break-even figures. The buses are comfortable, air-conditioned, suburban-type coaches.

(f) *Wayward Bus—San Francisco Mid-Peninsula:* A "reverse commute" subscription bus service carries two groups of workers from home to work in the San Francisco Bay area. A group of travelers negotiated with two bus companies to lease full-sized (40 to 50 passenger) buses for nonstop trips via freeways in the morning and evening. There are two routes:

- One home-to-work route is from San Francisco to the Palo Alto/Menlo Park area, a one-way distance of about 35 miles. The bus is leased from Peninsula Transit Company at $1,500 per month (1.9 to 2.4 cents per productive seat-mile). The fare is $30 to $35 per month depending on the number of subscribers.

- The other home-to-work route provides service from Berkeley to the Palo Alto/Sunnyvale area (a one-way distance of about 50 miles). This bus is leased from Peerless Stages at $55 per day for two one-way trips (1.1 to 1.4 cents per productive seat-mile). The fare for the service is $1.65 per one-way trip or $11 per week.

The costs of these services have been relatively low compared with the Reston Express, perhaps because the service is "reverse commute" for which the companies can use an otherwise dead-heading vehicle.

(g) *National Geographic Society:* In 1968 the National Geographic Society moved its bindery plant from northeast Washington, D.C., to suburban Gaithersburg, Maryland—a distance of approximately 20 miles. The Society, faced with the difficult problem of getting their low-skilled, low-income workers (who live in northeast Washington and its vicinity) to the new plant, worked out a network of 10 routes in contract with D.C. Transit. Since around the beginning of 1973 the Society has been leasing most of the buses from the Atwood Gold Lines—a charter bus company—because WMATA, which took over the D.C. Transit Company in early 1973, had indicated intentions of substantially increasing the leasing charges.

Bus stops were established so that most of the prospective riders (determined by a survey of 1,150 employees, out of which 450 had indicated a willingness to use such a service at 50 cents per day) were within a block and a half or two blocks of the stops. The service attracted 580 riders (approximately 50 percent of the employees) on inception, with a round-trip fare of 50 cents per day. The fare was raised to 60 cents per day in October 1970 and the Society started deducting this amount directly from the salaries of the employees. The service is not financially self-supporting, however, and the Society subsidizes it to the amount of approximately $170 per rider per year. Assuming about 240 working days per year, the subsidy amounts to approximately 70 cents per rider per day. The total cost, therefore, is about $1.30 per rider per day for the 40-mile round trip, or about 3.2 cents per passenger trip-mile. The riders pay only 1.5 cents per passenger trip-mile.

(h) *COM-BUS:* Since around 1967 COM-BUS, a private corporation, has been providing commuter bus service in the greater Los Angeles area.[27] Over 40 runs are made daily to transport workers between their homes and places of work. COM-BUS handles all aspects of operating the commuter bus system, including matching the passengers, establishing the routes and schedules, collecting fares, leasing buses from charter companies, and negotiating with the Public Utilities Commission for certification and the setting of fare levels. The services are provided on a weekly subscription basis. The routes are between 20 and 65 miles long and the weekly fares were between $8.75 and $11.50 in 1972. There are enough subscribers to make this a profitable operation.

In addition to the subscription operations already discussed in this section, there are several cooperative van and bus operations:

- Two consumer-owned cooperatives provide fixed-route service in the small urban areas of Fond du Lac (Wisconsin) and Stevens Point (Wisconsin).

- Two other consumer-owned cooperatives provide bus service to rural areas—one in Harwood (Maryland) and the other in Fulton (Missouri). These services are provided only to the members.

- A workers' cooperative provides bus service in the mid-sized urban area of Wheeling (West Virginia).

- A nonprofit corporation based in Burlington (Vermont) serves a four-county area in northwestern Vermont with nine 10- to 12-passenger vans. This demand-actuated private service is ori-

---

[27] See, for example, COM-BUS (1972) and U.S. Department of Transportation (1974).

ented toward participants in senior citizens and community action programs. There are no actual membership requirements. Another similar, but fixed-route van service is provided in Troy (New York) to county residents who are more than 55 years of age.

SUMMARY

In this chapter, we have described some of the more notable examples of car pool, van pool, and subscription bus operations. These operations provide service almost exclusively for peak-period work trips between a residential neighborhood and a large employment center, such as a manufacturing plant or a complex of federal offices. Many of the operations are self-supporting in that the costs are fully met by the fares. In providing these carefully tailored services, the private sector has responded to certain types of travel demand with reliable, comfortable, and reasonably inexpensive transportation conducted in a club-like atmosphere. Specifically, experience to date permits the following important observations:

- The car pools, the Monarch and 3M van pools, and subscription bus operations such as the Specialty Transit, Reston Express, and COM-BUS have shown that for some forms of public transportation all the costs *can* be met by the fare revenues. These operations need no subsidies. A primary reason for this financial success appears to be that the costs per passenger trip-mile have been substantially below the cost of making the same trip by automobile, while overall service has been maintained at a high level.

- Subscription buses have a greater chance of success for long trips because they can provide service that is comparable to the automobile in terms of door-to-door trip times. In addition, the comfortable journey is free of driving chores and allows sufficient time to settle down and do other things such as read, write, or sleep. These advantages of subscription buses are not fully realized on short trips and they can seldom compete with the service provided by an automobile. The experiences of Reston Express and Specialty Transit show how well the subscription bus can compete with automobiles over long trips: they have been able to attract a large share of the market and the costs are fully met from the fare box.

- A large concentration of employment in a small area, together with uniform work schedules, will favor car pools, van pools, and subscription buses. The larger the employment center, the better the chances of forming a sizable pool of people with common residential locations and time of travel.

- The success of these operations also seems to depend on socio-economic homogeneity within the potential market. The club-like atmosphere during the trip appears to be an important component of the service to many riders.

- Even though an overwhelming majority of the operations serve home-based work trips (for a variety of income groups), school trips, shopping trips in low-income areas, and social trips for senior citizens have also been served successfully by pre-arranged ride-sharing services.

- The Haddonfield dial-a-ride project (Chapter 8) indicates great potential for subscription services as feeders to line-haul systems in residential areas.

- The experience of Little House van pools in Menlo Park (California) and of the B&B Minibus in Long Island suggests that such services may be a viable means of providing mobility for low-income groups and the aged who are poorly served by conventional transit systems. That these two services have been provided at overall costs of 3 to 4 cents per passenger trip-mile should be encouraging to those concerned with this problem.

- A large number of car and van pool riders were formerly automobile drivers, while the subscription bus riders were predominantly former auto and car pool users. This observation implies that these services have increased vehicle occupancy and reduced the number of vehicles on the roads, probably resulting in a net positive effect on congestion, pollution, and fuel consumption.

- Results of recent ridership surveys for the 3M van pool and Reston Express indicate that such services may have significant long-range impacts in reducing auto ownership and influencing residential location.

Most of the large scale car pooling operations mentioned in this chapter were organized at large-employment institutions such as NASA, U.S. Department of Transportation, and McDonnell Douglas. Attempts to broaden the scope of car pooling even further to areawide or citywide levels have not been very successful to date, however. For example, in mid-1973, radio station WBZ in Boston started a free community service to help people form car pools. The experiment was less than successful and was dropped. More recently, the Metropolitan Washington Council of Governments has been preparing to organize a similar experiment in the Washington metropolitan area with the help of a local radio station. It will be interesting to monitor the progress of this and other attempts at large scale matching of riders for prearranged ride-sharing services.

The overwhelming success of the few organized attempts to "market" car pooling, as described by Pratsch (1973), suggests that the true potential of the prearranged ride-sharing modes has yet to be realized. The major reason for this may be the lack of information and of the coordination needed to accomplish the effective matching of persons with similar origins and destinations—match-boards, computer matching, information on the availability of alternative car pools, and so on. There appears to be a need to disseminate information on the wide range of incentives that may be offered to the car pool, van pool, and subscription bus riders at the origin, along the way, and at the destination—low cost close-in parking, toll-free rides, priority access to expressways, the use of exclusive lanes, etc. In addition, the prospective riders could use information on the incidence of ride-sharing costs for each member. Such information is being disseminated by a few organizations—Operation Oxygen (Los Angeles), the Federal Highway Administration and the Urban Mass Transportation Administration (Washington, D.C.), and the Connecticut Department of Transportation—but much greater effort is warranted. In particular, guidelines on the organization and operation of subscription bus services need wide exposure so that communities can plan the kinds of services best suited to their requirements.

Chapter 12

Ronald F. Kirby

A Comparative Study of Para-transit Modes

INTRODUCTION

The term *para-transit* has been used to describe a collection of transportation modes which are *like* conventional transit (scheduled bus and rail) in many respects but are not generally referred to as such, including taxi, dial-a-ride, jitney, daily and short-term rental car, car pool, and subscription bus. Chapters 7 through 11 of this volume have dealt in some detail with the special characteristics of these modes which essentially determine, at least for the present, their respective roles in urban transportation systems. The purpose of this chapter is to examine these modes as a group by comparing their service and operating characteristics, and developing cost and performance estimates for some selected services.

A comparison of the characteristics of the different para-transit modes under consideration here reveals that the modes are perhaps not as "different" as they might appear at first. As has been pointed out in earlier chapters, we define each mode in terms of its service characteristics, rather than in terms of the particular vehicle used or the type of labor employed in providing the serv-

251

ice. When defined in this manner, the differences between the para-transit modes are reduced essentially to differences in one or two significant service characteristics. Of course, substantial variations in service characteristics are possible within each para-transit mode. For example, such aspects as comfort, average wait time, travel time, and so on may vary from one taxi system to another.

The present roles of para-transit modes in urban transportation systems are not necessarily representative of their potential. A number of quite artificial limitations on the operation of para-transit modes have been identified in earlier chapters—limitations which, if lifted, could lead to immediate expansion of the services offered. Another major consideration is the likely effect of different pricing policies or restrictions directed at congestion, pollution, and energy consumption, which might make high capacity or low polluting modes relatively more attractive to travelers. Part One of this book identifies segments of the transportation market which could be served efficiently by para-transit modes and recommends the next steps which need to be taken to encourage the provision of these services.

DEFINING SERVICE CHARACTERISTICS

The predominant service characteristics which need to be considered in describing para-transit services are the following:

- *Directness of route—*
  Para-transit modes may provide direct route service from origin to destination (taxi, rental car); essentially direct route with minor route deviations at either the origin end or the destination end (jitney, subscription bus, car pool); or indirect route with potentially substantial route deviations at both ends of the trip (dial-a-ride).

- *Places of access to and egress from the mode—*
  Some para-transit modes provide door-to-door service (taxi, dial-a-ride, and car pool), while others usually have to be reached or left at a terminal (rental car, jitney, and subscription bus).

- *Manner in which travel time is spent—*
  An important service characteristic to many travelers is undoubtedly the manner in which they spend their travel time—working on business documents or reading is quite a different

proposition from driving in heavily congested traffic, for example. In some para-transit modes travel time is spent as a passenger (taxi, dial-a-ride, jitney, subscription bus and—sometimes—car pool) while for others (the rental car) the traveler must drive himself.

- *Degree of privacy—*
  For some para-transit modes the traveler essentially has the vehicle to himself or chooses his traveling companions (rental car, taxi), while for others he shares the vehicle with other travelers (dial-a-ride, jitney, subscription bus, car pool).

- *Permissible routes—*
  The system of routes over which para-transit modes travel may, from the traveler's viewpoint, be essentially fixed with minor variations (jitney, subscription bus, car pool) or may be completely variable in the sense that the vehicle will go to whatever destination the traveler wishes by the best route available (rental car, taxi, dial-a-ride).

- *Method of requesting service—*
  Service may be requested of para-transit modes in several ways: by prior arrangement with other travelers (subscription bus, car pool), by telephone request (taxi, dial-a-ride), by hailing in the street (taxi, jitney), or by obtaining the vehicle from the nearest terminal as needed (rental car).

- *Need for vehicle parking—*
  Taxi, dial-a-ride, jitney, and, usually, subscription bus services have the advantage that the traveler does not have to unpark and park a vehicle at the beginning and end of his trip.

- *Baggage convenience—*
  Rental car and taxi services are convenient for baggage, other para-transit modes may be, but conventional transit generally is not.

These different service characteristics are displayed in Table 56 for each of the para-transit modes. For comparison, the private auto and conventional transit have been included in the same table.

Other major service characteristics which are not as useful for distinguishing between para-transit modes but are certainly very significant from the traveler's point of view are the following:

- *Safety* (accidents and crime)

Table 56

General service characteristics by mode

	Private auto	HIRE AND DRIVE SERVICES	HAIL OR PHONE SERVICES		Jitney	PREARRANGED RIDE-SHARING SERVICES		Conventional transit
		Daily and short-term rental car	Taxi	Dial-a-ride		Car pool	Subscription bus	
					PARA-TRANSIT MODES			
Direct route (DR) or route deviations (RD)?	DR	DR	DR	RD	RD	RD	RD	RD
Door-to-door?	Yes	Maybe	Yes	Yes	No	Yes	Maybe	No
Travel time spent as passenger (P) or driver (D)?	D	D	P	P	P	P/D	P	P
Ride shared (S), or personal (P)?	P	P	P/S	S	S	S	S	S
System routes fixed (F), semi-fixed (S), or variable (V)?	V	V	V	V	S	S	S	F
Access determined by prior arrangement (A), fixed schedule (F), phone (P), street hailing (H), or at user's discretion (U)?	U	U	H/P	P	H	A	A	F
Vehicle parking required (PR) or not (NP)?	PR	PR	NP	NP	NP	PR	PR/NP	NP
Convenient for baggage?	Yes	Yes	Yes	Maybe	Maybe	Maybe	Maybe	No

- *Reliability* (schedule, susceptibility to breakdown, and effects of congestion)

- *Comfort* (noise, temperature control, seating, passenger space, and package space)

- *Information*

- *Travel time* (access, egress, and in vehicle)

- *Courtesy of operator* (service refusal, and fraud)

- *Advertising*

- *Price*

It could be argued that price should be compared from one mode to another, but prices are influenced so much by subsidy and regulatory policies that they are often difficult to relate to the costs of providing service. For comparison purposes it will be much more meaningful later in this chapter to look directly at costs and the reasons why they vary for different forms of a particular para-transit mode and from one para-transit mode to another.

CATEGORIZING PARA-TRANSIT MODES BY SERVICE CHARACTERISTICS

Table 56 shows the similarities and significant differences in service characteristics between the modes represented. The modes are arranged so as to make the transition across the table (with each change in a service dimension flagged by an arrow) as gradual as possible. Examination of the table leads to the following general observations:

- In the sense that private automobile and conventional transit differ on every service characteristic listed, and that para-transit modes have some service characteristics in common with each, para-transit can be considered to lie "in-between" these two more common modes. This is not to imply, however, that the trend across the table is strictly one of declining level of service; scheduled bus service with short headways may be regarded by many travelers as superior to a car pool service with an inflexible schedule, for example.

- Within the para-transit portion of the service characteristics spectrum, certain subgroupings appear:

Daily and short-term rental cars have identical service characteristics even though the operating schemes and locations might be quite different.

Taxi, dial-a-ride, and jitney are all hailed or phoned by the user, and differ essentially with respect to the door-to-door service feature, and the degree of route deviation and ride-sharing.

Car pool and subscription bus have very similar service characteristics; a subscription bus can be thought of as a large car pool, particularly where the driver is also a passenger and parks the bus during the day while working at his or her regular job.

These three groups can be conveniently labelled as hire and drive services, hail or phone services, and prearranged ride-sharing services respectively.

- Regulations permitting, the same vehicle and driver can provide different para-transit services at different times of the day. A small bus can provide subscription bus service, scheduled bus service, or jitney service during rush hours, and offer dial-a-ride service during off-peak hours. In addition to providing regular taxi service, a taxicab can offer jitney, dial-a-ride, or subscription services.

- Rearrangement of some of the service characteristics in the table shows that several "hybrid" services can be defined which are realistic (if uncommon) forms of urban transportation. If in moving from dial-a-ride to jitney, for example, we retain the door-to-door and variable route system of dial-a-ride but change from phone to hail as the means of access to the mode, we have a form of shared-ride service which might be termed "hail-a-ride." Similarly, by changing the hail characteristic of jitney service to access by prior arrangement and making the service door-to-door, we have the service characteristics of a subscription taxicab.

Careful consideration of the above observations has resulted in the formal *definition* of para-transit as those forms of intra-urban passenger transportation which are available to the public, are distinct from conventional transit (scheduled bus and rail), and can operate over the highway and street system. This definition excludes strictly private services such as the private automobile and systems such as personal rapid transit which require their own guideway. The definition does include however, such hybrid services as hail-a-ride and subscription taxicab.

LABOR ISSUES

It has become a common complaint of transit operators in the U.S. and elsewhere that the labor component of transit operations is an increasingly large part of the total cost of transit systems, to the point where efficiencies suggested in hardware components (particularly in bus transit, where the cost of the guideway is hidden) are dismissed because they affect only a relatively small part of total cost. For example, driver costs account for almost 50 percent of the bus-mile costs of $1.34 for buses operated by the Washington Metropolitan Area Transit Authority.[1] The labor aspect is an important component of para-transit operations also, and is likely to be the critical factor in determining the viability of para-transit modes under a number of demand conditions. Several types of labor conditions apply to the different para-transit modes under consideration here.

Drivers

Para-transit drivers can be:

- *Unionized bus drivers* with strict union regulations (work rules) regarding shifts, salaries, and fringe benefits, who work for a salary with no tips.

- *Unionized taxi drivers* with union regulations which are less strict than those for bus drivers, but which still restrict length of shifts and percentage commission to be taken by the driver from the total revenue. Tips are not regulated, of course, and it is typically much easier for a taxi driver to take fares without reporting them than it is for a bus driver. For this reason the true earnings of taxi drivers are rather difficult to estimate, but as discussed in earlier chapters these earnings appear to be well below those for bus drivers.

- *Free-lance drivers* who drive many of the taxicabs in the country and earn whatever they take in over the cost of operating the cab. They may own their own cab or rent or lease a cab, and they usually work their own hours. These jobs constitute a very flexible part of the labor market and attract many people who wish to work only part-time or for a limited period, such as retired people, students, or moonlighters.

- *The traveler himself* in the case of daily or short-term rental car, car pools, and sometimes subscription bus. Here virtually

---

[1] Washington Metropolitan Area Transit Authority (1973).

none of the cost is attributable to the driver, but at least one
traveler must be a driver rather than a passenger during the trip.

- *Part-time or volunteer drivers* in the case of school bus services,
some home-to-work subscription bus services, and a variety of
specialized services for health care agencies, hotels, and social
service organizations.

The cost of providing these different types of drivers varies
considerably; a cab driver may cost on the order of $3 per hour
(excluding tip) while a unionized bus driver is likely to cost around
$6 per hour including fringe benefits, vacation, and so on (see
Table 28)—a difference which makes dial-a-ride bus service typically much more costly to provide than shared taxi service. The
passenger who becomes the driver incurs an opportunity cost consisting of the difference between the value he or she places on
time spent as a passenger and time spent as a driver. This would
almost always be less than the cost of a bus driver and probably
also less than the cost of a taxi driver.

The two para-transit services for which the labor question is
most crucial are dial-a-ride and subscription bus. The Amalgamated Transit Union (ATU) has long seen dial-a-ride as a new
form of *bus* service which offers employment opportunities to the
city bus driver at union wages and conditions; it has opposed
suggestions that dial-a-ride should be provided by taxicabs. Section 13(c) of the Urban Mass Transportation Act virtually ensures
that the ATU view will prevail in any dial-a-ride project which has
financial support from UMTA, by prohibiting federal support for
services which might worsen the employment situation of transit
workers. For its part, the International Taxicab Association (ITA)
seems rather reluctant to become involved with publicly supported
dial-a-ride services (presumably because of the labor question),
and apparently prefers to view dial-a-ride as just one form of taxicab service which has existed for many years. As a result, the
current trend in the planning of dial-a-ride services appears to
favor bus systems (for which federal funds are available) over less
costly taxicab systems.

Subscription bus services have a related but somewhat different problem. As a peak-period service, the subscription bus mode
requires drivers only for short periods during the peak hours.
Where part-time drivers are employed, as for the Specialty Transit
service in St. Louis, costs are remarkably low at about 1 cent per
productive seat-mile (Table 48). Full-time bus drivers are provided
for the Reston (Virginia) service by the Washington Metropolitan
Area Transit Authority (WMATA), however, and costs exceed 3.5

cents per productive seat-mile—more than three times the cost of Specialty Transit. Because these drivers are not needed by WMATA for off-peak services, the subscription bus service must pay a full week's wages for each driver it uses.

For both dial-a-ride and subscription bus services, then, costs can be kept down by using part-time or low-cost drivers, and several services are currently operating successfully in this manner. If these services are to be implemented on a larger scale, however, they will apparently have to operate without assistance under the Urban Mass Transportation Act, and they may face opposition from conventional transit systems. Whether or not these disadvantages will seriously inhibit the expansion of low-cost dial-a-ride and subscription bus services is unclear at present, and experience which is accrued on this topic should be studied carefully in future para-transit research efforts.

Management and control

Management and control costs vary greatly for different para-transit services, ranging from essentially negligible values for simple forms of car pooling and subscription bus services to almost 25 percent of the operating costs of dial-a-ride (Table 28) and rental cars (Table 40; note that fuel and tolls are excluded). The comparison of bus-based and taxi-based dial-a-ride services in Table 28 suggests that management and control costs for the former are likely to be more than double those of the latter due to greater operational experience accrued by taxicab systems. Estimates of expenses for fleet cabs providing regular taxi service in New York City place management and control costs at about 9 percent of total costs (Table 10), while for the Atlantic City jitneys the portion appears to be less than 4 percent (Table 35).

Several questions will be of interest with regard to para-transit management and control costs in the future. For minicars, for example, they have been estimated very conservatively at 20 percent of total costs (Table 41), with the acknowledgment that it will take "drastic innovations" to bring management and control costs below the 25 percent currently paid by daily rental car services. Whether or not these reductions can be achieved in practice remains to be seen, and indeed is likely to be crucial to the viability of the minicar concept. For dial-a-ride, the important question is whether or not computerized dispatching will significantly reduce management and control costs. Until a large-scale system is implemented and computer software is fully developed, this question will remain unanswered, although forecasts are optimistic (Table

29). For the car pool and subscription bus services, the potential for low management and control costs seems to be good as long as the services are kept in the hands of small, private operators with much of the organization done voluntarily by the travelers. If subscription bus services are operated by transit authorities, however, these costs will go up substantially—to perhaps 10 to 15 percent of total costs.

REGULATORY CONDITIONS

A wide spectrum of regulatory environments can be found applying to para-transit modes in the U.S. At one extreme we find that jitneys have been regulated practically out of existence, while at the other extreme we have car pools and daily rental cars operating in a completely unregulated environment. Between these two extremes are taxis, which are generally regulated with respect to entry, financial responsibility, service standards, and fares. Dial-a-ride, where it exists, is typically regulated as a public utility, rather like regular taxi service, and subscription buses are usually regulated by public utility commissions in a manner similar to conventional bus services. Conventional transit services are typically regulated with respect to the routes and schedules on which the service must be operated, and, in the past, para-transit services such as jitney have been explicitly forbidden to offer service along the same routes as conventional transit.

All the para-transit modes are also subject to regulation, implicit or explicit, resulting from the control and pricing of highway and parking facilities. Car pools are often given preferential parking treatment by firms providing employee parking; both car pools and subscription buses may be permitted to use lanes reserved for high-occupancy modes; subscription buses may be given priority movement at traffic intersections; and so on.

A number of studies have suggested that present regulatory structures for transportation modes are not acting in the interest of the traveling public or in harmony with overall urban objectives.[2] Eckert (1968) points out that the objectives of regulatory commissions are largely a function of what the commissioners see as the most rewarding outcomes for themselves, and that many regulatory agencies were set up as a result of pressure from existing transit operators whose main goal was to suppress competition.

---

[2] For example, Banks and Associates (1972).

Given these conclusions, how should we go about establishing regulatory structures which are more responsive to urban goals? The discussion of taxicab regulation in Chapter 7 demonstrates clearly how complex a question this is, and we do not propose to tackle any specific issues here. We do suggest, however, that pricing, subsidy, or restrictive policies should be sought which reflect accurately the effects of operating each transportation service, and within these policies all forms of transportation service should be encouraged to seek their full role in serving urban transportation demand. Unless this approach is taken, it seems that some para-transit modes will continue to be inhibited from playing their proper role in urban transportation systems by overly restrictive regulation.

VEHICLE TECHNOLOGY

Little attention has been paid in earlier chapters to the types of vehicles which are best suited for offering para-transit services, since, in our judgment, minor variations in vehicle design have less effect on the quality of service than do regulatory and operating procedures, for example, and also have less effect on operating costs than labor factors do. This is not to say that vehicle design is unimportant, however. It has been reported, for example, that acquiring suitable vehicles at reasonable cost is such a problem for Atlantic City jitney operators that no new vehicles have been bought for over six years. And the New York City taxi commission has sponsored research projects directed specifically at vehicle design. (For taxi service, the London Austin cab is often cited as far superior to the standard vehicles used as New York cabs.) Considerable research has also gone into the design of small nonpolluting vehicles for use in a minicar or public automobile system.

Federal expenditures for research in vehicle technology can, in principle, be justified on several grounds. First, the operators of para-transit modes are many and are not organized in a manner which would permit joint research undertakings. Second, the number of vehicles involved throughout the United States may not be large enough to stimulate a great deal of interest on the part of private vehicle manufacturers; this is particularly true, of course, for jitney vehicles at present. Third, most safety and pollution standards are specified by the federal government, so some federally funded research on the implications of these standards with respect to vehicle design and cost seems appropriate. Finally, the federal government is in a better position than most para-transit operators to see the full potential of improved vehicle design and should, therefore, support on a continuing basis research designed to assess the need for vehicle technology development.

The greater the potential application of para-transit modes, of course, the greater will be the interest of suppliers, both domestic and foreign, in developing improved vehicles at competitive prices. The difficulties of the Atlantic City jitney operators in finding suitable vehicles may be due largely to a quite justified feeling on the part of manufacturers that little potential exists under current regulatory conditions for jitney vehicles. Where research indicates that significant potential does exist for para-transit modes in urban transportation systems, interest by manufacturers in para-transit vehicle technology should follow as a matter of course; Ford Motor Company, for example, appears to feel that dial-a-ride services have sufficient potential to warrant developmental effort on vehicles and, indeed, some promotional effort for the service.

The recent increase in concern over pollution and fuel consumption has placed greater emphasis on the question of vehicle technology. To the extent that prices or restrictions are imposed in the near future on vehicles in accordance with their contribution to congestion, pollution, or fuel consumption, the roles of the private automobile, para-transit, and transit services in urban transportation systems may be changed significantly. Table 57

Table 57

**Congestion, pollution, and energy consumption
by passenger car and transit bus**

	Passenger car	Bus	Bus/passenger car
Congestion [1]	N.A.	N.A.	2.5
Pollution [2] (Environmental effect emissions in grams/vehicle mile)	11.41	54.83	4.8
Energy consumption [3] (BTU/vehicle mile)	103,000	250,000	2.4

[1] See Roth (1965).
[2] From Hanley (1971).
[3] Assuming 13.5 m.p.g. for passenger car, 5 m.p.g. for diesel bus, 1,390,000 BTU/gallon for diesel fuel and 1,250,000 BTU/gallon for gasoline (from American Petroleum Institute, 1971).

illustrates, for example, that a conventional city bus behaves in urban traffic conditions rather like 2.5 passenger cars in terms of congestion, 4.8 passenger cars in terms of pollution, and 2.4 passenger cars in terms of energy consumption. These vehicle values are, of course, averages over a wide range of traffic conditions and vehicle types, and are likely to change as research and development proceeds on vehicle technology. Such values would be crucial, however, to any scheme designed to price or regulate transportation services according to congestion, pollution, or energy consumption characteristics.

PERFORMANCE AND COST MEASURES

Certain quantitative measures will be useful in comparing the performance and cost characteristics of para-transit modes in this chapter. The following measures will be used to describe the performance of para-transit modes under particular conditions.

- *Vehicle seating capacity—*
  This measure gives the number of seated passengers which the vehicle can accommodate.

- *Average speed—*
  This measure gives the average vehicle miles covered per hour of vehicle operation.

- *Vehicle potential—*
  The vehicle potential describes the capability of the vehicle to transport passengers at the given average operating speed; measured in seat-miles per vehicle-hour, vehicle potential is given by the product of the vehicle seating capacity and the average speed.

- *Productivity—*
  Measured in passenger trips provided per vehicle-hour, this quantity is often used to describe the operation of dial-a-ride systems, and reflects the fact that for route deviation systems it is important to measure the number of trips completed per vehicle-hour rather than the passenger miles covered.

- *Average trip length—*
  Trip length refers to the direct over-the-road distance between the trip origin and trip destination. For direct route modes the distance covered by the traveler will be assumed to be equal to the trip length; for route deviation modes the traveler may

cover a greater distance than the trip length. Average trip length over a representative period is simply the average of the trip lengths for all the trips served by the mode during that period.

- *Output*—
  Output is defined here as the passenger *trip* miles produced per vehicle-hour by a transportation mode—that is, the sum of trip lengths for all of the trips served (as distinct from the total passenger miles covered). Output is the product of average trip length and productivity.

- *Utilization*—
  A measure of the extent to which vehicle potential is being used in any given situation is obtained by expressing output as a percentage of vehicle potential. This measure will be termed utilization.

- *Cost per vehicle-hour*—
  The cost per vehicle-hour of operation to the operator (as distinct from the social cost) of a transportation mode consists of three components: (a) the driver—wages, benefits; (b) the vehicle—vehicle capital cost, maintenance, fuel, oil, insurance, licenses, and taxes; and (c) management—communications, dispatching, and administration.

- *Cost per passenger trip mile*—
  This cost is obtained by dividing the cost per vehicle-hour by the output.

- *Level of service*—
  This term has been defined in the dial-a-ride literature as follows:

$$LOS = \frac{\text{total time from trip request to arrival at destination}}{\text{travel time by automobile}}$$

Note that the *variance* of this term may also be an important service measure and deserves greater attention in the evaluation of taxi and dial-a-ride services.

The effect of route deviation

In the above discussion, output has been defined as passenger trip miles produced per vehicle-hour of operation, where a trip mile is produced when a traveler is carried one mile of the *direct* over-the-road distance between his trip origin and his trip destination. For route deviation modes such as dial-a-ride, therefore, excessive route deviation may restrict output and raise the cost per passenger trip mile. In fact, there must be a point at which additional route deviation to pick up more passengers is, in this sense, not worthwhile. The following analysis suggests that this question should be considered carefully by operators and regulators of route deviation services.

Let us define a route deviation factor d as follows:

$$d = \frac{\text{total passenger miles produced}}{\text{total passenger trip miles produced}}$$

where the totals are taken over a representative period of operation. Then clearly the minimum value of d is unity, a value that is attained in the case of taxi operations where no route deviation is permitted to pick up additional passengers. Then since

$$\text{cost/passenger trip mile} = \frac{\text{cost/vehicle-hour}}{\text{passenger trip miles/vehicle-hour}}$$

it follows that

$$\text{cost/passenger trip mile} = \frac{\text{(d) (cost/vehicle-hour)}}{\text{passenger miles/vehicle-hour}}$$

Using this equation we can illustrate graphically the relationship between cost per passenger trip mile and passenger miles per vehicle-hour for different values of d.

Figure 3 is a graph of the above equation for values of d of 1, 1.2 and 2.0, assuming a constant cost per vehicle-hour of $6.00. Suppose that in a given situation taxi service is operating at an output of 15 passenger trip miles per vehicle-hour with a cost per passenger trip mile of 40 cents; that is, at point A on curve I. (Note again that for taxi operations with d = 1, passenger trip miles are equivalent to passenger miles.) Suppose also that dial-a-ride service is operating in the same environment and producing 25 passenger miles per vehicle-hour with route deviation d = 1.2 and at a cost per passenger trip mile of 28.8 cents: point B on curve II.[3] Finally, suppose it is noticed that the dial-a-ride operation could produce more passenger miles per vehicle-hour by a change in operation (such as a reduction in the number of vehicles) which would result in a route deviation d = 2. What would be the implications of such a change?

Clearly the level of service declines as d increases, possibly resulting in some loss of patronage. If the new figure for pas-

---

[3] Note that the average *price* or *fare* charged per passenger trip mile might be higher or lower than the *cost* per passenger trip mile; in the former case the service would be profitable, and in the latter case a subsidy would be required.

Figure 3

The effect of route deviation on cost per passenger trip mile

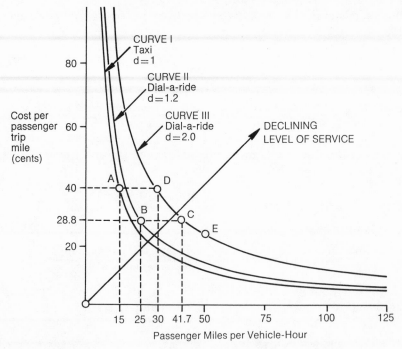

Passenger Miles per Vehicle-Hour

senger miles per vehicle-hour is less than 41.7 (that is, point C on curve III at which the cost per passenger trip mile is the same as at point B on curve II), then a much lower level of service will be provided at a higher cost per passenger trip mile. Thus, dial-a-ride operation at point B on curve II dominates operation at any point on curve III to the left of the point C, and the operator of such services should be motivated to move from curve III to curve II under these conditions. In fact, if fewer than 30 passenger miles per vehicle-hour are produced by a curve III dial-a-ride operation (that is, to the left of point D on curve III), a much higher level of service could be provided by the taxi service at a lower cost per passenger trip mile (assuming, of course, that the taxi service could continue to operate at or to the right of point A on curve I).

Notice that if the dial-a-ride service could operate at some point E on curve III to the right of point C, a lower level of service could be offered at a lower cost per passenger trip mile than at point B on curve II. If the prices or fares charged at point E were lower than those at point B, however, the revenue produced per vehicle-hour might also be lower,[4] which, under the assumption of constant cost per vehicle-hour, might result in either lower profits or higher subsidy requirements.

Jitney service as provided by a regular taxicab could also be represented on curves such as I, II, or III, depending on the extent of route deviation involved, and the same analysis could be applied to the question of additional route deviation. Most jitney systems presently operating in the U.S. and overseas are confined almost entirely to a fixed route with negligible route deviation, so that curve I would probably be the most appropriate for these cases. They usually operate substantially to the right of point A on curve I due to high vehicle occupancy, and consequently can offer service at a considerably lower cost per passenger trip mile than regular taxicabs.

Cost and performance estimates for selected services

Figure 4 illustrates the variation in cost per vehicle-hour values estimated for a number of para-transit services discussed in earlier chapters, and also includes estimates for the private automobile and conventional transit (costs generally exclude tips, profits, and fees). It is stressed that these estimates are based on rather uncertain data from earlier chapters, and on some broad assumptions, as documented in the notes accompanying the figure.

In Figure 5 the cost per vehicle-hour values are used with ridership and operating data to plot output and cost per passenger trip mile estimates for each of the services. The broken line shows the locus of cost per passenger trip mile and output points for a constant cost per vehicle-hour of $10.00. It should be noted that the units of output, passenger trip miles, will be provided at different levels of service by different modes, and for any one mode higher output levels are likely to correspond to higher vehicle occupancy and reduced passenger comfort.

Using the values in Table 57, we can estimate the effects on congestion, pollution, and energy consumption per passenger trip mile for each of the services shown in Figure 5. In Table 58 these

---

[4] For let the price per passenger trip mile and cost per passenger trip mile be p and c respectively at point B, and (p-d) and (c-e) respectively at point E. Then for a constant cost per vehicle-hour of $6.00, the number of passenger trip miles produced per vehicle-hour is 6/c at B and 6/(c-e) at E. Consequently, the change in revenue per vehicle-hour in moving from B to E is

$$\{(p\text{-}d) \times 6/(c\text{-}e)\} - \{p \times 6/c\}$$

Solution of an algebraic inequality shows that this change is negative if

$$d/p > e/c$$

Figure 4
Estimated cost per vehicle-hour for selected services

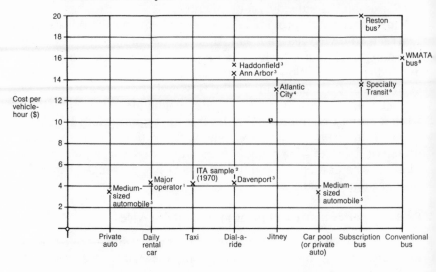

Notes:
1. Table 40. Assume 2000 miles per month, average speed 25 mph, fuel and tolls 5 cents per mile.
2. Table 10 (International Taxicab Association sample of 27 fleets). Assume an average speed of 15 mph.
3. Table 27.
4. From Chapter 9: Gross annual receipts of $10,500 for a total of 800 hours per year.
5. From Chapter 11: 14 cents per mile. Assume average speed of 25 mph.
6. From Chapter 11: 1 cent per seat mile (including profit), 41 seats. Assume average vehicle speed 33 mph (trip speed 30 mph in Table 46).
7. Washington Metropolitan Area Transit Authority (1973): $1 per bus mile operating cost (excluding fee). Assume average vehicle speed 20 mph (trip speed 15 mph in Table 46).
8. Washington Metropolitan Area Transit Authority (1973): $1.34 per bus mile. Assume average speed of 12 mph.

effects are expressed as a percentage of passenger car effects per vehicle-hour; a value of five means that the effect per passenger trip mile is five percent of the effect of a regular passenger car operating for one hour. In the absence of more precise data, all services have been treated as though they were provided by a passenger car vehicle except for WMATA bus, Reston bus, and Specialty Transit. This simplification presumably results in some underestimation of the effects for services operated with small

Figure 5

**Cost per passenger trip mile and output estimates
for selected services**

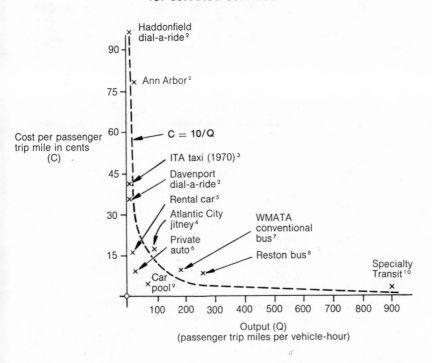

Cost per passenger
trip mile in cents
(C)

Output (Q)
(passenger trip miles per vehicle-hour)

Notes:

[1] All cost per vehicle-hour values taken from Figure 4.

[2] For Haddonfield, Ann Arbor, and Davenport dial-a-ride services: assume average speeds of 15 mph, and estimate output (Q) as the product of mean trip duration (Table 25), average speed, and productivity (Table 22). Note that this procedure may overestimate output slightly because it estimates passenger miles traveled per vehicle-hour rather than passenger trip miles per vehicle-hour.

[3] Assume 50 percent paid mileage and 1.35 passengers per cab trip (Table 9), and average speed 15 mph.

[4] From Chapter 9; assume average vehicle occupancy 4, average speed 19 mph. (15,000 miles per year, 800 hours)

[5] Assume vehicle occupancy 1.1, average speed 25 mph.

[6] Assume vehicle occupancy 1.5, average speed 25 mph.

[7] Assume daily average vehicle occupancy 15 (Hanley, 1971), average speed 12 mph.

[8] Assume 33 riders per bus (Table 55), 22 mile trip, cost per bus trip $57 (WMATA, 1973). Hence C = 8 cents.

[9] Assume vehicle occupancy 3.3, average speed 25 mph.

[10] As discussed in Chapter 11, the fare per passenger trip mile ranges from 1.25 cents to 1.76 cents. Assume C = 1.5 cents.

buses or vans, such as Haddonfield, Ann Arbor, and Atlantic City. Additional underestimation occurs for all the taxi, dial-a-ride, and jitney services because the effects of stops for passenger pickup and dropoff are ignored. On the other hand, effects for the Reston bus and Specialty Transit are presumably overestimated, because they operate at higher speeds and with fewer stops than conventional bus service.

Table 58

Congestion, pollution, and energy consumption effects for selected services

Services (ranked by cost per passenger trip mile)	Cost per passenger trip mile (C) (cents)	Output (Q) (passenger trip miles per vehicle-hour)	Congestion and energy consumption [1,2]	Pollution [2]
Haddonfield dial-a-ride	96	16	6.2[3]	6.2[3]
Ann Arbor dial-a-ride	77	19	5.2[3]	5.2[3]
ITA taxi	42	10	10.0[3]	10.0[3]
Davenport dial-a-ride	34	12	8.3[3]	8.3[3]
Atlantic City jitney	17	76	1.3[3]	1.3[3]
Rental car	16	28	3.6	3.6
Private auto	9	38	2.6	2.6
WMATA conventional bus	9	180	1.4	2.7
Reston subscription bus	8	250	1.0[4]	1.9[4]
Car pool	4	82	1.2	1.2
Specialty Transit subscription bus	1.5	900	0.3[4]	0.5[4]

[1] Listed together because the conversion factors from Table 57 are essentially identical.
[2] Measured in percent of passenger car vehicle-hour effects/passenger trip mile (see text).
[3] Probably underestimated (see text).
[4] Probably overestimated (see text).

Table 59 draws together the performance estimates for each of the selected services (all data are taken from Figures 4 and 5, and from earlier chapters). The utilization measure illustrates the extent to which each service is making use of its vehicle potential, reflecting the effects of load factor, deadheading, and route deviation. Services which are considered high occupancy, such as the Reston bus and WMATA bus, may have utilization values close to those of the private automobile primarily because of the deadheading problem, while services which are high occupancy with no deadheading, such as car pool and Specialty Transit, may have utilization values more than twice those for other services.

Table 59

Performance estimates for selected services

	Vehicle capacity (seats)	Average speed (m.p.h.)	Potential (vehicle capacity x average speed)	Output (passenger trip miles per vehicle-hour)	Utiliza-tion (output as per-cent of poten-tial)
Haddonfield dial-a-ride	17	15	255	16	6
Ann Arbor dial-a-ride	10	15	150	19	13
ITA taxi	5	15	75	10	13
Davenport dial-a-ride	7	15	105	12	11
Atlantic City jitney	10	19	190	76	40
Rental car	6	25	150	28	19
Private auto	6	25	150	38	25
WMATA conventional bus	50	12	600	180	30
Reston subscription bus	50	20	1,000	250	25
Car pool	6	25	150	82	55
Specialty Transit subscription bus	41	33	1,353	900	67

The extent to which the different services listed in Table 58 could actually substitute for each other at the output and cost values listed is clearly quite limited. The Reston subscription bus, car pool, and Specialty Transit services might serve the same kinds of trips, such as long work trips made on a regular basis. The dial-a-ride, taxi, and private automobile might also serve the same kinds of trips for some travelers, particularly short shopping and personal business trips. Specialty Transit clearly could not substitute for any of the dial-a-ride, taxi, or even conventional bus services, however. Some of the services might provide suitable complements for others, of course; dial-a-ride could act as a feeder service to conventional bus, for example.

Although the data values presented in Table 58 are specialized and in some cases rather uncertain, they do permit some rather important observations:

- Costs per passenger trip mile for dial-a-ride services in Haddonfield and Ann Arbor appear to be more than 50 percent above those for the ITA sample of regular taxicab services, and more than 100 percent above those for dial-a-ride services provided by regular taxicabs in Davenport. Even allowing generous tips for taxi drivers, these data suggest that regular taxi service could be provided to dial-a-ride patrons in Haddonfield and Ann Arbor more cheaply than existing dial-a-ride services.

- A private automobile with vehicle occupancy of 1.5 and operating at 25 miles an hour also produces more output than the average for any of the taxi or dial-a-ride systems listed (the U.S. Department of Transportation (1973a) reports average vehicle occupancies of 1.4 for work trips and 1.9 for all trips by private automobile).

- Car pools with an average occupancy of 3.3 perform well with respect to cost, congestion, pollution, and energy consumption relative to the Reston peak-hour subscription bus service (which involves considerable deadheading).

- Taxicabs are by far the worst of the services considered with respect to congestion, pollution, and energy consumption, and even the shared-ride operation in Davenport is worse in these respects than the rental car or private auto cases presented.

- Specialty Transit subscription bus service produces almost four times the output of its nearest rival, the Reston subscription service, with proportionate savings in cost, congestion, pollution, and energy consumption per passenger trip mile.

- A large range of potential operating points lies between car pool and Specialty Transit for the various forms of van pooling. Some of these services might operate more cheaply than conventional bus and with lower congestion, pollution, and energy effects.

Categorizing modes by performance and cost characteristics

The estimates presented above for selected services are sufficiently realistic to permit a coarse categorization of the different modes according to vehicle potential, output, cost per passenger trip mile, and utilization. By defining low, medium, and high ranges for each of these quantities as shown in Table 60, an overview of the capability and present usage of the different modes can be obtained. The choice of the ranges is of necessity somewhat arbitrary, and further experience in the analysis of para-transit potential may indicate more appropriate ranges. (Note that the short-term rental car has been omitted because we have insufficient experience to date with this service.)

Table 60
Categorizing para-transit modes by cost and performance characteristics

	Private auto	Hire and drive services — Daily rental car	Taxi	Dial-a-ride	Jitney	Car pool	Sub-scrip-tion bus	Conven-tional bus
			Hail or phone services			Prearranged ride-sharing services		
Vehicle potential	M	M	L	M	M	M	H	H
Output	L	L	L	L	M	M	M-H	M-H
Utilization	L-M	L	L	L	M	H	M-H	M
Cost/passenger trip mile	M	M	H	H	M	L	L-M	M

Definition of Terms:

	Low (L)	Medium (M)	High (H)
Vehicle potential (V) (seat miles/vehicle-hour)	$V < 100$	$100 \leq V \leq 500$	$V > 500$
Output (Q) (Passenger trip miles/vehicle-hour)	$Q < 50$	$50 \leq Q \leq 250$	$Q > 250$
Utilization (U) $\left(\frac{100 \times \text{output}}{\text{vehicle potential}}\right)$	$U < 25$	$25 \leq U \leq 50$	$U > 50$
Cost/passenger trip* mile (C) (cents)	$C < 5$	$5 \leq C \leq 25$	$C > 25$

As pointed out earlier, with respect to service characteristics the para-transit modes lie "in-between" the private automobile mode and conventional bus transit in the spectrum of transportation modes. In Table 60 the relatively low potential and high cost per passenger trip mile of taxis, and the high utilization and low cost of car pools, interrupt the otherwise steady increases in potential, output, and utilization and the steady decreases in cost per passenger trip mile as we move from private auto through the para-transit modes to conventional bus. The trend would be smoothed somewhat if taxi were moved to the left of private automobile, suggesting that the "in-between" concept is not as appropriate for cost and performance characteristics as it is for service characteristics.

For the dial-a-ride and subscription bus services the costs found for existing services span wide ranges, varying greatly with the way in which the service is provided. All the dial-a-ride services fall into the high-cost category, but the taxicab service in Davenport operates at less than half the cost per passenger trip mile of the other two services. For subscription bus the medium utilization and medium cost categories are listed because of the Reston type of service, where buses and operators are obtained from a transit authority. Where part-time drivers are used with no deadheading, utilization is likely to be high and cost per passenger trip mile very low.

The broken curved line in Figure 5 shows that the reduction in cost per passenger trip mile which can be achieved by an incremental increase in output (and hence utilization) is a decreasing function (the inverse square) of the output value at which the mode is operating. Consequently, the magnitudes of the changes which could be effected (through operating, pricing, or regulatory changes) vary considerably from one service to another. Table 61 shows the extent of reduction in cost per passenger

Table 61
Cost reduction from expanded output

Output range	Reduction in cost/passenger trip mile for an increase in output of one passenger trip mile/vehicle-hour
Less than 50 (Low)	At least .0004 × (cost/vehicle-hour)
Between 50 and 250 (Medium)	Between .0004 × (cost/vehicle-hour) and .000016 × (cost/vehicle-hour)
Greater than 250 (High)	At most .000016 × (cost/vehicle-hour)

trip mile resulting from an increase in output of one passenger trip mile per vehicle-hour. Modes operating in the low range (private auto, rental car, taxi, dial-a-ride) have considerable potential for savings in cost per passenger trip mile through even small increases in output. This potential decreases substantially as output increases, to the point where small savings obtained in cost per passenger trip mile for high output modes will have a significant effect on cost per passenger *trip* only if the mode is serving long trips (often the case for subscription bus service, of course).

Table 58 provides some illustrations for the above discussion. ITA taxi costs per passenger trip mile are 8 cents higher than those for the Davenport dial-a-ride service, which are in turn 17 cents higher than those for the Atlantic City jitney service, suggesting potential cost savings for taxicab services through increased ride-sharing. For the long trip case, suppose that the output of the Reston bus service could be increased by higher load factors, reduced deadheading, and the use of express bus lanes to increase operating speed and driver utilization. If a 50 percent increase could be obtained (the service would still only be operating at well under half the output of Specialty Transit), a savings of more than 2 cents per passenger trip mile would result, amounting to a daily saving of 88 cents per passenger for the 44-mile round trip.

PRESENT PATRONAGE OF PARA-TRANSIT MODES

To the extent that the limited data permitted, the nature of the travel demand currently served by the different para-transit modes has been discussed in the chapters dealing with the modes individually. Information is rather sparse on these trips at present for a number of reasons:

- Para-transit modes are operated almost exclusively by private operators who have little incentive to make detailed trip and cost data available to outsiders.

- Short-term rental cars are not operating as a system anywhere in the world. Jitneys are operating only in a very few situations in the U.S. (although many operations exist in foreign countries) and all these systems are privately operated. Of the few dial-a-ride systems in existence, none could be considered a large-scale system.

- Para-transit modes have not been analyzed in any detail in traditional transportation studies; virtually no data have been collected on para-transit operations and these modes have been largely ignored in the development of transportation plans.

A discussion of the *magnitude* of the travel demand being

served by para-transit modes must be tempered by recognition of the degree to which the private automobile dominates urban travel in the U.S. Table 62 drawn from the 1972 National Transportation Study shows that almost 90 percent of urban trips were made by the private automobile in 1970, and the forecast increase in these trips from 1970 to 1990 is greater than that for any other mode. Almost 94 percent of the urban passenger miles in 1970 were provided by the private automobile, having increased 74 percent from 1960, while passenger miles provided by conventional bus transit declined by more than 26 percent.

Table 62
Urban passenger travel by mode

	Percent of average weekday person trips (1970)	Forecast percent increase in person trips 1970-1990	Percent of urban passenger miles (1970)	Percent of change in passenger miles 1960-1970
Automobile	89.4	75.0	93.9	74.0
Bus transit	6.1	29.6	2.7	—26.3
Rail transit	2.8	60.7	2.2	— 8.5
Commuter rail	0.4	23.6	0.6	0.0
Taxicabs	1.3	41.2	0.6	30.8

Source: U.S. Department of Transportation (1972b)

While the conventional wisdom currently deplores this dependence of the urban traveler on the private automobile, for those who can use it the service characteristics of this mode are clearly superior to conventional transit service in most situations. Furthermore, data in the previous section suggest that from the point of view of cost, congestion, pollution, and energy consumption per unit of output, the private automobile may dominate all other existing services for short trips in low density areas, and can also be very efficient during rush hours if vehicle occupancy is high.

Some particular indicators of the magnitude of para-transit patronage relative to other services are as follows:

• Taxicabs account for almost 60 percent of passenger expenditure on intraurban public transportation in the U.S., for almost twice as many revenue vehicle-miles as the transit bus, rail, and trolley combined,[5] and for about 1.3 percent of the average weekday person trips.[6]

- Taxicabs and rental cars appear to play a significant role in serving airport access trips, and together account, for example, for about 28 percent of the trips to and from the Cleveland and Philadelphia airports, as shown in Table 63. It has been estimated that up to 85 percent of rental car business is conducted from airport locations (Chapter 10).

Table 63
Airport access trips

Mode	Cleveland	Philadelphia
Private auto	48.0	49.7
Taxi	17.6	15.9
Rental car	7.1	10.6
Airport limousine	15.7	12.9
Hotel-motel limousine	0.5	0.9
Airport bus	6.5	2.0
Other	4.6	8.0
Total	100.0	100.0

Sources: deNeufville et al. (1972), and Corradino and Ferreri (1969)

- Dial-a-ride and accompanying subscription services have been serving between 1 and 7 percent of the trips in the six areas listed in Table 22.

- The more successful subscription bus services such as Specialty Transit, National Geographic, and Reston have been serving between 20 and 70 percent of the home-to-work trips made along their service routes.[7] Surveys made in Reston indicate that the service is having a significant impact on auto ownership and even residential location; 21 percent of riders answering a questionnaire said they had reduced the number of automobiles they owned and 44 percent said they would not have moved to Reston had the bus service not been available.

- The Burroughs car pool service appears to be attracting up to 30 percent of potential trips.

---

[5] Table 6.
[6] Table 62.
[7] Table 51.

With respect to urban travel as a whole, the potential of para-transit modes appears to exceed their present utilization. Services such as dial-a-ride, jitney, organized car pool, and subscription bus have demonstrated their ability to serve urban travel demand efficiently and effectively in a few locations, but on a national scale they are relatively insignificant at present. Current urban goals for providing mobility with minimal congestion, pollution, and energy consumption strongly favor the expansion of these para-transit services, and it seems likely that they will play an increasingly important role over the next decade.

Chapter 13

Martin Wohl
Michael A. Kemp

Innovation in Para-transit Regulation

INTRODUCTION

Currently there is much talk about deregulating certain sectors of the urban transport system, about changing regulations for others, or about imposing new regulations for aspects not now under governmental control. Most of these ideas involve simplistic types of regulatory actions such as downtown automobile bans, congestion tolls, restriction of downtown auto usage to cars with more than one passenger, surcharge taxes for downtown parking, and so forth. Existing concerns of public regulation include entry restrictions for taxi and jitney services, rate regulation for these services, and the use of different types of pricing mechanisms (for example, the prescription of zone or meter fare systems for taxis or jitneys).

However, these are not the only types of regulatory actions which may, or perhaps will, result in innovation and rationalization for urban passenger transport systems. Not to be overlooked, for example, is the potential impact, on both the provision of service and the usage of para-transit modes, of recent government actions with respect to automobile safety, vehicle emissions

279

standards, and energy policy as well as to air quality standards for cities more generally.

The purpose of this chapter is to speculate on the impacts of these types of action, to make inferences about the pros and cons, and then to conclude what the wiser policy courses in the years ahead seem to be, particularly in the near term.

THE "CONVENTIONAL WISDOM" ABOUT FARE AND RATE CHANGES: SOME LESSONS TO BE LEARNED

One cannot help but be struck by the enormous, almost single-minded attention and concern which is devoted to fare and rate regulation, especially within the transit sector. Regulatory agencies, transit operators, and the news media seem to focus almost all of their efforts on appropriate fare and rate levels whenever public transport operations are faced with financial difficulties or with cost squeezes. It is almost as though they are unaware of the extent to which passengers, both current and potential, are sensitive to the *service* qualities of the operations in question. Their actions occasionally suggest that some of them even fail to understand the simple notion that fare or rate increases do not always lead to increases in total revenues, much less net revenues. Nor do they often devote more than scant effort to understanding what cost changes will accompany proposed fare or rate changes. It is hardly any wonder that most transit operations find themselves in the all-too-familiar "price increase/service decrease/passenger decrease/revenue decrease/price increase" spiral.

In this context, three points are in order:

- Urban travelers are especially sensitive to the service qualities of the various modes available to them and, proportionately, find service decreases more important in influencing their travel behavior than fare or rate increases.[1] As a consequence, when fare or rate increases are accompanied by service decreases (say by deliberately reduced schedule frequencies), an operator might well find that the revenue loss from the drop in ridership due to poorer service is greater than the additional revenues received through higher fares for the remaining customers, even when the demand is price-inelastic.

  Closely related to this point, the available empirical evidence indicates that urban travelers are much more sensitive to the difficulties and inconveniences associated with getting to, from,

---

[1] See, for example, Kraft & Domencich (1970) or Kemp (1973).

and onto transportation facilities (including waiting and transfer times and discomforts) than they are to the travel times incurred once they are inside the vehicle.[2]

- The "conventional wisdom" suggests that urban passenger travel demand is almost always price-inelastic. Since only fare or rate increases are virtually ever proposed as a means of alleviating the financial difficulties of public transportation or of overcoming wage or other cost increases, one must conclude that regulatory agencies and transit operators assume that a fare or rate increase will always result in a proportionately lower reduction in ridership.[3] However, it increasingly appears that the higher-service, more demand-responsive forms of public transportation (like taxi and dial-a-ride) exhibit price elasticities around or slightly above the unitary level.[4] Even for some high-grade conventional transit services, such as the rapid rail link to Cleveland's Hopkins Airport,[5] there is some evidence that ridership is relatively price elastic. That is to say, the demand for these services—even at current fare levels—is such that fare increases will reduce ridership by an even larger proportion, and thus reduce gross revenues.[6] Accordingly, if the operators in these instances want to increase gross revenues, then it appears that fare or rate increases can only work to their detriment.

- It should be apparent that more is at stake than gross revenue changes when considering fare or rate changes. To be sure, one should try to determine what increases or decreases in gross revenue totals can be expected when the price is raised or lowered. But two other factors should be considered concurrently. First, one must also consider the impacts of deliberate adjustments to service levels (either changes of schedule frequencies, or changes in the vehicle supply). Second, one should consider the cost as well as revenue impacts resulting

---

[2] This point is buttressed not only by the service and price elasticity values estimated by Kraft & Domencich (1970) but also by the demand models developed by Wong (1971) for taxi operations in Washington, D.C. This can be seen by comparing Wong's elasticities with respect to travel times with those with respect to taxi destination frequency, the latter being simply a proxy for the difficulties, discomforts, and time expended while trying to obtain a taxi.

[3] Purely aside, that is, from considering the deleterious effects of reducing service levels at the same time in order to maintain what operators regard as "efficient" load factors.

[4] See Chapter 7 and Wong (1971), Table 1.

[5] Wohl (1972), Table 3 and Figure 7.

[6] Again, without even considering further ridership drops that can stem from accompanying service reductions aimed at "stabilizing" load factors.

from the proposed fare (and service) changes. For instance, when a price increase is proposed and the demand is price-inelastic over the range of that increase (and when no service changes accompany the price increase), an operator can be assured of both total and net revenue increases, since the number of passengers, and consequently total costs, will decrease while gross revenues will increase. On the other hand, for price increases which range from the inelastic to the elastic portion of the demand curve (before and after the increase, respectively), or for price decreases when the demand is price-elastic over the range of that decrease, no conclusions about the resultant effect on net revenues can be made without individually examining both the cost and gross revenue changes resulting therefrom.[7]

From the foregoing, it is evident that if regulatory agencies or public transportation operators are to act either in the public interest or on their own behalf, they should have considerably more knowledge and understanding about travelers' sensitivities (as measured by demand elasticities) with respect to both price and service changes. Also, it is clear that one should not only understand the changes in ridership and gross revenue which result from price adjustments but should understand the probable cost changes as well. Without a clearer picture of both these aspects there can be no rationalization of rate regulation for urban transport systems.

These observations and remarks underscore the necessity for more experimentation and analysis which will shed light on the demand for and the costs of various transport modes. In suggesting this, however, we do not mean to endorse a continuation of the kind of demonstration program which has been so commonplace in the past. Rather, we suggest undertaking demonstrations which will provide analytically sound information about services not currently available or about price levels not now experienced. Further, the research should endeavor to provide a pattern of results which can, in turn, be used to test more sensible hypotheses than have been formulated in the past. Needless to say, these hypotheses should be formulated before the design of the demonstrations and the gathering of data have been undertaken.

Also, care must be taken to ensure that the demonstration is mounted for a period long enough to provide a sensible test of

---

[7] In the case of a price decrease when the demand is elastic, for example, the fare cut will increase total revenues but it will also lead to increased usage and thus higher total costs for the operation—the net result cannot be ascertained on an a priori basis.

the market response. Some types of responses—particularly those involving car ownership decisions—are not short-run in character, but will involve lengthy and rather permanent experiments. Given the fact that interest in both transit and para-transit modes is likely to continue over a long period of time, and that investments and grants are often of a long-run nature, it seems high time indeed to invest in this fundamental research activity.

SOME SPECIFIC REGULATORY ACTIONS

In the following discussion, we examine the impacts of various changes in regulatory postures (some of which affect para-transit modes directly and others indirectly), and we assess the advantages and disadvantages of those regulatory postures from various points of view. The discussion will necessarily be largely descriptive and will reflect informed judgments rather than comprehensive analysis. Even so, we will try to be objective, to identify the extent and incidence of the benefits and costs (both internal and external), and to indicate potential areas for additional study and experimentation. We will focus on three types of regulation: entry controls for taxi and jitney operations, fare regulation for para-transit modes, and indirect regulations affecting para-transit.

Entry controls for taxi and jitney services

In Chapter 7 we presented a fairly detailed discussion of the impacts of taxicab entry controls on the level and nature of the service provided to the public. In our judgment, as was stated there, the balance of available evidence suggests that the entry limitations found in most large cities are not in the public interest. To go further, we believe that in the short run as well as the long run there is probably no simpler or more effective way to alleviate some of our urban transportation problems than to relax present-day entry controls for both taxis and jitneys. A relaxation of those controls would entail other problems, to be sure—especially in the short run—but, on balance, the measure has genuine merit.

What would be the impacts of abolishing current license or franchise restrictions, and upon whom would they fall? They would be many, and they would vary from city to city. Free entry would break up the present publicly created monopolies in cities such as New York, Boston, and Chicago (to name but three) and would eliminate (or at least diminish) the present fare surcharge which is required to cover the monopoly rent. The monopoly rent does vary from city to city (and probably is higher for license-type restrictions than for franchises) and at present may form a significant part of the total passenger fare in some cities. Since the evidence suggests that demand for taxi services may be price-elastic, it is possible that substantial ridership increases could occur in some cities with the abolition of the entry limitations.

This increased usage and the substantial reduction of risk associated with entering the taxi market would probably increase the supply of taxis. That is, with the abolition of entry controls an individual would no longer have to risk the $15,000 to $25,000 necessary to buy a medallion, or to risk the capital necessary to operate a franchised fleet, or to have the necessary credit for either possibility. It would be relatively more easy to enter the taxi business. At most, for instance, the potential owner-driver might be risking the difference between the resale price of a taxi and the price of a private automobile. Moreover—in a free-entry market—the individual taxi owner can afford to use the vehicle for both business and nonbusiness purposes and can thus obtain the economies and tax advantages of multiple-use (according to individual tastes and preferences). Finally, since taxi users appear generally to be more sensitive to the *availability* of taxi service than to the trip travel times, the increased taxi supply can in itself be expected to generate additional ridership.

It is difficult to estimate with any precision the overall magnitude of these impacts. However, to provide some perspective on the matter and to indicate that one should indeed expect some rather substantial increases in taxi supply and usage, it might be well to point out some comparative statistics for San Francisco and Washington, D.C. These cities are of similar size—the 1970 populations both for the two metropolitan areas and for their central city jurisdictions are quite comparable. So too are the automobile ownership levels; transit ridership is slightly higher in San Francisco than in Washington. The supply of taxicab services, on the other hand, differs markedly. San Francisco, with numerical limitations on entry, supports between 700 and 800 cabs carrying some 22,000 passengers each day. In Washington, by comparison, there are some 12,000 licensed cabs—although this is a misleading figure since a number of vehicles with taxi tags seem to be rarely, if ever, used as cabs. There are roughly 8,700 taxi drivers' licenses extant; these drivers serve nearly 93,000 passengers each day, over four times the volume in

San Francisco. It seems likely that a very substantial increase in taxicabs and their usage would ensue if the San Francisco entry restrictions were eliminated.

Some problems could be anticipated if all U.S. cities were to adopt a free-entry policy for taxis and jitneys, especially in those cities where the number of licenses has been restricted and has led to the creation of paper capital.[8] In New York City, for instance, the medallions when first sold could be purchased for $10; in 1964 they were changing hands for up to $35,000; today, when sold on the open market, the individual medallions sell for around $20,000 and the fleet medallions for about $6,000 each. For those medallion holders who bought their licenses from the city at $10 or from others at low prices, the abolition of entry controls would represent no great investment loss; it would prevent them from making a windfall gain should they desire to sell their medallions. However, for those medallion owners who bought their licenses from others at substantially higher prices—which of course resulted from the publicly created monopoly—a considerable investment loss would be incurred if the city were to abolish the present restrictions without any compensation. While the economy overall would not suffer from a change in entry controls, the individual medallion owners who paid high prices would suffer to the extent of their capital loss, paper or not.

As a matter of fairness rather than one of efficiency, it can be argued that such individuals should not be burdened with the private losses which would stem from dissolution of the publicly created monopoly. It might appear more equitable for the city to assume the burden and to repurchase all outstanding medallions —possibly at the price actually paid at purchase by the present owner, or possibly at a fair current market value. Obviously, the date of purchase should be set to prevent certain owners from obtaining windfall gains at the public's expense. New York City, for example, might have to assume a total burden for paper capital losses ranging from $140 to $250 million; if amortized over a ten year period at (say) 6 percent, the annual tax burden might range from $19 to $34 million, on the order of $2.40 to $4.30 additional annual taxes per resident over a period of ten years. With the annual subsidies for transit in New York City now running more than ten times higher, the additional tax bite seems comparatively small. In San Francisco, the corresponding

---

[8] In Chapter 7 we examined in greater detail the position of established fleet owners on this issue, discussed some of their objections, summarized the probable impacts, and suggested how some of the problems might be surmounted.

extra tax required over ten years would be in the range of $3.10 to $3.60 per resident.

There would, however, be other options available to a public agency that wished to abolish numerical entry limitations while trying to preserve the financial interests of the current license-holders. For example, various types of medallion-splitting schemes can be envisaged, under which existing medallion-holders could be given (say) two new medallions for each one they currently own—to trade or to use as they see fit. These ideas have the disadvantage that they would increase the cab supply without really abolishing the monopoly protection, and medallion-holders could conspire to limit the supply by not using their additional licenses. Yet another possible method would be to phase the medallions out gradually by selling several dozen additional medallions each year to the highest bidder; the revenues from such an auction could even be distributed among the present medallion owners. Annual auctions would be continued until the market value of a license fell to zero. This method might avoid harming anybody unjustly and would not cost the public anything.

For cities having franchise rather than numerical restrictions, there would appear to be no similar type of financial problem in abolishing entry controls. Of course, strong objections would undoubtedly be raised by those who currently have the franchises and who now reap the benefits or monopoly profits by being allowed to restrict the taxi supply and increase prices above the levels which would prevail in a more competitive situation.

Other problems which deserve attention when one considers the abolition of entry controls stem from the increased taxicab supply and usage. For instance, what might happen to traffic congestion, to ridership of the scheduled transit services, and to pollution and other environmental problems? As we have argued in Chapter 7, it is very difficult to gauge beforehand what the net effect would be. While the number of taxicabs using city streets would undoubtedly increase, it also seems likely that some (and perhaps a substantial number) of the current private automobile trips would be displaced. Such a diversion would also tend to reduce the amount of parking space required in the core city and other congested areas, thus relieving another difficult urban problem. Moreover, if the abolition of entry restrictions were coupled with better peak-load pricing policies (to be discussed in a later section), it is possible that some commuter-only cars (that is to say, a second family car used almost exclusively for commuting to and from work) could be dispensed with entirely by some households. Given that taxis and jitneys probably could make at least two round trips between residential and work places during peak periods, it is quite credible that the number of families having exclusive home-to-work commuter cars could be somewhat reduced.

On balance, then, it is not clear that traffic congestion and the attendant energy consumption, pollution, and other environmental problems would be increased [9]—at least when viewed over a period long enough to allow commuting and car ownership patterns to shift in response to entry and fare regulation changes. Besides, congestion pricing schemes could be coupled with the abolition of entry regulations to restrict the total vehicular flow or spread the peaks.

It also seems likely that the abolition of entry controls would result in diversions not only from private automobiles but also from the existing conventional transit services. On the one hand, the revenues and costs of present transit operations would fall, but on the other hand, those for taxis and jitneys would increase. Given the extent to which transit systems typically suffer from too much peaking already, it is not clear that the transit operations would be worse off. On balance, it is difficult to judge the "goodness" or "badness" of these traffic diversions. But given that the great bulk of taxi and jitney costs are variable, that taxi patrons now pay more than the total costs for such a service, and that many if not most transit services are not currently covering even their variable costs, it seems very likely that such a regulatory change would result in a more favorable balance.

It should also be pointed out that the abolition of entry restrictions would tend to widen the number of different public transport service and price options which are available to the urban public. In the past, one of the problems with public transport modes has been that, except in a handful of cities, the public is generally provided with just one or two different service-and-price combinations—that is, either the bus or the taxi. The abolition of jitney restrictions, however, would tend to increase the number of public transport options available, and would tend to make these modes more competitive with the private automobile which has a wide range of price-and-service options (for example, chauffered limousine service, drive alone, and car pooling with from one to five other passengers, not to mention the choices among car sizes and degrees of luxury).

Two final points are worthy of brief mention. First, in cities like Los Angeles one would expect the abolition of entry con-

---

[9] By the same token, of course, there is no certainty that these problems would be ameliorated if taxicab entry controls were relaxed.

trols to expand the taxi and jitney services vastly, and to reduce significantly the rental car fleet and its usage, especially by non-resident travelers. Second, the employment market for low-skilled workers should be improved in a significant and immediate way.

Fare regulations for para-transit modes

It can be argued that no regulation of rates or fares is necessary since the market is fairly competitive and, by and large, the economies of scale are small.[10] On the other hand, one can argue that individuals operating their own cabs or small fleets might not have enough information to price taxi or jitney operations properly, either in their own interest or in the interest of the public. Further, with the prospect of literally thousands of taxis and jitneys serving central city areas, one can foresee that pricing would become chaotic. It seems important to provide the potential rider with as much information as possible about the trip price—preferably before starting the trip, and even before hailing a cab. This is particularly true for nonresident travelers who may easily be "taken for a ride" when they are not familiar with the town they are visiting. On balance, we favor the retention of public regulation for taxi and jitney fares.

As we have detailed in Chapter 7, several matters should be considered in setting taxicab rates. By and large, trips of equal quality and length should have uniform prices;[11] the pricing mechanism should be simple, fraud-proof, and cheaply administered; and the rate scheme should encourage drivers to make trips as quickly and efficiently as possible (that is, it should discourage circuitous driving merely to increase the meter total). Also, the rates should be regulated so that fare levels can be increased as variable costs increase. The latter will increase, for example, during periods of congestion and in denser central cities, when taxi and jitney trips will entail more driver time and higher operating expenses. Finally, in setting rates for taxis and jitneys it is important to consider both the supply and the demand components of the total trip-making. That is, at different prices and levels of supply how many taxi and jitney trips will be made? Similarly, how many taxis and jitneys will be needed and what pattern of operation[12] will result under different price

---

[10] Meyer et al. (1966).

[11] Fares for trips to very low density areas with problems of deadhead returns or to dangerous areas, however, might justifiably be set higher.

[12] For example, full-time as against part-time operations, and other such variations in operating procedures.

and usage levels? How do these aspects interact to produce an equilibrium in the transportation system?

In our judgment, such matters as these are ones which should properly fall within the purview of a public regulatory authority, as should the establishment of minimum mechanical and safety standards for vehicles, minimum driving standards, and the financial responsibility requirements for operators. Ideally, a proper regulatory authority would, as a high priority, gather and analyze basic information on the local market and supply conditions and on cost and demand, and would thus have a better basis for estimating the effects of adopting different price schedules, fare schemes, and so on.

Other transportation pricing policies affecting para-transit

Other kinds of pricing innovations for public transportation facilities have sometimes been suggested and have been widely discussed. Among them are fare-free public transport systems, congestion toll pricing for highways, parking surcharges for downtown areas, and so forth. The first two of these have received extensive coverage in the literature and merit little additional discussion here. Briefly, though, fare-free transit appears to be a less efficient means of achieving the social objectives which are espoused than other more direct means—such as improving transit services selectively or offering subsidized chits or passes for deserving riders. Moreover, para-transit modes seem much more suitable for helping certain population groups who are transportation-disadvantaged than the conventional bus or rail transit modes; this holds especially true for older and handicapped people who need more personalized service, less walking, less waiting, less jostling, no stairs, and so forth. Furthermore, these groups of people will be less afraid of using para-transit modes, in all likelihood, than of using the normal transit modes.

Congestion toll pricing for highways, while clearly having its merits,[13] would probably require expensive and time-consuming toll gate operations since electronic metering systems are not yet fully operational, and would also possibly result in a regressive income transfer.[14] On the other hand, the institution of congestion tolls should improve the market for para-transit modes, especially for jitneys and shared taxis. While some experimentation with congestion tolls seems in order, it would be unfortu-

---

[13] Especially as a long-run proposition and when coupled with good investment planning. See McGillivray (1973).

[14] That is to say, the less well-to-do who cannot afford the congestion tolls are "tolled off" the facilities and are thus left to fend for themselves.

nate to settle for purely short-run experiments rather than view the problem as a long-run one in which the expansion of facility capacity and price, as well as increased trip-making, are also properly considered and evaluated.

The use of parking surcharges as a means of reducing congestion (especially in downtown and other congested areas) and also of increasing the market for para-transit services, has merits and demerits, broadly considered.[15] This kind of policy has sometimes been proposed as a proxy for congestion toll pricing, and as a means of partially internalizing the difference between the private and social costs of automobile travel. Others, of course, view parking surcharges simply as a means of reducing pollution and congestion, and as a way of diverting riders from private automobiles to transit.

The use of such charges, if extensive enough, should achieve all these objectives. At the same time, though, some detrimental impacts would also be expected to stem from their usage. First, the amount of travel to and from downtown—and thus the overall economic viability of the downtown area—would probably decline. That is, the private automobile and the public modes, even with an increased supply of properly regulated para-transit services, cannot be regarded as perfect substitutes, and thus the total amount of trip-making to downtown areas for work, pleasure, and business would decline. Second, the less well-to-do could be more adversely affected by the surcharge than the more well-to-do. Third, to use parking surcharges as a means of imposing congestion pricing can be unfair, since in many large cities up to 65 percent of the total traffic on central business district streets is through-traffic, going neither to nor from downtown. One survey of the available empirical evidence[16] concluded that, even if parking restrictions were applied to most of the downtown section, in many cities some 15 to 30 percent of automobile trips into the area do not involve parking and hence would escape the parking surcharges. So while it is difficult to say, on balance, whether the long-run impacts of parking surcharges would result in a net benefit for society, if one simply wants to improve the market for para-transit modes (and simultaneously reduce congestion and pollution) then parking surcharges or congestion tolls would do the trick.

However, a warning must be sounded against the adoption of pricing or regulatory actions of this sort on a short-term experimental basis. A far wiser policy would be first to remove the entry

---

[15] Kulash (1973b).
[16] Kulash (1973a).

controls on the major para-transit modes; to experiment with different fare systems and with peak and off-peak pricing for these services; and then to begin considering the long-run effects of developing more rational pricing for the entire urban transport system.

Other regulations affecting para-transit modes

Most attention pertaining to the regulation of para-transit and to its improvement has been directed specifically at regulation of entry and rate making for the para-transit modes *per se*. But there are other regulatory standards and controls which will affect—perhaps markedly if not significantly—the market for para-transit. A few of these come readily to mind—for example, the 1970 Clean Air Act Amendments; standards for both automobile emissions and air quality in cities; actions arising out of the energy crisis; the National Highway Traffic Safety Administration standards for automobiles; and driver licensing standards, whether at federal, state, or local levels.

Rather than comment on the *overall* appropriateness of the existing controls and regulations in these areas, we will discuss the effects on para-transit of the continuance of such actions, and of possible new standards for the future. The emission and safety standards already in force have surely increased the price of owning and operating private automobiles and have thus played a role in increasing the market for para-transit, relative to what it would have been without their imposition. Further, and more importantly, if the proposed 1975-1976 standards for both emissions and safety are enforced as currently proposed, it appears that the additional costs will range from $900 to $1,400 per automobile for 1975 models.[17] While no definitive studies are available to indicate the elasticity of the market to price increases of that magnitude, it seems evident that it will not be trivial, and that it should—everything else being equal—significantly enhance the opportunities for para-transit modes. This will be particularly true if entry restrictions are abolished, if diversification of the para-transit market is allowed (for example, by allowing jitneys and shared taxis to operate), and if rates are formulated soundly.

Energy concerns are also likely to affect the para-transit modes. Many proposed public strategies in response to gasoline shortages —such as gasoline rationing, gas tax increases, fuel economy taxes on vehicles, or simple price increases by suppliers—will

---

[17] RECAT Committee (1972).

serve to make para-transit modes that much more attractive compared to the private automobile.

It also seems probable that over the next several years there will be changes in driver licensing standards. Two kinds of changes could easily affect the market for para-transit modes. First, it is likely that more stringent controls for those driving "under the influence of alcohol or drugs" will be enacted. Such a move should reinforce the need for para-transit services. That is, if suitable alternative modes are available for those who wish to indulge, it is likely that indulgence will continue to take place but that travelers will simply switch their travel modes when they expect to be drinking.[18]

Second, it is also entirely possible, if less likely, that more stringent driving standards will be imposed upon those whose reaction capabilities or driving records place them in the "dangerous" or "near dangerous" driver category. A more rigid set of standards in this regard would tend to inhibit both the young or inexperienced and the old. If such restrictions are enforced, para-transit offers the kinds of service-price conditions which will permit these people to continue their former urban travel patterns and yet not be seriously inhibited or disadvantaged. It is difficult to imagine, though, that most conventional bus and rail transit modes (as presently operated) can even begin to substitute for the private automobile for these people.

---

[18] Ross et al. (1970).

A Para-transit Bibliography

This bibliography includes all of the sources cited in the text, together with a number of other sources which are primarily concerned with the operation of para-transit modes.

Aex, R. P. (1973). "B-Line Dial-a-Bus System in Batavia." *See* Highway Research Board (1973).

Alexander, D. (1972). "Commute Club May Buy Own Marin Buses." *San Francisco Examiner,* March 30, 1972.

Altshuler, A., and Melone, T. (1971). "Site Selection for a Dial-a-Ride Demonstration." Report USL TR-70-16. Cambridge, Mass.: Massachusetts Institute of Technology Urban Systems Laboratory.

American Academy of Arts and Sciences (1968a). "Conference on Poverty and Transportation—Summary and Conclusions and Papers Presented." Brookline, Mass.

———— (1968b). "Conference on Poverty and Transportation—Edited Transcript." Brookline, Mass.

American Academy of Transportation (1972). *Final Project Report: Maxi-Cab Commuter Club.* Flint, Mich.: Flint Transportation Authority.

American Petroleum Institute (1971). *Petroleum Facts and Figures, 1971 Edition.* Washington, D.C.

American Transit Association (1972). " '71-'72 Transit Fact Book." Washington, D.C.

Ann Arbor Transportation Authority (1973). *Ann Arbor Dial-A-Ride Pilot Project Final Report.* Ann Arbor, Mich.

Archer, E., and Shortreed, J. H. (1971). "Potential Demands for Demand-Scheduled Bus Services." *Highway Research Record 367.* Washington, D.C.: Highway Research Board.

Atkinson, W. G. (1973). "Telebus Project in Regina." *See* Highway Research Board (1973).

————, Couturier, R. P., and Ling, S. (1971). *Regina Telebus Study.* Regina, Sask.: Regina Transit System.

Automotive Fleet (1973). *Annual Fleet Fact Book Issue, Automotive Fleet* 12, no. 5.

Bain, H. (1970). "The Reston Express Bus." Washington, D.C.: Washington Center for Metropolitan Studies.

Banks, R. L., and Associates, Inc. (1972). *Study and Evaluation of Urban Mass Transportation Regulation and Regulatory Bodies.* Springfield, Va.: National Technical Information Service.

Barbera, K. G. (1972). "Introduction to the City of Boston Taxicab Industry." *Traffic Quarterly* 26, pp. 277-88.

Barden, S. A., and Nip, K-f. (1968). "The Level of Service Provided by Taxis in March, 1968." Technical Report TR54. Hong Kong: Traffic and Transport Survey Unit.

Bauer, H. J. (1971). "Case Study of a Demand-Responsive Transportation System." *See* Highway Research Board (1971).

Beesley, M. E. (1973). "Regulation of Taxis." *The Economic Journal* 83, pp. 150-72.

Beimborn, E. A. (1969). "Characteristics of Taxicab Usage." *Highway Research Record* 283. Washington, D.C.: Highway Research Board.

Belknap, R. A. (1973). "The San Francisco Jitneys." Unpublished mimeograph. Berkeley, Calif.: University of California Institute of Transportation and Traffic Engineering.

Bendixson, T. (1972). "Coin-Operated Taxis." *Transportation* 1 pp. 100-101.

———— (1973a). "Self-Drive Mini Hire-Cars Proposed for Amsterdam." *Transportation* 2, pp. 97-101.

———— (1973b). "A Japanese Self-Drive Urban Hire Car." *Transportation* 2, p. 102.

Berla, M. J. (1973). "Dial-a-Ride Project in Ann Arbor: Public Response." *See* Highway Research Board (1973).

Blurton, M. A. S. (1968). *Mass Transportation Demonstration Projects III— MTD—3, 4.* Urbana, Ill.: University of Illinois.

Board, C., and Goddard, J. B. (1970). "A Survey of Taxicab Availability in London." London, U.K.: London School of Economics Geography Department.

Bonsall, J. A. (1971). *Dial-a-Bus—The Bay Ridges Experiment.* Toronto: Ontario Department of Transportation and Communications.

———— (1973). "Dial-a-Bus Experiment in Bay Ridges." *See* Highway Research Board (1973).

Bruck, H.; Piret, M.; Melone, T.; and Little, F. (1971). "Topics in the Design of Dial-a-Ride Demonstration Experiments." Report USL TR-70-12. Cambridge, Mass.: MIT Urban Systems Laboratory.

Business Week (1969). "Rent-A-Car Roars Ahead." *Business Week*, November 1, 1969, pp. 84ff.

———— (1971). "Now Avis Thinks It Can Become Number 1." *Business Week*, February 6, 1971, pp. 46ff.

Car and Truck Renting and Leasing Association (1973). Statement of R. Denkmann before the U.S. Senate Interior and Insular Affairs Committee, May 9, 1973. Reprinted in U.S. Congress, Joint Economic Committee Subcommittee on Consumer Economics, *The Gasoline and Fuel Oil Shortage*, May 1, 2, and June 2, 1973. Washington, D.C.: Government Printing Office.

Carbajal, M., Jr. (1970). "Insuring Non-Medallion Taxicabs in the New York City Area." Unpublished mimeograph.

Chard, J. (1971). "Availability of Taxicabs at Night, on Weekends, and on Holidays." New York, N.Y.: Taxi and Limousine Commission.

Cherry, R. C. (1973). "Computers, Taxis, and Grass Roots Transportation." *See* Highway Research Board (1973).

Chow, P-t., and Nip, K-f. (1970). "Taxi Passenger Waiting Times in July 1970." Technical Note 36. Hong Kong: Traffic and Transport Survey Division.

COM-BUS (1972). "About Private Commuter Buses." Mimeograph publicity material. Long Beach, Calif.

Corradino, J. C., and Ferreri, M. G. (1969). "In-Flight Origin-Destination Study at Philadelphia International Airport." *Highway Research Record* 274. Washington, D.C.: Highway Research Board.

Curry, D. A., and McGillivray, R. G. (1971). "Urban Transit Regulation and Planning in the San Francisco Bay Area." Palo Alto, Calif.: Stanford Research Institute.

DeLeuw, Cather and Company (1971). *Draft Summary Report: Contra Costa County Needs Study*. San Francisco, Calif.

deNeufville, R.; Wilson, N. H. M.; Moore, H. L.; Landau, U.; and Yaney, J. (1972). "Airport and Air Service Access." Research Report R72-35. Cambridge, Mass.: MIT Department of Civil Engineering.

District of Columbia Government (1971). "District of Columbia Register, Special Edition: D.C. Rules and Regulations, Title 14." Washington, D.C.

Douglas, G. W. (1972). "Price Regulation and Optimal Service Standards." *Journal of Transport Economics and Policy* 6, pp. 116-27.

Eckert, R. D. (1968). "Regulatory Commission Behavior: Taxi Franchising in Los Angeles and Other Cities." UCLA Ph.D. Thesis. Ann Arbor, Mich.: University Microfilms.

———— (1970). "The Los Angeles Taxi Monopoly: An Economic Enquiry." *Southern California Law Review* 43, pp. 407-53.

————, and Hilton, G. W. (1972). "The Jitneys." *The Journal of Law and Economics* 15, pp. 293-325.

Elliott, J. M. (1973). "Demand-Responsive Transportation as Seen by the Transit Worker." *See* Highway Research Board (1973).

Fargier, P. H., and Cohen, M. (1971). "Study of a Collective Taxi System." Unpublished mimeograph. Arcueil, France: Institut de Recherche des Transports.

Farmer, R. N. (1965). "Whatever Happened to the Jitney?" *Traffic Quarterly* 19, pp. 263-79.

———— (1967). "Middle Eastern Jitney Services." *Traffic Quarterly* 21, pp. 219-28.

Frederich, K. G. (1972). "Sammeltaxis im Linienverkehr?" *Verkehr und Technik*, November 1972, pp. 454-58.

Fried, J. P. (1970). "Taxi Fares Are Up in Many U.S. Cities." *New York Times*, November 22, 1970, p. 79.

Friedman, D. (1972). "Public Vehicle Rental System: Determination of Feasibility." *See* University of Pennsylvania (1972b).

Gilman, W. C., and Company (1957). *St. Louis Metropolitan Area Transportation Study*.

Glick, I. (1971). "Service Refusal and the Taxi Industry." New York, N.Y.: Taxi and Limousine Commission. Chicago, Ill.

Golden Gate Bridge, Highway, and Transportation District (1973). "Monthly Statistical Summary: November-December 1973." San Francisco, Calif.

Golob, T. F., and Gustafson, R. L. (1971). "Economic Analysis of a Demand-Responsive Public Transportation System." *Highway Research Record* 367. Washington, D.C.: Highway Research Board.

Gramza, K. R.; Paik, I.; and Willyard, J. (1969). "Estimates of Taxi-Driver Income and Operating Costs." Bethesda, Md.: Resource Management Corporation.

Grava, S. (1972). "The Jeepneys of Manila." *Traffic Quarterly* 26, pp. 465-83.

Growald, P. J., and Custer, M. M. (1973). "Bug-eyed Bus Line—It's Free." *San Francisco Chronicle*, February 26, 1973.

Guenther, K. W. (1971). "Incremental Implementation of Dial-a-Ride Systems." *See* Highway Research Board (1971).

———— (1973). "Ford Motor Company's Role in Dial-a-Ride Development: 1972 and Beyond." *See* Highway Research Board (1973).

————, and Augustine, R. G. (1972). "Radio Teleprinter Test—Batavia, New York Dial-a-Bus System." Dearborn, Mich.: Ford Motor Company Transportation Research and Planning Office.

Gurin, D., and Wofford, J. (1971). "Implications of Dial-a-Ride for the Poor." Report USL TR-70-18. Cambridge, Mass.: MIT Urban Systems Laboratory.

Gustafson, R. L.; Curd, H. N.; and Golob, T. F. (1971). "User Preferences for a Demand-Responsive Transportation System: A Case Study Report." *Highway Research Record* 367. Washington, D.C.: Highway Research Board.

Gustafson, R. L., and Navin, F. P. D. (1973). "User Preferences for Dial-a-Bus." *See* Highway Research Board (1973).

Gutknecht, R. (1974). "Alternative Fares System." In *Symposium on Public Transport Fare Structure: papers and discussion.* TRRL Supplementary Report 37UC. Crowthorne, U.K.: Transport and Road Research Laboratory.

Gwynn, D. W., and Simpson, A. V. (1973). "Dial-a-Ride Demonstration in Haddonfield." *See* Highway Research Board (1973).

Habig, W. C. (1973). "Model Cities Dial-a-Ride System in Columbus, Ohio." *See* Highway Research Board (1973).

Hanley, G. P. (1971). "Comparison of Emissions per Passenger Mile—Private Car versus City Bus." Unpublished mimeograph. Detroit, Mich.: General Motors Corporation.

Harel, R. (1965). "Organization of Public Transport in the Developing Countries." Thirty-sixth International Congress. Brussels, Belg.: Union Internationale des Transports Publics.

Harris, E. E. (1963). "A Report on Area Taxis." Pittsburgh, Pa.: Pittsburgh Area Transportation Study.

Heathington, K. W.; Davis, F. W.; Middendorf, D. P.; and Brogan, J. D. (1974). "An Example of Demand-Responsive Transportation Systems in the Private Sector." *Transportation Research Record* 522. Washington, D.C.: Transportation Research Board.

Heathington, K. W.; Miller, J.; Knox, R. R.; Hoff, G. C.; and Bruggeman, J. M. (1969). "Computer Simulation of a Demand-Scheduled Bus System Offering Door-to-Door Service." *Highway Research Record* 251. Washington, D.C.: Highway Research Board.

Henderson, C. (1971). "Seminar on System Evaluation." *See* Highway Research Board (1971).

Herr, P. B., and Fleisher, A. (1968). "The Mobility of the Poor." *See* American Academy of Arts and Sciences (1968a).

Highway Research Board (1971). *Demand-Actuated Transportation Systems.* Special Report 124. Washington, D.C.

———— (1973). *Demand-Responsive Transportation Systems.* Special Report 136. Washington, D.C.

Hines, J. M., and Sloan, D. W. (1971). "Legal Analysis of Transportation Regulation and Innovation: The Dial-a-Ride." Report USL TR-70-19. Cambridge, Mass.: MIT Urban Systems Laboratory.

Howson, L. L., and Heathington, K. W. (1970). "Algorithms for Routing and Scheduling in Demand-Responsive Transportation Systems." *Highway Research Record* 318. Washington, D.C.: Highway Research Board.

Hupkes, G. (1972). "Buxi: Demand-Responsive Bus Experience in the Netherlands." *Highway Research Record* 397. Washington, D.C.: Highway Research Board.

Institute for Defense Analyses (1972). *Economic Characteristics of the Urban Public Transportation Industry.* Washington, D.C.: Government Printing Office.

Katz, S. B. (1971). "Citizen Complaint Hearing Procedures." New York, N.Y.: Taxi and Limousine Commission.

Kemp, M. A. (1973). "Some Evidence of Transit Demand Elasticities." *Transportation* 2, pp. 25-52.

Khleif, A. K. (1972). "The 'Service-Taxi' Cab Transportation System in Beirut; A Case Study for Washington, D.C." Washington, D.C.: Consortium of Universities Urban Transportation Center. Unpublished.

Kitch, E. W.; Isaacson, M.; and Kasper, D. (1971). "The Regulation of Taxicabs in Chicago." *The Journal of Law and Economics* 14, pp. 285-350.

Kraft, G. (1973). "Free Transit Revisited." *Public Policy* 21, pp. 79-105.

————, and Domencich, T. A. (1970). *Free Transit.* Lexington, Mass.: D.C. Heath and Company.

Krasnowiecki, J. (1970). "Legal and Organizational Aspects." *See* University of Pennsylvania (1970).

Kudlick, W. (1969). "Carros por Puesto—The Jitney Taxi System of Caracas, Venezuela." *Highway Research Record* 283. Washington, D.C.: Highway Research Board.

Kulash, D. J. (1971). "Routing and Scheduling in Public Transportation Systems." Cambridge, Mass.: MIT Ph.D. thesis. Unpublished.

———— (1973a). "Parking Taxes for Congestion Relief: A Survey of Related Experience." Paper URI 67000. Washington, D.C.: The Urban Institute.

———— (1973b). "Parking Taxes as Roadway Prices: A Case Study of the San Francisco Experience." Paper URI 68000. Washington, D.C.: The Urban Institute.

Lasson, K. (1971). *The Workers.* New York, N.Y.: Grossman Publishers.

Lax, J. (1973). "Dial-a-Ride Project in Ann Arbor: Legality." *See* Highway Research Board (1973).

Lazar, M. J. (1971). "The Non-Medallion Industry: A Transportation Phenomenon." New York, N.Y.: Taxi and Limousine Commission.

Lee, B.; Falcocchio, J. C.; and Cantilli, E. J. (1972). "Taxi Usage in New York City Poverty Areas." *Highway Research Record* 403. Washington, D.C.: Highway Research Board.

Marbury, D. (1972). "Uncle Dede is a Jitney Driver." *QED Renaissance* 3, no. 5, pp. 37-39. Pittsburgh, Pa.: Metropolitan Pittsburgh Public Broadcasting.

Marlowe, M. (1967). "Effect of One Day's Withdrawal of Taxi Service on Traffic in the West End of London." Report LR114. Crowthorne, U.K.: Road Research Laboratory.

Massachusetts Institute of Technology (1969). "CARS—A Prototype Dial-a-Bus System." Research Report R69-56. Cambridge, Mass.: MIT Urban Systems Laboratory.

Medville, D. M. (1973). "Dial-a-Ride Demonstration in Haddonfield: Planning and Initial Operation." *See* Highway Research Board (1973).

Meyer, J. R.; Kain, J. F.; and Wohl, M. (1966). *The Urban Transportation Problem.* Cambridge, Mass.: Harvard University Press.

Meyer, R. A., Jr. (1971). "Seminar on Pricing and Economic Evaluation." *See* Highway Research Board (1971).

Mid-Ohio Regional Planning Commission (1973). *Report on the Columbus, Ohio Model Cities Second Year Transit Project.* Columbus, Ohio.

Mikofsky, A. J. (1973). " 'Alternative Transportation' in City." *Washington Post,* February 19, 1973.

Milwaukee Department of City Development (1971). "Milwaukee Taxicab Controls and the Public Interest." Unpublished.

Milwaukee Municipal Reference Library (1969). "The Licensing and Regulation of Taxicab Companies in 15 Major Cities." Unpublished.

Morin, D. A.; Lindsey, L. C.; and Riemer, R. (1972). "A Report on the Reston Bus Passenger Survey." Unpublished mimeograph. Washington, D.C.: U.S. Department of Transportation Federal Highway Administration.

Motor Vehicle Manufacturers Association (1972). *1972 Automobile Facts and Figures.* Detroit, Mich.

McGillivray, R. G. (1973). "On Road Congestion Theory." Paper URI 69000. Washington, D.C.: The Urban Institute.

McLeod, M. G. (1972). "The Operation and Performance of a Taxi Fleet." Cambridge, Mass.: MIT Ph.D. thesis. Unpublished.

Nakpil, C. G. (undated). "The Jeepney—A Product of Filipino Ingenuity." Unpublished.

National Capital Region Transportation Planning Board (1970). "Characteristics of Taxicab Service in the District of Columbia." Information Report 31. Washington, D.C.: Metropolitan Washington Council of Governments.

National Safety Council (1973). *Accident Facts.* Chicago, Ill.

Nelson, J. P. (1971). "Group Riding and Central Dispatch." New York, N.Y.: Taxi and Limousine Commission.

New York City (1971). *Charter of the City of New York.* Chapter 65. New York: City of New York.

New York City, Mayor's Commission on Taxicabs (1930). "Report of the Mayor's Commission on Taxicabs." Unpublished.

New York City, Mayor's Committee on Management Survey (1953). *Modern Management for the City of New York.* New York: City of New York.

New York City, Mayor's Committee on Taxicab Survey (1934). "Report of Mayor's Committee on Taxicab Survey." Unpublished.

New York City, Mayor's Taxi Study Panel (1966). "Recommendations to John V. Lindsay, Mayor of the City of New York." Unpublished.

Noortman, H. J. (1971). "The Effect of the Organisation of Transport Facilities," In *Fourth International Symposium on Theory and Practice in Transport Economics.* Paris, France: Conference Européenne des Ministres des Transports.

Oka, N. (1973). "Public-Use Private Transport." *The Wheel Extended* 2, no. 4, pp. 17-19.

"Origin and History of Jitneys in Atlantic City" (1967?). Unpublished mimeograph provided by the Atlantic City Department of Revenue and Finance.

Orr, D. (1969). "The 'Taxicab Problem': A Proposed Solution." *Journal of Political Economy* 77, pp. 141-47.

Oxley, P. R. (1973). "Dial-a-Ride Application in Great Britain." *See* Highway Research Board (1973).

Ozdirim, M. (1973). "The Problems in Big Towns Created by Traffic Increase." In *Techniques of Improving Urban Conditions by Restraint of Road Traffic*. Paris, France: Organization for Economic Cooperation and Development.

Pang, H-c. (1968). "The Level of Service Provided by Taxis in July 1968." Technical Report TR59. Hong Kong: Traffic and Transport Survey Unit.

Peck, M. J., and Meyer, J. R. (1965). "The Determination of a Fair Return on Investment for Regulated Industries." In *Transportation Economics*. New York, N.Y.: National Bureau of Economic Research.

Pratsch, L. W. (1971). "A Successful Private Bus Company Serving Rural U.S." Unpublished mimeograph. Washington, D.C.: U.S. Department of Transportation Federal Highway Administration.

————— (1973). *Carpool and Buspool Matching Guide*. Washington, D.C.: U.S. Department of Transportation Federal Highway Administration.

Price Waterhouse and Company (1967). "New York City Fleet Taxicab Industry Financial Survey." Unpublished.

————— (1970). "New York City Fleet Taxicab Industry Financial Survey." Unpublished.

Rainwater, L. (1970). *Behind Ghetto Walls: Black Families in a Federal Slum*. Chicago, Ill.: Aldine.

Rattien, S., and Duckett, E. J. (1971). "The Pittsburgh Taxicab Study 1970." Pittsburgh, Pa.: University of Pittsburgh Graduate School of Public Health.

Read, A., and Pill, J. (1973). "Strengths and Weaknesses of the Current Metropolitan Toronto Transportation System. Part 6: The Taxicabs." Toronto, Ont.: Metropolitan Toronto Transportation Plan Review.

RECAT Committee (1972). *Cumulative Regulatory Effects on the Cost of Automotive Transportation*. Washington, D.C.: U.S. Office of Science and Technology.

Roberts, J. (1969). "An Auto-Taxi System." *Official Architecture and Planning* 32, pp. 173-76.

Roos, D. (1971). "Dial-a-Bus System Feasibility." *See* Highway Research Board (1971).

————— (1972). "Operational Experiences with Demand-Responsive Transportation Systems." *Highway Research Record* 397. Washington, D.C.: Highway Research Board.

Rosenbloom, S. (1968). "Characteristics of Taxicab Supply and Demand in Selected Metropolitan Areas." In General Research Corporation, *Systems Analysis of Urban Transportation*, vol 4. Santa Barbara, Calif.

————— (1970). "'Taxis, Jitneys, and Poverty." *Transaction* 7, pp. 47-54.

————— (1971). "Taxi and Jitney Service in the United States and Recent Transportation Trends in the Inner City." Internal Memorandum IMR 1346. Santa Barbara, Calif.: General Research Corporation.

————— (1972). "Taxis and Jitneys: The Case for Deregulation." *Reason* 3, no. 11, pp. 4-16.

Ross, H. L.; Campbell, D. T.; and Glass, G. V. (1970). "Determining the Social Effects of a Legal Reform—The British Breathalyser Crackdown of 1967." *American Behavioral Scientist* 13, pp. 493-509.

Roth, G. (1967). *Paying for Roads.* Harmondsworth, U.K.: Penguin Books.

Saltzman, A. (1973). "Para-transit: Taking the Mass out of Mass Transit." *Technology Review* 75, no. 8, pp. 46-53.

Samuels, R. E. (1971). "Samuels Reviews Taxicab Industry Regulations." Part 1. *Taxicab Management* 19, no. 12, pp. 9ff.

———— (1972a). "Samuels Reviews Taxicab Industry Regulations." Part 2. *Taxicab Management* 20, no. 1, pp. 5ff.

———— (1972b). "Samuels Reviews Taxicab Industry Regulations." Part 3. *Taxicab Management* 20, no. 2, pp. 6ff.

Schmidt, J. W.; Arnold, R. K.; and Levy, S. (1972). "Specification and Evaluation of Alternative Feeder and Local Transit Systems in a Suburban Area." *Highway Research Record* 417. Washington, D.C.: Highway Research Board.

Schwartz, H. (1973). "Manhattan Without Cars?" *New York Affairs* 1, no. 1, pp. 46-59.

Smith, Wilbur, and Associates/Padilla and Gracia (1968). *Metropolitan Area Transportation Studies* (4 volumes). San Juan, P.R.: Commonwealth of Puerto Rico Department of Public Works.

Solomon, R. J., and Saltzman, A. (1971). "History of Transit and Innovative Systems." Report USL TR-70-20. Cambridge, Mass.: MIT Urban Systems Laboratory.

Stafford, J.; Urbanek, G.; Plourde, R.; Soolman, A.; Kutner, S.; Pecknold, W.; and Robinson, R. (1971). "Economic Considerations for Dial-a-Bus." Report USL TR-70-11. Cambridge, Mass.: MIT Urban Systems Laboratory.

Stanford Research Institute (1968). *Future Urban Transportation Systems: Descriptions, Evaluations, and Programs.* Menlo Park, Calif.

Stevens, R. D., and Smith, R. L. (1971). "Demand Bus for a New Town." *See* Highway Research Board (1971).

Suomala, J. B. (1971). "Dial-a-Ride Vehicle Specification." Report USL TR-70-17. Cambridge, Mass.: MIT Urban Systems Laboratory.

Tomazinis, A. R. (1972). "Forecasting Travel Demand for New Urban Transportation Systems." *Highway Research Record* 392. Washington, D.C.: Highway Research Board.

Toyota Motor Sales Company Ltd. (1972). "The Town Spider System." *The Wheel Extended* 2, no. 1, pp. 31-35.

Transport Central (1972). " 'When Does the Bus Leave?' 'When Can You Make It?' " *Transport Central,* 26 June 1972, pp. 6-8.

Transportation Association of America (1973). *Transportation Facts and Trends.* Ninth Edition (July 1972, as updated by the quarterly supplement of April 1973). Washington, D.C.

Tri-State Transportation Commission (1969). "Who Rides Taxis." *Regional Profile* 1, no. 11. New York, N.Y.

Turvey, R. (1961). "Some Economic Features of the London Cab Trade." *The Economic Journal* 71, pp. 79-92.

Tye, W. B. (1973). "The Capital Grant as a Subsidy Device: The Case Study of Urban Mass Transportation." In U.S. Congress Joint Economic Committee, *The Economics of Federal Subsidy Programs—A Compendium of Papers Submitted to the Subcommittee on Priorities and Economy in Government of the Joint Economic Committee. Part 6—Transpor-*

tation Subsidies, February 26, 1973. Washington, D.C.: Government Printing Office.

U.K. Home Office (1970). *Report of the Departmental Committee on the London Taxicab Trade* (the "Maxwell Stamp Report"). Cmnd. 4483. London, U.K.: Her Majesty's Stationery Office.

U.K. Ministry of Transport (1953). *Report of the Committee on the Taxicab Service* (the "Runciman Report"). Cmnd. 8804. London, U.K.: Her Majesty's Stationery Office.

———— (1967). *Cars for Cities.* London, U.K.: Her Majesty's Stationery Office.

U.K. National Board for Prices and Incomes (1968). "Proposed Increase in London Taxicab Fares." Report No. 87, Cmnd. 3796. London, U.K.: Her Majesty's Stationery Office.

U.S. Department of Commerce (1972). *Statistical Abstract of the United States, 1972.* U.S. Department of Commerce Bureau of Census. Washington, D.C.: Government Printing Office.

U.S. Department of Labor (1965). *Dictionary of Occupational Titles.* Washington, D.C.: Government Printing Office.

———— (1968). "Union Wages and Laws: Local Transit Operating Employees." U.S. Department of Labor Bureau of Labor Statistics, Bulletin 1589. Washington, D.C.: Government Printing Office.

———— (1970a). "Employment Outlook—Driving Occupations." U.S. Department of Labor Bureau of Labor Statistics, Bulletin 1650-94. Washington, D.C.: Government Printing Office.

———— (1970b). "Union Wages and Laws: Local Transit Operating Employees." U.S. Department of Labor Bureau of Labor Statistics, Bulletin 1667. Washington, D.C.: Government Printing Office.

U.S. Department of Transportation (1972a). "Cost of Operating an Automobile." U.S. Department of Transportation Federal Highway Administration. Washington, D.C.: Government Printing Office.

———— (1972b). *1972 National Transportation Report.* U.S. Department of Transportation Office of the Secretary. Washington, D.C.: Government Printing Office.

———— (1972c). *Sixth Annual Report, Fiscal Year 1972.* Washington, D.C.: Government Printing Office.

———— (1973a). *Nationwide Personal Transportation Study: Report 8, Home-to-Work Trips and Travel.* Washington, D.C.: U.S. Department of Transportation Federal Highway Administration.

———— (1973b). "Selected Data on Research, Development, and Demonstration Activity since 1966." Private communication from the Urban Mass Transportation Administration Office of Administration, August 24, 1973.

———— (1974). "Buspools." Washington, D.C.: U.S. Department of Transportation.

U.S. House of Representatives (1957). Committee on the District of Columbia, Subcommittee on Public Utilities, Insurance and Banking, *Taxicab Industry in the District of Columbia.* Hearing of June 24 - July 24, 1957. Washington, D.C.: Government Printing Office.

University of Pennsylvania (1968). "Minicar Transit System: Final Report of Phase 1, Feasibility Study" (2 volumes). Philadelphia, Pa.: University of Pennsylvania Transportation Studies Center.

———— (1970). *Minicar Transit System Final Report.* Philadelphia, Pa.: University of Pennsylvania Center for Urban Research and Experimentation.

————— (1972a). "A Minicar Transportation System in an Urban Low-Income Group." Philadelphia, Pa.: University of Pennsylvania Transportation Studies Center.

————— (1972b). *Selected Proceedings of a Conference on Methods and Concepts of Forecasting Travel Demand for Future Systems.* Philadelphia, Pa.: University of Pennsylvania Transportation Studies Center.

University of Puerto Rico (1972). "Publicos Study: Final Report." Mayaguez, P.R.: University of Puerto Rico Transportation Institute.

Urbanek, G. (1969). "Jitneys and CARS." Unpublished memorandum CARS-EC-16, Project CARS. Cambridge, Mass.: Massachusetts Institute of Technology.

—————, and Guenther, K. (1969). "Atlantic City Jitney." Unpublished memorandum CARS-EC-33, Project CARS. Cambridge, Mass.: Massachusetts Institute of Technology.

Urbanik, T. (1973). "Dial-a-Ride Project in Ann Arbor: Description and Operation." *See* Highway Research Board (1973).

Verkuil, P.R. (1970). "The Economic Regulation of Taxicabs." *Rutgers Law Review* 24, pp. 672-711.

Vickrey, W. (1973). "The Pricing of Urban Transportation: Economic Desiderata, Technological Possibilities, and Political Constraints." Paper presented to the 1973 Intersociety Conference on Transportation. New York, N.Y.: American Society of Mechanical Engineers.

Vidich, C. (1973). "Union Taxies and Gypsy Cabbies." *Society* 10, no. 5, pp. 43-49.

————— (1974). *The New York Taxicab Driver.* Cambridge, Mass.: Schenkman Publishing Company.

Vidich, P. (1972). "The Economic Regulation of Taxicabs." Middletown, Conn.: Wesleyan University A. B. thesis. Unpublished.

Vitt, J. E.; Bauer, H. J.; Canty, E. T.; Golob, T. F.; and Heathington, K. W. (1970). "Determining the Importance of User-Related Attributes for a Demand-Responsive Transportation System." *Highway Research Record* 318. Washington, D.C.: Highway Research Board.

Voorhees, Alan M., and Associates Ltd. (1973). "Luton, Dunstable and Houghton Regis Transportation Study—Phase II: Attitudes to Carpooling." Unpublished mimeograph. London, U.K.

Vuchic, V. R. (1970). "Minicar Transit System—Description and Evaluation of a New Concept." *Highway Research Record* 318. Washington, D.C.: Highway Research Board.

Wallace, E. (1972). "Confessions of a Cabbie." *Washingtonian Magazine* 8, no. 3, p. 20.

Ward, J. E., and Rausch, R. G. (1971). "Vehicle Communications for a Dial-a-Ride System." Report USL TR-70-15, Cambridge, Mass.: MIT Urban Systems Laboratory.

Washington Metropolitan Area Transit Authority (1973). "Notice of Metrobus Public Hearing No. 9, and Price of Reston Service Contract for Period August 1, 1973 through July 31, 1974." Washington, D.C.

Wells, J. D., and Selover, F. F. (1972). "Characteristics of the Urban Taxicab Transit Industry." *See* Institute for Defense Analyses (1972).

Wells, J. D., and Thomas, S. (1972). "Economic Characteristics of the Urban Bus Transit Industry, 1960-1970." *See* Institute for Defense Analyses (1972).

White, M. (1973). "Model Cities Jitney Transportation in Buffalo." *See* Highway Research Board (1973).

Whitlock, E. M., and Cleary, E. F. (1969). "Planning Ground Transportation Facilities for Airports." *Highway Research Record* 274. Washington, D.C.: Highway Research Board.

Wilson, N. H. M. (1967). "CARS—Computer-Aided Routing System." Research Report R67-12. Cambridge, Mass.: MIT Department of Civil Engineering.

———, and Higonnet, B. T. (1973). "General Purpose Computer Dispatching System." *See* Highway Research Board (1973).

———, and Roos, D. (1968). "An Overview of CARS." Research Report R68-60. Cambridge, Mass.: MIT Department of Civil Engineering.

———, Sussman, J.; Goodman, L.; and Higonnet, T. (1970a). "Simulation of a Computer-Aided Routing System." *Highway Research Record* 318. Washington, D.C.: Highway Research Board.

———, Sussman, J. M.; Wong, H-k.; and Higonnet, T. (1970b). "Scheduling Algorithms for a Dial-a-Ride System." Report USL TR-70-13. Cambridge, Mass.: MIT Urban Systems Laboratory.

Witkin, R. (1971). "Nixon Aides Score Taxi Setup Here." *New York Times,* April 14, 1971, p. 1.

Wohl, M. (1972). "An Analysis and Evaluation of the Rapid Transit Extension to Cleveland's Airport." *Highway Research Record* 417. Washington, D.C.: Highway Research Board.

Wong, H-k. (1971). "Some Demand Models for the Taxicab System in the Washington, D.C. Area," Working Paper 708-39. Washington, D.C.: The Urban Institute.

Zettel, R. M., and Carll, R. R. (1964). "The Basic Theory of Efficiency Tolls: the Tolled, the Tolled-Off, and the Un-Tolled." *Highway Research Record* 47. Washington, D.C.: Highway Research Board.

Index

SUBJECT INDEX

In the subject index, subentries are heavily concentrated under primary entries for the various modes and classes of transportation. Therefore, two types of cross-references have been introduced: those in bold-face refer to primary entries, while those in light-face link two subentries under the same main entry.

Air pollution
daily rental car, 24-25, 197
para-transit services, 9-10, 37-40 passim, 45, 54, 252, 261-63, 267-70, 278
prearranged ride-sharing, 4, 249, 272
private automobile, 3, 261-63, 267-70, 276, 279-80, 290-91
short-term rental car, 23-24, 26, 28, 187, 197-98, 200, 204, 210
taxicab service, 16, 97, 272, 286-87
conventional transit, 261-63, 267-70, 278

Airport service
daily rental car, 43, 191-93, 195, 197, 277
jurisdictional disputes, 69-70
limousine, 59, 277
short-term rental car, 212
taxicab service, 14, 59, 69, 95, 115-16, 120, 122, 277
conventional transit, 277, 281

Automobile. See **Private automobile, Daily rental car, Short-term rental car**

Baggage, 8, 58, 133, 153, 168, 222, 253-55

Car pools. See **Prearranged ride-sharing**
Central business district, 114-15, 117-18, 120, 140, 200-201, 203-6, 210, 213-14, 290
Charter service, 129, 148, 154-55, 165
Clean Air Act of 1970, 3, 97, 291
Common carriers, 195, 231-32, 234, 236. See also **Transit service**
Computerization
communications, 127, 147, 155
daily rental car reservations, 195
dispatching, 18, 22, 54, 127, 130-31, 147, 149, 151-54, 163, 259
matching of ride-sharers, 35, 218, 250
short-term rental car system, 7, 23-24, 211-12
Congestion. See **Traffic congestion**
Congestion pricing. See **Fares and Charges**
Contract carriers, 195, 231-32. See also **Charter service**
Conventional transit
costs, 223-24, 257, 267-75 passim, 280-82, 287
and dial-a-ride service, 13, 129-33, 135, 138-39, 142-44, 149-55 passim, 164, 292
demand for, 40-41, 114, 116-24 passim, 135, 177, 181-85 passim, 228, 276-77
elasticity of demand, 6, 280-82
employment level, 61
fares and charges, 6, 37, 74, 125, 153, 173, 179-80, 184, 201, 280-82, 289
headways, 7, 280-82
industry size, 60-61

and jitney service, 13, 166-68, 172-74, 176, 179-85 passim, 286-87, 292
labor, 19-20, 88-89, 144, 149-50, 176, 233, 257-59
market share, 276-77
and para-transit services, 7-9, 36-37, 43, 45-54, 251, 253-59 passim, 262-63, 267-74
passengers, 61, 135, 142-43, 157, 164
and prearranged ride-sharing, 30-34 passim, 215-16, 218-29 passim, 233-35 passim, 238-42 passim, 292
and regulation, 63-65, 74, 98, 260, 280-83, 286-87
revenues, 60-61, 98, 155, 157, 164, 280-82, 287
service characteristics, 58, 133, 168, 254-56, 276
and short-term rental car, 26, 199, 201, 207, 213-14
subsidization, 4-6, 10-11, 19-20, 34, 48-49, 64, 129, 143, 152-53, 285, 287, 289
and taxicab service, 4, 18, 60-61, 63-65, 98, 114, 116-24 passim, 286-87, 292
U.S. transit industry, 60-61
Costs
administrative, 27, 83, 85-86, 144, 146, 152, 156, 194-95, 197, 203-4, 224, 259-60, 264
amortization, 84, 146, 174-75, 203, 224
capital, 17, 19, 83-84, 86, 146, 156, 174, 179-80, 194, 200-201, 224, 264, 284-85
depreciation, 63, 83, 86, 101, 155, 174-75, 179, 194-95, 203
dispatching, 62-63, 83, 85-86, 146-47, 149, 179, 264
economies of scale, 62, 85, 288
and fare changes, 280-82, 288
fuel, 83, 146, 175, 194, 203, 205-6, 210, 223, 237, 259, 264
garaging, 62, 83, 86, 194, 203
insurance, 14-15, 27, 61-62, 69-70, 76, 83-86, 101, 146, 175-76, 179, 194, 203, 223, 264
interest, 61-62, 74, 83-84, 175, 179
labor. See **Labor**
licenses, 61, 66-67, 83-84, 92, 107-8, 146, 169, 175, 177, 264
maintenance and repair, 61-63, 83, 107, 146, 175-76, 194, 202-3, 223, 264
medallion, 14, 66-67, 83-84, 92, 107-8, 285-86
and output, 264, 267-76
rent, 62, 83, 195, 203, 222-23
taxes, 62, 74, 146, 169, 177, 223, 237, 264
See also **Conventional transit, Daily rental car, Dial-a-ride service, Jitney service, Prearranged ride-sharing,**

307

NAME INDEX

The name index lists all proper names, personal or corporate, appearing in the text; however, names which appear only in the Bibliography are not indexed. Numbers in italics denote pages in the Bibliography.

Aex, R. P., 154, *293*
Airways Rent-A-Car, 191
Allen, Sir Roy, 123-24
Amalgamated Transit Union, 144, 150, 258
American Academy of Arts and Sciences, 119, *293*
American Academy of Transportation, 241, *293*
American Automobile Leasing Association, 188
American Honda Motor Company, Inc., 198
American International Rent-A-Car, 191
American Petroleum Institute, 262, *293*
American Taxicab Association, 60
American Transit Association, 61, 223-24, *293*
Ann Arbor Transportation Authority, 139, 148, 158, *293*
Arnold, R. K., 199, *300*
Atkinson, W. G., 155, *293*
Atlantic City Jitneymen's Association, 167, 170, 173-75
Atwood's Transport Lines, Inc., 246
Augustine, R. G., 155, *296*
Automotive Fleet, 189, *293*
Avis Rent A Car System, Inc., 23-24, 28, 190-91, 193, 195, 206, 214

Badger Cab Company (Madison), 13, 158-59
Bain, H., 217-18, 229, 244, *294*
Banks, R. L., and Associates, Inc., 64, 260, *294*
Barbera, K. G., 116, *294*
Bauer, H. J., 137, *294*
Bay Area Rapid Transit District, 199
B & B Minibus Company, 217, 219, 226, 229-33, 235
Beesley, M. E., 90, *294*
Beimborn, E. A., 113-16 passim, 118, 120, 122, 124, *294*
Belknap, R. A., 176, 178-79, *294*
Bendixson, T., 209, *294*
Berla, M. J., 158, *294*
Bhatt, K. U., 126-65, 215-50
Bi-State Transit Authority (St. Louis), 181
Blurton, M. A. S., 217-18, 228, 238, *294*
Bonsall, J. A., 139, 143, 157, *294*
Brandeis University, 119
British Leyland Motor Corporation, 261
Brogan, J. D., 152, *296*
Budget Rent-A-Car Corporation of America, 23, 28, 191
Burroughs Corporation, 217-18, 225, 229, 234, 277
Business Week, 191, *294*

Cab Research Bureau, 60
Calumet Mutual Insurance Company, 70

Campbell, D. T., 292, *300*
Cantilli, E. J., 111, 113, 117, *297*
Caplovitz, D., 119
Car and Truck Renting and Leasing Association, 188, 191, *294*
Carll, R. R., 38, *303*
Caterpillar Tractor Company, 238
Checker Motors (Chicago), 65
Checker Motors Corporation, 152
Cherry, R. C., 152, *295*
Chrysler Corporation, 174, 190, 205
Chrysler France, Simca Division, 25, 205
Chrysler Leasing Corporation, 190, 193
City Coach Lines (Flint), 241
City Mutual Insurance Company, 70
City Transit Company (Peoria), 218, 238-39
Cleary, E. F., 116, *303*
COM-BUS, 232, 247-48, *295*
Corradino, J. C., 277, *295*
Curry, D. A., 177, 217-18, 235, *295*

Davis, F. W., 152, *296*
D.C. Transit System, Inc., 219, 246
DeLeuw, Cather and Company, 199, *295*
deNeufville, R., 277, *295*
District of Columbia Government, 123, *295*
Dollar-a-Day Rent-A-Car Systems, 191
Domencich, T. A., 280-81, *297*
Duckett, E. J., 69, 111, 113, 115-17, 123, *299*

Eckert, R. D., 64, 66, 68, 166-67, 260, *295*
Econo-Car International, Inc., 191
Elliott, J. M., 149, *295*

Falcocchio, J. C., 111, 113, 117, *297*
Farmer, R. N., 183, *295*
Fellman, G., 119
Ferreri, M. G., 277, *295*
Fleisher, A., 117, *296*
Flint Transportation Authority, 241
Ford Motor Company, 126, 190, 194, 235, 262
Fried, J. P., 104, *295*
Friedman, D., 194, 202-4 passim, *295*

General Bank of Holland, 209
General Motors Corporation, 126, 174, 189-92, 241-42
Gilman, W. C., and Company, 181, *295*
Glass, G. V., 292, *300*
Glick, I., 111, 125, *295*
Golden Gate Bridge, Highway, and Transportation District, 33, 217-18, 220-28 passim, 232-33, 245-46, *295*
Golob, T. F., 137, 141, *295, 296*
Gramza, K. R., 82, 88-89, 103, 146, *296*
Grava, S., 183, *296*
Greyhound Lines, Inc., 32, 232

317

DATE DUE

DEMCO 38-297